RISE, MY SETTING
SON

RISE, MY SETTING SON

GEORGE J. BARNES

Tampa, Florida

The views and opinions expressed in this book are solely those of the author and do not reflect the views or opinions of Gatekeeper Press. Gatekeeper Press is not to be held responsible for and expressly disclaims responsibility for the content herein.

Rise, My Setting Son

Published by Gatekeeper Press
7853 Gunn Hwy., Suite 209
Tampa, FL 33626
www.GatekeeperPress.com

Copyright © 2023 by George J. Barnes

All rights reserved. Neither this book, nor any parts within it may be sold or reproduced in any form or by any electronic or mechanical means, including information storage and retrieval systems, without permission in writing from the author. The only exception is by a reviewer, who may quote short excerpts in a review.

ISBN (paperback): 9781662940996

eISBN: 9781662940989

DEDICATION

To those who raised me and mentored me in the classrooms, in the hallways, on the blocks, and on the pulpit. To school employees, pastors, coaches, OGs and drug dealers, to the entertainers and athletic icons, and to the authors and social movement leaders of the past. To the father, the father figures, the brother and the brothas, to the uncles and my nephew, the cousins and to the play cousins. To my boys that I have the privilege of calling my sons, to the young men I have been and will be father figures to, to those who called me mentor and uncle. Men of different shades and cultures, you have all made me better. To my mother and my sister, to my aunts and my niece, to the other mothers that have attempted and the few who were successful in guiding me. To the mentors who remain a voice of wisdom as needed. To the sisters I have attempted to be a good male representation for in my various professional roles and to the one I have accepted like my own. To the sisters that have become family and blessed me with being present in my life. To the woman that accepts every part of me, lifts me up, steals my every breath and whom I would trust with my last. I thank you all.

PROLOGUE

I consider the raising of a child. This opportunity to see yourself in this tiny being from the womb. You look at this little person in amazement and, in most cases, I assume, see yourself in the little nuances in this person before they can walk, talk, or do much of anything besides lay there and sleep, consume nutrients, and cause you to lose sleep or clean up after them (that may only go away in increments). You watch this little person get older and they begin to speak and act. They have their own identities, but still you see so much of yourself in them. You do your best to protect them and love them. You want them to have the world and you want to offer all that you have that is "good" and defend them from all that is inherently "bad." Yet, there is free will. Your little person gets to make decisions and you do your best to sow seeds into them so they can make decisions that you think are "right" vs. "wrong." The days turn to months and months into years. You begin to see that you are running out of time, and soon this little person that you wish you had more time with, to protect, to teach, to guide, is eighteen years old and they profess their adulthood and legally can pronounce themselves "grown."

I know there are battles before then in many cases. Some of us may have or had children that thought they were "grown" way before eighteen as they *allowed* you to pay bills and put food in the refrigerator. Somebody is reading this and their twenty-five-year-old is still at the house requiring the same support, but they are "grown." In any event, we watch, we cry, we pray, we worry. We want what is best for our children and our children believe they know what is best. We have wisdom to impart and we hope the lessons that our children must learn are not too hard, because we love them.

In some of us there is also a sense of pride. That is my kid! That little person is a part of me and I have the DNA make-up for greatness. I have the answers. I have either gotten some part of life really right or really wrong and I want you to do what is "right," little person, so we (I) can be successful. I don't want to be embarrassed. I want us to win at whatever life is. It hurts to watch your little one fail and choose the "wrong" path. To defy all that you have to offer and accept a "counter-culture" that does not connect with your specific brand. To throw away all that you have worked for and all that you have given them. You continue to give with love with hopes that they "see the light" and "come back home" because you know what is best for them and in some cases, *you* don't want to fail.

People offer you advice. Some try to keep "family business" with the family. Some get into fights with total strangers at the grocery store because they are trying to tell you how to raise your child. Outsiders offer judgment and pity. I don't want your help. I just want my child to be "better." My child refuses my help at various levels as I ask God for strength. I see myself in them and I just want a better life for them. I want them to have all of the good things I had to break my back to afford, and I want their children to enjoy life without the stress that I have to endure to build a family. Ah, free will. We pray for their choices.

I offer these pages to our sons and daughters. This narrative is, in a sense, an opportunity to tell my sons everything I have. To offer both Elijah and Isaiah all that I have in this moment to give them as a father. To offer them any information and wisdom I have been blessed with for them to read, digest, and use when they are ready. There is no hope that this will ignite a fire the instant it is read. I pray for at least a slow burn that will lead to an eternal flame for a passion to be the best man they can be for their future children and all those that may see my sons in action, whether they are being seen as Black men, fathers, sons, husbands, workers, scholars, citizens, and/or more. Yet, this is an opportunity for more.

I wish a writing such as this was not needed. I wish we realized in the past that we were living in a society where there has been a problem in our realities. I wish people didn't want to ignore that the social construct of race still divides us. I wish more understood that, at least in the vast majority of the Western Hemisphere, African blood runs through many of our veins. I wish there was no hate in this world based on some concept of individuals and communities fighting for security or fear of losing their sliver of tangible peace, whether it is job security, education, homes, and/or other material objects. Today, the census tells us there are 15 percent of Americans that consider themselves Black. What decisions would be made if all who were brown accepted that they were also African? How many of those who denoted "White" actually have more than a European nation running through them? What if people were "colorblind" and had no implicit bias? What if we could all accept each other as love as the cornerstone of humanity and see our diversity as an added value?

However, wishing does not make something so.

This is not a call to get angry. This is not a call for separatism or racism. This is a call to action for Black people, specifically Black men, to move toward getting past what divides us. As long as we are separated by Crips, Bloods, Vice Lords, Gangster Disciples and their current-day factions, the various Greek fraternities, religion, political affiliations, socioeconomic levels, and paradigms that make some of us believe we have been accepted and we "got ours," coasts and regional areas of America, and even countries, we are missing the power that we own. We are to turn to our neighbors and return to our communities and lead. We can no longer wait for another politician, federal or otherwise, to provide pennies from heaven. We need to love each other. We need to build each other. Then, and only then, can we offer the love needed to other parts of society that need our leadership. The same leadership that puts fashion on the backs of others across the globe, that puts rhythm in ears and taught the world how to groove their bodies when the music hits. The leadership and passion that moves athletes, entertainers, orators, and artisans. The power we see in action when we create and run businesses, hold office, and lead in various opportunities is the same power that is needed to mentor and build the next generation. This movement needs to occur at the base and the base is where you are needed. This writing is not to miss the sisters of the Black communities, or those who cannot and do not directly connect with the race we call "Black." It would be ridiculous to think that Black men were only needed in this struggle. My call is that Black men are not doing enough on our own collectively to lead the movement. As a person that identifies as a Black man, I call to others that identify as the same to step up and lead for the good of our homes, communities, cities, and, as we look at the solution through a Pan-African lens, countries. Lead to step with the Black sisters, women that have felt the sting of systematically being held back, the Latinx community that bleeds our blood, the Indigenous people of the lands in America and across the globe, Asians, various peoples of the Greater Middle East, the Irish, Jewish, and Italian cultures that have had their times of being oppressed. Learn to see people for their heart and actions and offer love as you focus on building yourself and our community. The struggle is not a color issue, but a specific cultural issue that uses and compounds race while leveraging a false empowerment to manipulate our "truth" to a social acceptance. We must think differently.

Finally, this is a call against a "them" and "they." This "they" is a spirit that has permeated through various races and ethnicities. It is the mindset that often rests with a power or opportunity to use force to take something from others. Or to use fear or subjugation to put themselves in a frame of reference or vantage point as others see them as "powerful." A position that allows "them" to control the narrative and dictate what is "truth." We have seen "them" on many lands with various skin tones, I am sure. Historically, or at least based on the history that is written by "them," "they" are men. Men who take what "they" desire for some glory or some "noble" cause for a land "they" represent or belief or value "they" hide behind. "They" have used this power against those that do not look like "them" and those that do. Thus, it is not about skin, ethnicity, gender, belief in God, or any easily identifiable feature or category. There is a spirit in "them" that runs deep that fears a decrease in power "they" believe exists and "they" must hold onto and protect. This fear and desperate attempt to oppress and control has had quiet times like the whispers heard in laws that have been quietly passed that affected certain types of people. The attempts of control have also been evident through overt transparency, such as times of imperialistic land grabs, slavery, and censorship of historic facts. I offer these writings not to create anger toward the face of one group of people that have had dominance through centuries of the spirit that runs rampant with this spirit, but as an opportunity to recognize the spirit, unite, and rise above through acknowledging people and offering love to humanity.

Since I started these writings there have been several cases in the media and riots and protests regarding the wrongful deaths of Black people. These issues were brought to light and some practices may have been altered. There has been a cry out to defund the police, but it is not all police that have the spirit of "they" that misses the value of people. The argument is missed even more when we dehumanize the officers and forget they want to go home at the end of the day and also may have families. We miss that, due to lack of funding and proper practices, most police have not been trained to deal with the social ailments that have been created by "them" in their ability to ignore the oppressed people to secure wealth and false power. We forget that this spirit of the oppressor can infiltrate all jobs and careers and we need to be mindful of the responsibilities we offer others without supervision and systems of support. We miss that faces that look like ours tend to terrorize our communities in their organizations far more frequently and worse than the police, and there are no uprisings or marches that push back against our own atrocities against human kind.

If it were about race and ethnicity, it would be simple. We could say absolute statements and it would be easier to define and maybe there would be an easier rally cry to defeat "them." However, this same oppressive spirit uses all methodologies to keep "them" in positions of control and influence. "They" are masters of tapping into emotions of the majority that vote and keep "them" in positions of control and leadership all while sustaining and/or increasing themselves financially. If "they" cared about any lives, stricter gun laws would not be an issue. "They" had a war on drugs that put thousands of Black and brown people in jail, but a war on guns? There was support for a taxation on cigarettes and there were strategic moves that influenced that industry, but not guns? Murder is wrong, "they" say, and overturn Roe vs. Wade and states run to ban abortions while guns flood the streets and children are murdered in schools.

Perhaps it's not the guns, but the people who use them incorrectly. Has there been conversation about federal dollars for mental health and social support? The government is passing a $1.7 trillion-dollar budget with $858 billion being spent in defense and $45 billion toward the Ukraine and Russia War in 2023 alone. Has there been conversation regarding the social welfare of the support in raising students through public funds? If only there was a publicly funded system that could help train human beings to be empathetic, emotionally cognizant, and logical with the ability to be more analytical. Schools? Offer schools more money to create thinkers and leaders outside the community of "they"? Nope. "They" have made the conversation about gun rights and not about social development to help support the wellbeing of citizens who may purchase guns and make heinous choices. "They" have made abortions about "saving lives" as opposed to saving lives by making sure we have appropriate programs for the youth so they have a chance at life success. "They" keep the curriculum in schools very basic while the children in "their" homes are taught "family values" and are influenced by cultural capital that perpetuates the struggle for equity for all.

This is not a book about a race or color, but about the false notion of power and how it has been used against a specific group of people over time. My hope is that the book is read and all reflect on the possibility of respecting each person and the promotion of self-awareness, accountability, and action in the understanding that there is a false reality written by this oppressive spirit that we chose to obey despite the fact that we have the choice to live beyond promoted "realities" as we stretch toward our own "truths." My vision is that we continue to see these individuals in our community, in the media, in their businesses and networks, and in their elected positions as people who are infected with a spirit that runs rampant through them. As we see their anger and their tantrums on television, as we see their frantic efforts to lean into yelling and emotions to catch more attention and misguide followers, and as they slip into becoming more irrelevant, I ask that we forgive and move past them and grow into the humankind that we are destined to become. Let us love.

INTRODUCTION

Son, I see you daily and I hope for what is best for you. I give you space at times because I do not want to push too hard on that day because something tells me that today and now is not the "right" time. I am running out of time. I have watched you grow over the years now and, at times, I grow angry when I see what you have been turned into on my watch. I see you as a king. I know you have heard that from more than just me. There are many of those I see around you that attempt to sow seeds. The voices and the predicaments you have been in remind me of my journey. However, in you, I don't see an element that, in bias, I believe is needed for your success. You get tired of my voice. My long winded speeches. My moments of pulling you to the side to remind you how great you are. Some days you tolerate me more than others. Some days you come looking for me to hear the words or perhaps you just need a break from whatever else is causing you pain and frustration. Whether you are hiding or coming to the fighter's corner, I appreciate the blessing to invest in you. You parrot the words back on good days and there might be just enough consciousness in some of your music that trickles in positivity and an insightfulness to who you are meant to be versus who society at large is trying to mold you to become. Yet, there are some days we don't speak. You have a scowl on your face or have already been set off and no words of wisdom is going to bring you down from that point. Or is that what I tell myself because I am busy. I am busy jumping through hoops or other "pressing issues." I am trying to find that thing that gives me a false sense of security. I am trying to "stack" or grab the bag. I am working to put food on the table, but not protecting the ones who sit at it. Yet, I know we have had this talk and we should possibly talk about it again, often. How many times can we talk about the issues until you realize how mighty and powerful you are. Why don't you get that you are gifted regardless of your past circumstances? Then I grow angry and wear the same scowl you do. I see you lost. I see you broken. I see not enough resources in the richest country in the world to fix this lost person who could offer so much. I see an investment lost and I see us all waiting for something to change. Still in the fields. Still in shackles.

There are several researchers and vast amounts of people that speak of our plight. It took decades for people to have conversations regarding the trauma and the damage of generations of oppression. Some of that matters now because more than just one segment of the population has gun violence that is affecting them and their safety. However, now there is dialogue around the love you need to bring you back to the root of humanity. Yet, the conversation is often missed on the fact that you have been dehumanized. That you are who you are not by accident. That you stand before a judge, in the back of a police car, suspended and expelled from school, addicted to weed and vape juice, perhaps dealing with harsher chemicals such as prescription drugs based on the trends and what is the "escape" of choice, and perhaps having the occasional drink or too much, trained to be who you are. You are short-sighted and reactive to the now, but isn't that just being young? Sadly, you may not have the same time to be "young." You cannot be only instinctual and not the thinker you were born to be. You have to be aware of all that is happening and you cannot be apathetic to the larger concept of the struggle. You should notice the "saviors" that have come to "rescue" you while you are being researched and gawked at in schooling laboratories to save the "poor kids" for profit through book deals and speaking engagements for those same saviors. Catch phrases and trends like specific mindsets and your lack of grit. Others used phrases like "deficit thinking" to counter where you allowed yourself to remain. All the answers on how we can save the poor little broken kids from "that community" and forgetting to connect with your mindset of survival and your already present grit to overcome the odds to continue to exist daily and show up to school...ever. A school that on average has less quality facilities and less qualified teachers, but you persist in life. You leave the harsh realities of home to travel past gangs, drug dealers and deals, prostitutes, and violence and still make it to school, even if you are late. You get past the voices in your mind that explain to you how easy it would be to make fast money or focus on the flash and glamour of music or the lifestyle that is promoted by the lyrics and still sit in a classroom that doesn't speak to your need for success immediately and in the future.

    I see you daily. I see what you could have been and what we made you. I see the leader you still are. I see the greatness within you and the lack of direction to use that leadership. I see your potential and your gifts at work daily. I have become angry. Angry at circumstances that have you where you are even though there were other options for you. Angry that even in your highest level of success, you have to fight harder and lift most in America. You have to learn to be Black and successful while others just have to be successful. There is so much more. You are so much more. We are so much more. It didn't start with your birth. This was before you. This was before me.

KNOW YOUR HISTORY

It wasn't always this way. The "American Way" has only been so since the colonization of the country. Relatively, the United States of America is a young country in comparison to other empires that have come and gone and the countries that still stand. Yet the concept of the social construct of what we call power has been around since time itself. The idea that you have to possess something that others want in order for you to be more important has been established in our very DNA for survival. This desire to have more in the efforts to create a false sense of safety to protect the "more" you already have is interwoven in your biological necessity to survive. Historically, the more physical strength you had meant you could do what you wanted. The gathering of more items meant you were "safer" in times of drought or famine. Wealth, in whatever means calculated, meant you could buy or barter whatever you needed to keep you secure or healthy. This desire for "more" perpetuates a cycle that some blame capitalism, however this is a human, worldly flaw. To offer what you have in a sense of vulnerability and selflessness is an evolution that must be taught, modeled, respected, and nurtured. This need for "security" is the power of what many cultures of the past sold out for in collective efforts to have what "they" had. Cultures existed in our human history where the good of the whole was more than the good of the one. Quite often, based on history that was written, these open, sharing cultures, were "primitive."

Enslaving people in their own lands was not easy and Europeans struggled to trek into Africa to meet resistance of warriors to defend strangers in their lands. We sold our brethren into bondage for shiny objects and weaponry to "advance" our tribes as the Europeans were crafty enough to play our natural desires of greed and power against ourselves as the spirit of "they" is in us all. This code is ingrained in us still today as we as men will chase a vision at all cost to provide a sense of safety for our families, to build a sense of security for our people, to wear the latest fashions, drive the latest cars with the best rims, and have the newest phones all concerned with our emotional lie of safety as we forget to look toward sustainable security as a people. We innovate and create for the "people" only to sell out to the highest bidder to dance on the leash of investors and bastardize our creative gifts. Worse still, we stand silently by while cultural appropriation allows the newest generation of teens to "find themselves" for a few years and cash in on their privilege. We work to obtain something we cannot buy; the respect of others. All of our artists, athletes, and entrepreneurs that set trends and become popular with the influence of mass media in the eyes of America means nothing in comparison to those in perceived power's ability to change laws as they see fit and break them with even more ease. We hoped for the melting pot, but our specific flavor was never quite kept. We are allowed in the pot just long enough to add something special, but never good enough to partake in the digestion of what America was or is. As America's bay leaves, we have built the industries and the economy, we have added to the American dream a soundtrack worth listening to as other nations lean in close to sample what we offer and our royalties are past due. I digress.

My son, I see your struggle. I see that you try to remain tied to "our culture" that was defined for us in our efforts to etch out a life from their scraps. Much like the chitlins from the swine from our masters' fine cuts, we have created our own way of life. Our soul food is who we are. Our clothing, our music, our walk, our swagger. Good, bad, or "ghetto" the soul of who we are is rooted in the parts of life that many are not proud of or even scared to be. Our slang, our inflection, our "attitude," our anger. We have been raised over the centuries and created what America loves, but can't bring home. The world loves our rhythm and our blues. The world loves our jump and our jive. So many imitate our strut and stroll as we define "cool" in action and in word. There are many who are amazed and drawn to our fight and spirit. There are those who cheer and desire our ability to win in the spirit of battle. We are who we are because we have not only survived, but thrived in creating our ways.

This is our history.

Our ability to play chess in our lives. The strategy and fight and the refusal to give in and give up over the centuries. Our ancestors were enslaved because, to an extent, we didn't perish. Our Indigenous brothers and sisters in the Americas and islands fought in their ways and defined their paths and added to the Americas their flavors. Yet, our destiny was to fight from within and survive. Survive the beatings and the breakings. We endured the belittling of our men and rape of our women. We wiped away our tears and stood on our feet despite the nights of sobbing as our children were sold. We watched our kinsmen hang like strange fruit from the trees of the south. We marched for freedom. We protested with nonviolence and others of us took up arms in self-defense. We stood and created this definition of "blackness" that has indefinite depths.

Being "Black" cannot define who we are as much as works of art cannot be simply described as just a painting or sculpture. Sure, in its simplest form, a mountain is "just that" and a sunset is the rotation of the universe and the Earth. However, to those who truly understand that creation stirs the soul, being defined as "Black" is, at best, a lazy way to describe exponential layers of depths.

What I tell you in these next pages wasn't taught to me in history classes growing up through high school. Not even did we discuss these items in my Afro-American History elective that I was so proud to take in high school while watching the Autobiography of Malcolm X being presented on the big screen in the theaters and brothers and sisters wearing "X" hats and African colors infused with our hip-hop trends. I didn't learn this while obtaining my history undergraduate degree while buying into how "smart" I was sitting in the primarily white institution of my choice at the time. I learned this through my personal interest and effort to find a better "truth" to believe in as a Black man. Being more drawn to what "feels" right and what spoke to me, I worked through and continued to dig to learn more because our history is buried. Is there some old, white man with white hair and a red face purposely rejecting our history? I think there is some fear about offering full facts, but besides a few politicians who have become outspoken "heroes" for some, I do not buy into that particular conspiracy theory of oppression by design when it comes to hiding our history. I do believe wholeheartedly in bias, whether explicit or implicit, choices were made based on comfort and a specific perception. That comfort still remains among even those "woke" individuals fighting for "our" justice, but still keep us ignorant through schooling in the classrooms with filtered history. I also know there is a percentage of Americans with a certain mindset that are very comfortable with the status quo of "America" being the hero of its own story. I have never seen such a fear of open communication in our country than the newest trends of a section of Americans who rallied after the election of President Obama in his first run for presidency and mobilized since the Trump administration. There may be only one version of the "truth" that continues to be taught in schools if current and future generations do not take action with their votes on all levels of government. I digress again.

America was once young and was developing a "brand." We still see the efforts to retain that "brand" in various ways today. Police brutality is a fight for that "brand." Reverting back to a *great* time is a call to that "brand." A mob attacking the capital is a call to that brand. Creating legal obstacles to voting through government procedures is a call to that "brand" and the list continues. That "brand" is one of heroic tales of white men gambling their lives on a dream to start off on their own in a new land. These "heroic men" fought through brutal conditions to develop the land and established a government built by their will and their own two hands as they made powerful decisions in their *great* leadership. They too who resonate with this specific culture of America need something to believe in as well. Their fairy tales are filled with kings and queens, scholars and philosophers, Roman soldiers, Greek Spartans, and Italian voyagers. This sense of pride spills over into brave men "finding" a "new world" and carving out a new destiny against tyranny and oppression to follow a vision. This was the culture that controlled the narrative and the "truth." This "truth" is the "reality" this country thrived on religiously for centuries and the "reality" we still see so many cling to. The idea and teachings of these men setting out to start a new life in a strange land in the Americas has a place in the conversation of courage and boldness, yet we know the history doesn't start there.

Often glazed over through an argument of evolution versus creationism, is a fact that regardless of how humans arrived on the planet, our earliest remains of human skeletons were discovered in Africa. We also know that migration patterns have taken those earlier civilizations across the globe. Whether one wants to believe that our skin pigment and face, body, and hair features evolved over time to adapt to the various geographic locations such as Africa in comparison to Europe is an argument to be had, but we cannot argue the fact that the start of it all was Africa. Past being the birthplace of humanity, your classrooms and the curriculum agreed upon by the state does not spend ample time to discuss the history of African empires and the voyages of black-skinned navigators across the oceans. Perhaps it is government compliance, the ignorance of history teachers, or implicit bias that causes a primary focus on Eurocentric topics, but we miss the opportunity to talk about the development of math, architecture, science, and medicine in these Black empires. Maybe we just don't have the time in our classrooms to discuss the coincidental influences of temples and statues on the other side of the globe from Africa, yet we make time to mention Ferdinand Magellan, Amerigo Vanspuci, Christopher Columbus, etc.

Odd that your history did not begin until 1619 with the first arrival of Africans with the Dutch. Asians migrated to the Americas and traveled to the lands possibly over a thousand years before the Europeans and America's history books could start there. There are enough records to enter a conversation in the high possibility that African peoples also made the trip to the Americas in efforts of their exploration. We also have enough research to support that Vikings made the trip several times, but the American brand couldn't align with the Viking narrative in history books because Vikings weren't known for their civility. There are the Indigenous people of the land that in the last ten years or so have started to pop up for a chapter or so in school history books even though they lived on the lands called the Americas in its purest form centuries before European influence. Somehow, the American history we are taught and schools emphasizes starts with English colonialism in the late 1500s as we discuss social and government decisions that helped finance "exploration" from the British.

We are taught that in the early 1600s the first set of "indentured servants" who were African came to the first colonies of what would later be the United States of America. Yet we also know that African slavery in the New World started with the use of slaves brought from Africa to what later would become the Caribbean islands and Central and South America. Does shaving off 100 years allow us to minimize the effects of American enslavement of Black folks? Perhaps we don't want to teach the larger picture of the African slave trade in the United States of American because it isn't "our" history? However, if we are telling the story of America and its people, we should tell the entire story.

I could spend time here talking about the lack of people of color in general when it comes to your average history classes growing up as a student in the third grade to your senior year. I can say without reservation that there are teachers that do their best to squeeze in some sort of equitable effort to offer more color to the canvas as they paint their pictures of "truth" around the scope and sequence of the designed curriculum for the state. Yet I know these efforts are "work arounds" and cause teachers to work harder on specific areas of passion projects while the majority of teachers teach to the letter of the law and, more than likely, their own bias. Frankly, the Anglo-Saxon male is the protagonist and more often the "hero" in the curriculum offered in historical based classes for the American schooling system.

Would you think of yourself differently if you had access to different information? Would you think of others differently if an alternate version of the "truth" was offered? We know the process of schooling was developed to help train the American youth to be "good" Americans. We know this schooling design was originally designed for males of European descent. What I offer you son, is not a complete historical representation, but an opportunity to make sure you are offered a different version of the "truth" that you have been offered. There are deeper versions of this "truth" than this and wiser, more informed people than I am about the past. My goal is to stir your curiosity to help you dig deeper or at least know there is so much to who you are.

I want you to know that the Africans were not random tribes or uncultured people. Your ancestors were not uncivilized "beasts" that the Europeans had taken in the African to develop and free them of ignorance through use of the "Good Book." The very least of what was West Africa, where our ancestors were ripped away from, was a place of intricate tribal people that existed with rules and honor, traditions, and belief systems, economies, and laws. However, at its peak, the continent of Africa was a place with some of the strongest empires of our planet's history. Your history courses probably didn't offer much information of the Carthage empire that had a harbor for 220 ships for trade and sailing and discovery. Your teachers perhaps failed to mention the Aksum empire that was one of the first to adopt Christianity because this new knowledge to you would argue with the theory that Africans were uncivil and enslavers were bringing religion. The images in your classes perhaps did not connect with Mali, Songhai, and Ghana empires that were all west African and all were known for culture, art, music, knowledge, science, medicine, political advancement, and remarkable wealth. Indeed, we gave our brothers and sisters away in Africa to the slave traders because of our greed and ignorance. However, these people of Africa were not barbarians, heathens, or animals.

America will offer history in museums and teachers will speak of pharaohs, pyramids, and the process of embalming as if Egypt is not in Africa. Perhaps teachers that offer learning in schools are not aware of the Ethiopian empires that were in full civilized operation 1600 years before colonization of America by the British. An empire that accepted Christianity fourth century AD and an empire that also was ruled by a queen during a time during their existence. Historically, these empires were advanced before their time and even in the rural areas of Africa and places of tribes, these people were grounded, caring, people in their own right. The people of these lands had a well-established government, advanced architecture that included advanced mathematics, and a version of water flow that emulated plumbing before plumbing was invented. Would that have made a difference to you if your classmates in your primarily white classes learned of your people with these descriptors? Could that be a powerful lesson for schools filled with faces like yours? Would you see yourself differently if you saw your people's past as more than captured slaves from the jungle of Africa?

The "truths" continue as we miss the Moors in Spain, we don't mention the main character in Othello was darker skinned based on Shakespeare's writing, and the fact there are many shades of melanin in Michelangelo's The Last Judgment painting on the altar wall of the Sistine Chapel in the Vatican City of Rome. Perhaps if we see that Black folks were being saved during the rapture based on a 1400s painting we could start to agree that this demonizing of slaves was a made up opportunity to purposely subjugate, oppress, and almost destroy a people. Rhetoric was created to base a false sense of power by these traders and business owners to give birth to a free labor source and a new commodity in the trading of human beings. A triangular trading system that led to the near thirteen million Africans being torn from their families, homes, traditions and customs, languages, safety and sanity in being brought to the Americas and neighboring islands.

As we talk more about slavery, I want you to think about the definition of genocide. In 2021, we were fortunate enough to have a president in President Joe Biden to address the Ottoman era Armenian genocide. During a statement President Biden stated, "... one and a half million Armenians were deported, massacred, or marched to their deaths in a campaign of extermination." Based on the definition of genocide found in the agreement via the United Nations:

As presented in the Convention, genocide means any of the following acts committed with intent to destroy, in whole or in part, a national, ethnical, racial or religious group, as such:

- Killing members of the group;
- Causing serious bodily or mental harm to members of the group;
- Deliberately inflicting on the group conditions of life calculated to bring about its physical destruction in whole or in part;
- Imposing measures intended to prevent births within the group;
- Forcibly transferring children of the group to another group.

Mind you though, as I write this to you in 2023, the United States of American nor the United Nations have admitted that slavery was genocide. My son, I offer you information for you to form your own "truth."

Data approximates that there were two million slaves lost during the voyages. Consider, all of the records were not recorded as it would be almost impossible to dissect the "collateral damage" of the capture, trade, travel, and embarking with the "curious cargo" of the Negro. However, to the best historical account two million slaves perished in the migration from their original land to the "New World." Which allows us to further accept, based on cargo records, that approximately ten million slaves from Africa were brought in shackles to North, Central, and South America and the neighboring islands. I want you to understand the important distinction that has been created for us in our schooling. Slaves were brought to the south to be used as forced labor in the fields and "domestic" help. Our "truth" is as if the northern colonies did not profit from this "peculiar institution." Furthermore, "our" history of the United States of America does not offer the details of the African slave that was forced onto the lands of Jamaica, Puerto Rico and the various Caribbean islands, Hispaniola which later became the Dominican Republic and Haiti, and the regions included in Central and South America. A fact that is often missed in your history courses is that approximately 400,000 slaves in the colonized areas of what is now the eastern coasts of the United States of America and millions more were transported to the variety of other areas I mentioned earlier. This fact is further solidified as we see that the US has a current population of 15 percent with those that identify as "Black" or Afro-American" and Brazil has the largest "Black" population outside of African countries. Would the color of your skin be seen differently if you were connected with a "truth" that your bloodline is directly connected with so many "other" cultures around these United States? That the beauty that is all around us in the islands and Mexico, Central and South America also runs in your DNA? Could it be possible that "power" would be perceived differently if the 15 percent was united with not only those considered of African descent of the Western Hemisphere, but those who have African genes at higher percentages that would denote a Black person a slave in the US in the 1600s? What if we embraced all of the brothers and sisters globally in a Pan-African movement? Would Black History month be seen differently?

I believe you have seen enough of the enslavement of the African to have a shallow understanding of the atrocity of the practice of African slavery by the European peoples. Though, I fear the conversation of the enslavement of African people to bring to the New World will one day become a passing paragraph in a history book. I can see how the details will become watered down as the events now have been decreased in conversation in classrooms and in time spent regarding the topic in several states. I remember there was a strong campaign when I was growing up regarding the Holocaust and seeing the phrase "Never Forget" on posters and t-shirts and I asked, "How would forgetting such a horrific event in history be possible?" If you control the schools and what is learned, you control the "truth" and what is reality. There are plenty of resources to get a glimpse into the torture African slaves endured in the New World of North, Central, and South America and the various surrounding islands. You can perform a quick search on your phone to see dreadful images that are being muted by politicians because of their shame. I won't spend time talking about it, but an image forever stained in my imagination comes from the Autobiography of Frederick Douglass as he speaks of particular beating he witnessed in his youth as a slave:

Before he commenced whipping Aunt Hester, [the master] took her to the kitchen, and stripped her from neck to waist, leaving her neck, shoulders, and back, entirely naked. He then told her to cross her hands, calling her at the same time a d——d b——h. After crossing her hands, he tied them with a strong rope, and led her to a stool under a large hook in the joist, put in for the purpose. He made her get upon the stool, and tied her hands to the hook. She now stood fair for his infernal purpose. Her arms were stretched up at their full length, so that she stood upon the ends of her toes. He then said to her, "Now, you d——d b——h, I'll learn you how to disobey my orders!" and after rolling up his sleeves, he commenced to lay on the heavy cowskin, and soon the warm, red blood (amid heart-rending shrieks from her, and horrid oaths from him) came dripping to the floor. I was so terrified and horror-stricken at the sight, that I hid myself in a closet, and dared not venture out till long after the bloody transaction was over.

Even prior to the recent heightened concern of an exposure to the facts of all things nonwhite history in America, we missed telling a full list of information to students in schools. I am sure they didn't teach that the same types of Africans that are the descendants of Black Americans also landed in Jamaica and Hispaniola (Haiti and the Dominican Republic). If you knew that, perhaps it would have mattered more to you that Jamaica was able to remove itself from British rule recently freeing itself from colonization after all of this time. Maybe it would matter more to you that Haiti was the land of a slave revolt that struck fear in the heart of all plantation owners in the colonies, was later taxed by the French and occupied by America less than 100 years ago which continues to be one reason for their inability to become a stronger country. The country was once known for its remarkable natural resources and easily could have remained a wealthy nation without the economic oppression placed by larger, wealthier, and whiter countries. Countries that are occupied by darker skinned citizens are more likely to be oppressed and suppressed by outside nations and disregarded by the United Nations although these same countries of darker skinned have the natural resources from which outside countries and governments are profiting.

Could the Black and brown communities form better relationships if we were taught that the bloodlines in what are considered "Latin" countries are filled with African DNA? Perhaps it is too much truth to offer by noting that colonists from Spain were free to have sex with the local Indigenous people, but were forbidden to marry? The colonists in actuality did both thus creating the bloodlines that we see today throughout the islands and South and Central America. Would it be worth knowing that Cuba was once so Black dominated that America feared the lands during the era of slavery because the slave to owner ratio was so uneven? Would it be worth knowing that Spain shipped thousands of men to the country of Cuba for "free land" and to "whiten" the peoples in the early 1900s? Brazil, Portugal, Columbia, Mexico and more all had slaves with rebellious histories with uprisings and later Black citizens and communities that lived as equals and the African bloodline flows through all of the countries and its citizens. Yet, there is division in an attempt to define ourselves more like those who have oppressed us because their identity is the identity of perceived power and security and safety.

I trust that you have seen movies and images of pain and suffering of slaves traveling across the Atlantic and the conditions of slave life in the Americas. You have some understanding of the auction blocks, the beatings, the murder, the rape, and the overall dehumanization of the African peoples in the western civilization. I had once seen some schooling effort to do better with offering more lessons on these practices as the United States started to peel back more layers of the trauma it has caused on several cultures. Yet, I have also seen a fear recently growing in speaking with too much honesty in classrooms and the fear of parents dealing with the awkward truths of the guilt of this country's labor pain carried by so many various peoples other than the colonists and settlers.

Hence the need, we of the Black community need to have these conversations with each other and future generations and allow others who have the intentions of equity to join the conversations in the movement we create. Even if you have to get these "facts" to consider that are coming to you in the form of memes and blurbs in social media, that is more than what I was taught as a historian in the classroom.

I will say again, this is not about harboring resentment against a people or building on a premise of separatism. This is for you to better understand the lift that is needed to achieve what you may perceive as success. All the things you have been taught, "....don't be on time, be early...be the hardest workers in the room...don't quit...hard work pays off...if you want it, you have to go after it..." still remains, but the reality is, you are competing in an inequitable system. A system that clearly says, based on empirical quantitative research, that white males have an advantage in America based on explicit and implicit bias and the psychology having a "home field" advantage. Were all white males born with silver spoons and silk bibs? No. Have ancestors of Anglo-Saxon communities struggled? Yes. Your history books have told you all about the immigrant Europeans from various countries and cultures who have "made it" despite the odds. Are there poor white people, uneducated white people, white people in jails? Yes, yes, and yes. However, whether it is the trailer park, the Appalachian south, a rural community, or a white brother or sister sharing residence in the "hoods" of America, the white male has the better odds to turn their life for the better. This is not my opinion, this is based on numbers and averages. Whether this systemic situation across the globe against African people is conscious or subconscious, whether America has an open bias against people of African descent, specifically Black people of the Americas, or the American race problem is implicit, our collective lack of response to the evils set before us generations ago is on purpose because as a human race we cannot agree to love.

All of the complications in the external world that we call society in the Americas, the Black people of America have an internal conflict. There are several struggles that are happening within the minds and spirits of Black people as they wrestle with the various stereotypes that we will talk about later in regard to Black men. Unlike those who have physical features that have been characteristically identified as our American forefathers, Black people have to wrestle with a psychology that connects with a list of reactions from trauma, past and current media messages creating an unfavorable narrative, and the lift of making choices that may not be aligned with what has been accepted by popular Black culture. There is just more weight on the bar as we try to lift ourselves up out of the hole we were tossed in centuries ago. However, it is our weight to lift to become stronger and help others with our positions of strength.

This is a "Black Community" problem as our murder, drug use and sales, and imprisonment rates all grow in trends. Meanwhile, Black men remain in the lowest percentile to complete a post high school program to improve our individual living opportunities which include trade school of any kind. Our communities have higher rates of infant mortality and lower averages of years of life. While we live shorter than average life spans, we have a higher potential for diabetes, heart disease, stroke, obesity, unemployment, and various types of physical abuse. Again, not opinions, but quantitative data that tells the averages based on hard facts on the 15 percent of the American population. The lift is hard. The lift is inequitable. Yet, as much as you have to work twice as hard to have half of what they got, you can do it.

A disconnect from the tribes, a geographic challenge, and a refusal to teach us has been an impactful tool for the status quo for

500 years. Your history is more than that of a United States slave and your people are vast, not monolithic. However, I don't want you to know these not so random facts and alienate you from those that don't share your skin complexion. Afterall, the majority of whites in America didn't own slaves because they could not afford them. The wealthy owned slaves and that is a fact that is often forgotten. Racism was and still is taught. The masses accepted racism because those who were perceived to have power and security and safety used the color of our skin to push an agenda to build more wealth through evil subjugation. There is no single race that is controlled by this mindset or spirit. This greed and fear runs rampant in a system of capitalism with no conscience. You should know that people identified slavery as a status symbol connected the practice with being wealthy, which connects to security and power. The Negro was bought and sold by Indigenous tribes of America and free Black people of the early colonial times were trying, as all were, to figure out their perception of the peculiar institution and social norm. To many, owning a slave was an advancement and step up in the social ladder. Various people including, but not limited to, white landowners who were not rich, who struggled feeding their families, who had dreams, aspired to have all that the wealthy had. However, whiteness was marketed as a social advancement as well and in this mode of survival the weak needed to be determined and the color of the skin was the identifier because those who controlled the message could use it to create a narrative of influence and authority. This concept of "might makes right" is barbaric and continues to be the cornerstone of oppression.

Would it affect you hearing as a young person that the same countries that have faces that look like yours still suffer from social and economic oppression from faces and sentiment that had established slavery? People with your bloodline are still picking cotton for pennies on the dollar from sunrise to sunset. Does it resonate with you at all that, regardless of ethnicity, much of the world treats those with more melanin in their skin as a far lower class citizen? Is it odd to you that a color based class system remains in places where darker skin affects the mindsets of those of the more European type skin complexion into the belief that they are the chosen people? One could say the world has been manipulating minds against the browner and blacker skin types since exploration of the lands began.

I know your American History classes in school have only 185 days or so to squeeze in the most important information. I also know you take American History and/or a Social Studies curriculum throughout the majority of your schooling years so there is plenty of time. Plenty of time to discuss that this beautiful country is remarkably diverse. Plenty of time to acknowledge the history of the descendants of Europeans with a slight introduction into the early ages of Europe including the empires of the Greeks, Romans, and British while also offering insight of the Celtic cultures and Vikings. Teachers could discuss the evolution of government and economy while having a conversation regarding the caste system and the divisions in society. There would be a time to discuss the royalty of the times to the indentured slaves and even the barbarians, pirates, and savages of the years to allow students to see there were more than philosophers, scholars, and kings and queens in the land of one of our mother continents. We could spend time discussing with students the prehistory of Asia and the vast empires that led for over a century and their advancement in war and art. We could spend time in American History classes speaking of the Asian dynasties and the culture of the land that our students should broaden their horizons to and our Asian family members could celebrate.

Our classrooms could take time in their American History to learn about the Aztec and Incan empires and their stretch into what we call the United States of America now down into the tips of South America and acknowledge the architectural advancements and their use of agriculture based on a calendar before the modern day calendar and time system. Dare I say, we could discuss in American History courses the people of the land before we colonized which would include the various peoples of the land including the native people of Hawaii that were displaced less than 100 years ago. We can talk about the kings and queens of these nations, the people's connection with community and their environment and their systems of trade and coexistence with nature with its destruction.

And yes, we could talk about Africa during the pre-colonial and colonial times of what we call the United States today. We could talk about the government, the economy, social systems, the kings and queens, and even their use of "slaves." We could talk about the beauty that European travelers were mystified by and the fact that many of the traditions we see in historical African tribes were remarkably similar throughout the globe besides Europe which leans into the theory of African travel as we see symbolic identifiers in the Americas connecting to African interaction. We could even talk about the fact that some of the earliest fossils and artifacts of mankind have been found in Africa.

We are a people of mixed ancestry and American history did not start in the 1600. The experiment of the colonies started at a specific time and we have grown into a mighty nation with many advancements as a people, but we also have our points of reflection and areas of darkness in which we hope to truly grow from in our further development.

Yet, as I watch and read the news about how we are struggling in America with the concept of Critical Race Theory, I am not surprised. I am not surprised that there is an actual uprising from the vast majority of those who historically held what has been perceived as power in this country to do all they can to limit the voice of the oppressed. There is a strategic effort to limit our truth to be told in America's classrooms. Much as the American slaves were to be kept ignorant of the success of Toussaint Louverture due to a fear of a larger slave rebellion, you are to be kept ignorant of the various historic facts of the African diaspora. While reading about the Holocaust and atrocities that occurred in Germany, we should also learn of the ten million Africans murdered in Congo by the regime of Leopold II. How would your mindset be changed or the mindset of all Americans be changed if they learned slavery wasn't abolished one day and we were free and united as a country the next? How would America change if while sitting in the classrooms of schools students learned that at one point after slavery various communities in various states had thriving Black-owned businesses and for the first time ever in American history there were Black politicians in the south? Would education matter to the Black community more if we knew one of the first efforts of our free people was to establish public schools that were taught by both white and Black educators? Would it matter that poor whites were taught based on propaganda and sensationalism of rich, white men that the free Black person was a threat to the American dream for the average white person? What if students were reading in history books that after slavery was abolished, it was basically a crime to be Black and we found ourselves being jailed for years for various crimes such as not having a job and walking next to train tracks and then, as slavery loophole, due to the 13th Amendment in the United States Constitution reads, "Neither slavery nor involuntary servitude, except as a punishment for crime..." ?

Are you thinking now, son? Allow me to help you as I also offer you the fact that states in the south gained what would be today millions of dollars per year based on "Convict Leasing" with the stronger the Negro equating a higher rate. Yet, your history books say America "freed" the slave and abolished this stain on our country. Yes indeed, this occurred under the Union with the North fully aware...our saviors. Perhaps there weren't enough lawyers to argue in the southern states who owned the responsibilities of the court systems. Perhaps free labor and regular steel development lined enough pockets in both the North and South to turn a blind eye to the Black men enduring the new slavery. Yes, chains were used to shackle these men. Yes, they were beaten with whips. Yes many died from the work. Some historians theorize that this was worse for the Black community as slaves had more value to the individual slave holder than Black men did to the businessmen involved in Convict Leasing. The philosophy of this specific type of business man was to "use up" the Negro and backload with the next batch at no cost to the company. In addition to the steady supply of "criminals" in the Black community there was also the Black boy, as a third of these camps were made of brothers under the age of sixteen. I could rest here and make a connection to the present date percentage imbalance in our current prison system, but I will leave that to you to continue the research. To engage in the empirical data that states that our low percentage of citizenship in America at 15 percent is represented by almost triple in the prisons today which is the same ratio of imprisonment in the conditions of Convict Leasing. This system that I have offered you today only changes to Chain Gangs and then to what we call now our efforts of behavior reform. Crime is wrong. Justice should be offered and there should be a form of accountability. However, keep an eye out for equity in sentencing. Read the data on the inconsistencies of charges for the same crime involving different races.

    1865 did not free the Negro after the end of the Civil War, but it did end legalized slavery. Know that the majority of our entire population lived in the most oppressive and violent areas for the Black person well into the 1940s, which opened, eventually, to the Civil Rights Movement with the next chapter of challenges. Your grandparents were born in the south in the 1950s. Slavery started 500 years ago in the Americas. Forms of slavery were legal through loopholes almost half way through the 1900s. We are not that far removed from what America tries to run from which means there are people alive today that are a generation removed from slavery and perhaps even remember a "good," Black house worker or farm hand that was "like family." Redefine your "truth."

Know that the Black family for generations has been torn apart, yet we still strive to come together. Black men were ripped from their families to work like a slave regardless of the laws being bent. It was the Black man that was sold off to another plantation with no regard to a "marriage ceremony" that occurred with the slave master present on their grounds earlier. Black men and women that were ripped from the shores from Africa to work in the strange and foreign lands across the waters. Black women were forced to lay with white, male slave owners, overseers, and traders only to have their "illegitimate" children shipped away or in some cases beaten for their representation of a white husband being unfaithful. Black women found strength to work in the fields and in the house and still try to lift up their own families and the Black man on the plantation. This is all compounded on the fact that we were originally from several different tribes from Africa with separate languages and traditions. The lift is hard and you should know what is ahead. Definitely not like our past, but we are still far from free. There is work to do.

I walk every morning to the Mississippi River and sense the spirits of the past. I walk by to see the sun rise over the very courthouse that legally, based on American law, declared Black slaves as property and not people. I read several other signs that clearly mark the similar location as the crux of trade and westward expansion. I touch the river and remind myself that we were sold and bought in Missouri to be shipped down that river to other plantations. I touch the river to remind myself of the blood that was shed and sweat and tears that dripped through those waters as slaves worked in these waters as well as used the waters in efforts to be free. I am reminded that as far as we may have come, our gains have been incremental and only allowed by our oppressors. I will tell you as much as I was excited to see President Barack Obama as our president for two terms, I am glad we had someone like Donald Trump represent a truth that rests in America's DNA. To see the ability of that dormant gene in our country to ring true with the slightest push has been difficult, but needed. To see that the same lever that was pulled during the times of slavery, during Reconstruction, and during the Civil Rights Movement is still there allows us to see that the struggle continues. The subculture of a certain type of person that has perceived power and can cause others to rally behind a rhetoric because they also want that perception of power much as the rallies in history that lead to so much misery, pain, and death still lives and is very strong. We cannot rest as if we "made it."

 I read hate and fear in between the lines of the argument of Critical Race Theory. The same ignorance that caused rural white men, women, and children to hate the Negro is being born again in plain sight. There are children and teenagers that are bringing the fear and hate that they are picking up from home conversations or perhaps they see it as all good fun as they yell slurs at their classmates. Our history cannot be taught without posing a threat to the comfort of others. There is a fear that if we were to offer all students options in their decision-making with a full glimpse into our country's history, all of our children might find common ground and see each other as human beings. I have seen a growing understanding in the youth and there are opportunities in our evolution of our country through generations. Collectively, we are understanding that this is less about color and race and more about a specific percentage of the population controlling the narrative and opportunities to own a specific track to life wellness. Moreover, the freedoms were set aside only for white men and typically for white men with financial resources in which they wanted to keep for themselves. A fear that is real and almost understood as the status quo that is possessed by this oppressive spirit is concerned with all Americans discovering a truth that divisions such as race and color and gender is used as a tool to keep us separated and distracted while the color green tends to be the color of utmost importance for those in perceived power.

Why else would we refuse to dig into the various facts that we have to offer in American history and the happenings throughout the centuries? Not enough time in the classrooms perhaps? Ah, but the states decide the standards and school boards determine the curriculum in their adoption and school districts develop the scope and sequence that sets the pace. Yet in virtually all-Black districts, we teach the same rhetoric. As we sit in footprints that are liberal and "woke" with "diversity" waved as a banner, students sit in classrooms and are taught that America has always been "right" and always will be and we dare not question the status quo. We spend time on George Washington Carver and peanuts in middle schools and we discuss Manifest Destiny as the growth of our mighty nation opposed to imperialistic land grabs and the displacement of entire civilizations.

We speak of Christopher Columbus and Hernan Cotez in our American History courses. Both of these men were heavily involved in the exploration of the Americas from Europe which is important to those who adopt the curriculum. However, we cannot read that the slaves in Mexico were able to rebel and create perhaps the first African based town in the western hemisphere as Cortez could not overcome the slave rebels' guerrilla warfare. We don't speak about the Arawak, their demise brought on the newcomers from Spain, and the birth of African slavery in the Americas including the various islands. Are we to believe these conversation of conquest were pleasant agreements and there was no murder, no rape, no captives of locals and plundering of goods? We know by the writings of Bartolome De Las Casas of the 1500 exploits that the "..natives were easily subdued, but perished quickly and were not ideal for work desired...." The establishment of the new lands in the Americas was founded on pain, blood, and deaths of entire groups of people yet we cannot agree to that as it would lead to a conversation of genocide, an issue of guilt connected to a particular spirit, and perhaps even talks of restitution.

Making it "Black" or "white" has made it easier for the categorization of the struggle. The lie that the "blacker" the skin the deeper the sin has been perpetuated around the globe and accepted by various cultures because "white made right." Yet, the ideals are shifting with each generation. As those historically in power cling onto every fiber of their rope they can, we are coming out of the noose we have been hanging by since the birth of the Transatlantic trade of Africans to the New World. An evolution of culture 500 years plus to create an opportunity where we can sit and listen to one another and respect the challenges before us and appreciate the strengths we all offer as intellectual beings that can be rational among our ability to empathize and analyze.

The lies "they" used as propaganda to manipulate the emotions of other individuals to create a "reality" in which we still fight to free ourselves from today should be compared to any other ruthless dictator and/or authoritarian that we typically, rightfully, shake a finger toward. We read in our World History textbooks of those evil empires and their heinous acts, but because there is no one person to blame, a system of persons to share the charge, we ignore the murders and mass murders, rape, mutilation, deliberate subjugation, psychological destruction, etc. that continues to hinder our country to grow as a people. I see your anger and it is righteous. You should be angry, but your frustrations and emotions are mismanaged. Your anger comes from generations of creating lives out of situations not worth living. Situations that created our food, our style, our music, our art, our culture over the decades and generations that we gracefully shared while offering America soul.

Since the drum beats, singing, and dancing from slaves, to spiritually connected ballads from the heavens in hymns we built the rhythms of the country into the development of the blues, to rhythm and blues and jazz that was bellowed from New Orleans through major cities into the clubs in Harlem. It was during these "free times" where "Black" people gained more layers to the archetype that was built for them during slavery. Specifically, for our conversation, the "Black" male gained a variety of new identities that more often than not were not to our favor. During slavery times the Black male ranged from the jungle animal with beast-like strength and endurance to slothful oaf. The Black man was not intelligent, yet in some circumstances crafty and smart enough to plot and scheme as needed. We were "rhythmic" people that loved a good song or "jig" and if we were to be gifted with an instrument we could play for the entertainment of the farm or in some cases the guests in the "big house." Our talents were often portrayed for the entertainment of whites of both the south and north. Yes, as a reminder during times of slavery, northern parts of America was not a magical place where racism and prejudice were left behind in all of the "progression" of the North. Negros were "brought out" to sing a tune, dance a jig, and even fight for the entertainment of white onlookers in both the south and north. True indeed there was a layer of patronage in the North, but reality, in both the South and the North we were aiming for the approval of those in perceived power and saying "no" wasn't always an afforded freedom for the Negro in the North either. The "Good Nigger" was the one that respected their role and the "kindness" of the white people offering our people "opportunities" to show talent and make promoters and slave masters proud.

In all that we did as Black men, our goal was to define our worth. We knew we had something of value to offer and despite the brutal beatings and taunting that we saw our grandfathers, fathers, uncles, and otherwise male role models take, we knew that we were talented and gifted with something to offer human kind. There was strength in the spirit of the Black men throughout history. Proper reflection could allow schools and scholars to dig into the strengths our collective human spirit has in the ability to overcome adversity toward a utopian vision of peace and joy. Black men would go on to find various angles to prove their worth and the military eventually would be an early opportunity outside of manual labor and periodic entertainment.

Black men have been in the military as long as America needed defense which is before we were considered America. You may or may not remember the French and Indian War or the Seven Year War from your history class. Same war, but different names and something you probably didn't care about during class if they spent any time on it. It was a war directly connected to a larger battle between the French and the British in both of their efforts to conquer the globe. The French and the British were fighting over land they were both stealing from the original Indigenous peoples which were various tribes located in North America. The Indigenous tribes sided with the French for the most part believing the French were the lesser of two evils and the British, being outnumbered by the French and their tribe allies, recruited both free Black men and the enslaved to fight a war in a country that had no desire to see them as equals in the various colonies. Arming Black men who were stolen from their country of origin to fight against tribes of people in efforts to steal their land is an amazing feat developed by the British that causes me to shake my head as I tell you this, but also it connects to the resolve of Black citizens once again. We did this to prove our quality and hopefully gain equality. Sure some took off when the chance allowed and ran for whatever the direction we thought "freedom" presented itself, but the majority of the Black men enlisted and drafted into the French and Indian War fought and fought hard in all circumstances as laborers and soldiers. We fought with less in our hands, on our backs with less clothes, and in our stomachs with less food offered to us. We fought for our dream. Yet, when the war ended with a peace treaty and the British laid claim to more North American land based on the colonists' conquest, Blacks folks just offered colonists more land for us to exist on as less than human in the eyes of the "owners." Black men went back to work as slaves in most cases, but with a new understanding for what a person can do when given the opportunity.

More and more history teachers and history lessons in schools offered the new "truth" of Crispus Attucks in the American Revolution so I am sure you were proud to know that a Black man was shot in a war for the freedoms of white slave owners and others who mostly did not see Black people as equals. Yet, there probably wasn't time in those history lessons to mention the interesting struggle colonists had with once again arming Black men, specifically slaves. The decision was basically made in desperation as we were used to help increase the manpower for the colonists. Once again, we rose to the occasion through all-Black infantry and even integrated units united to overcome our "oppressors." Indeed, during these times, colonists started to sniff out the hypocrisy and energy for equality for all in philosophy grew in their minds as the thought of being more human evolved in the minds of more white colonists. Yet, slavery persisted as political and economic underpinning for colonies including the northern ones. However, the Black man continued to define himself in the eyes of all. Becoming more of a threat to some as our abilities were becoming more evident, to others, the Black man was evolving before the eyes of all. Black men were fighting with strength of the body and spirit alongside white men. Men of all colors were carrying each other to safety and soldiers were fighting to win the war, but more importantly, see another day. Black men were more dispensable, but their valor later earned such respect that a percentage of those enslaved gained their freedom for their efforts. However, transforming the "reality" takes time.

As you may be asking, "what does all of this have to do with me as someone who is considered by society to be a Black male in the present times?" I want to help you understand not just the events of the past, but how the events of the past formed the mindsets of so much in today's world. I am hoping that if you read this, you and others like you who want a real change can have the bold conversations to shift our bias in regards of Black males. The equality we seek won't happen from tipping over police cars and looting when we are angry or outraged. Our equality comes when we all consistently grow and unite as a people and hopefully your generation can strategically stay on the right path.

It is important to know that with each war time effort, Black men inched toward a shift in the minds of western civilization and in some cases the world. It's necessary for you to understand that from the times of slavery when we were not considered human beings in the eyes of many in what would be America through the Civil Rights Movement which was occurring during the Vietnam War, Black men were called upon to fight for the rights of those that believed in the American dream even though we did not have access to it. Our sacrifice added to the image of the Black man, yet we still were not enough to be valued as people.

War after war, we came back to a country with a government that could not fully support our dreams. Our desires to be men and provide for our wives and for our children remained unfulfilled. To be able to look other men, regardless of color or social status, in the eyes should be a simple request for fighting for the advancement of the country that we share, but it was not afforded to us regardless of Crispus Attucks of the Revolution, the Free Men on Color of the War of 1812, and almost 200,000 Black soldiers in the Civil War. We were used as tools or dogs to aid oppression and imperialism through a dream to be like our oppressors. As the Buffalo Soldiers fought in Indian Campaigns and we battled in the Spanish American War to expand territories for economic gain, we were only setting up opportunities for more wealth that we would not see. Our Black soldiers were dying on the front lines in battles for land that we would later work on, but not freely walk through with our heads held high and definitely not own.

We continued to fight generation after generation for "our country" as Black men. As we fought, our self-confidence grew as men and as a people as we learned more of our abilities and refuted lies that were told to us and we believed. Lies that made us believe that we were not intelligent enough to equal the abilities of white men were dispelled in the battle fields and Black men had a stronger sense of pride with the new evidence witnessed. Additionally, as there are no atheists in foxholes during times of battles of war, white men directly and indirectly involved with our armed forces efforts continuously witnessed the abilities and spirit of the Black soldier. The Black man was growing in value as a human being in the eyes of a percentage of Americans. A percentage that grew in our country and in the eyes of the "enemy" in other countries as well as more and more as both sides of the battle lines witnessed the efforts of the Black male soldier despite them typically receiving less food, shelter, less clothing, and the less likelihood of survival in specific battles. As World War I continued with America joining the armed forces in 1917, Black people were still not equal and free to live as true citizens of the United States of America. Even though we were "free" by 1865, had a constitutional right to vote by 1870, and had fought in every war effort of America, our armed forces still met the Black soldier with racism, oppression, and aggression. Fighting for more of our dignity and respect from our own country, we signed up as Black men to fight in other nations against those that had more respect for our ethnicity than America at that time. Your history books may not offer you information regarding the group of Black troops that left for battle. You should know that Black men enlisting in the war efforts of World War I were brought on for labor and kitchen work and not as soldiers. To reduce racial tension based on a brutal attack from white American soldiers assaulting a fellow Black soldier, several all-Black regiments were sent to France's aid to battle the Germans. Although almost half of the 3000 Black soldiers were killed in battle, none were captured, and the group never gave up their ground. This group saw more continuous combat than any other troops during the war and also had the most casualties. However, their ferocious fighting led to the Germans calling these troops the "Hellfighters."

There is much more to be said about the efforts of Black men and women in the armed forces, but to learn more if you are interested, you will need to continue the research on your own. I will offer you a little more insight about our soldiers in the following pages, but I wanted you understand a little of the efforts to fight for "our" country since we were still considered property and into later times for you to start to consider our love for the country that would not collectively offer freedoms we were dying for in the wars. You will find an increasing amount of Black participation both men and women as you research World War II, the Korean War, and the Vietnam War all before there was a further push for our "equality" in America. Amazingly, the battle the soldiers fought regardless of opposition in the wars was about fighting for a position of equality in the minds of others. Over the centuries soldiers of color have proven time and time again the value and abilities of Black men and women. Today, we know that one path to the middle class for any Black man is more viable with serving in the armed forces, yet we rarely take the opportunity perhaps because we refuse to have someone yelling at us in bootcamp or perhaps we are afraid of the discipline and the expectations placed before us. However, my goal here was to make sure you understood a fraction of the history of what helped determine the "reality" and image of the Black man in America through the Reconstruction era of 1863 to 1877 to the early 1900s. There is much more history to the development of Black men, but my point made here was for you to recognize perhaps what you did not know based on missed lessons from school and our missed conversations.

 Yet, by 1865, we were "free" to become all that America would allow us to be as men. Men who could not read. Men who could not earn wages to feed himself let alone his family. Men who could not look authority, anyone white, in the eye. Men who had to "mind their tone." Yes, let's celebrate our "freedom." In our pain, trials, and tribulations, the culture of Black men continued to be defined. As

Black families struggled because the Black man was being jailed for laws created for free labor and wandering the lands to find the American dream, there was rising sentiment about the Black male. Fear is a vacuum that interrupts the opportunity for love. Fearful of losing positions of power, those of the status quo, politicians, media, and those with wealth needed to caricaturize and demonize the Black male to galvanize lower class whites as pawns in a strategy to oppress Blacks to hold them as cheap labor options. Thus, there was more energy to create the Black man as a "brute" and a savage. A fierce animal that hunts white women, the former male slave known as a "Buck" was now free to prowl and violate the peace of mind of white people.

Yet, just like we have taken so much and made it our own, Black men did the same with the images that were forced upon us. Somehow, in the shadows of being stereotyped as being too simple and childlike to learn, lazy, coonish, dimwitted, barbaric, knee-slappin', singing, and dancing Negroes, we figured a way to have style and swagger. We took what we were given and connected it with our ancestral DNA and made our struggle a part of our own culture as we walked and talked in society and created what would become who we were as Black men. As much as there was a narrative of our negative traits, we forged an identity through our tenacity and endurance in all the facets of society we could force ourselves into and we ran with every opportunity not only as individuals, but representation of our entire race of people in America.

The Reconstruction era ended for many reasons, but they all take root in the fear of losing "power." That very same false sense of security I spoke of earlier crept into politics and in the minds of voters, specifically Democrats. Remember, Republicans were historically the champions for the removal of slavery. We could spend time here and talk about the fact the British ended their support of the slave trade in 1807 and almost 60 years later America was trying to play with the major players of the world such as the countries in Europe that evolved the concept of owning another person and the new cool thing was industry, machines, automation, and "progressive thinking," but I don't want to distract you from the development of the Black man during these times. However, you should know that there was an Enlightenment period in Europe that also influenced the thinking of those considered in power throughout both the continent of Europe and the young country of America. Dangerously, the concept of slavery was being challenged and the experiment of questioning authority and freedom to all was starting to occur. Our very country was founded based on the Enlightenment, but losing free labor was a different conversation. This small seed of thought in the minds of the right people led to offering Black people opportunities in small corners of Europe and the colonies that would become the United State of America. These opportunities led to our early Black scholars, inventors, artists, and athletes prior to the Civil War and helped advance Black people after the Civil War into the 1900s. I want to pause here and make sure I remind you that the right spirited, minded, and hearted white people helped move us forward in these efforts. An opportunity to unite and move people in the spirit of love is a marvelous thing to witness.

It was during these times that Black men such as Marcus Garvey, Booker T. Washington, W.E.B. DuBois, George Washington Carver, Carter G. Woodson, and more were able to question America on its values and what it considered a Black man was. I should also remind you that these are times when several Black women excelled despite the odds that were greater in some ways being both Black and woman. Overall, the Negro was a part of society and as a component of society we continued to add our flavor to the American way. I often wonder how much further we would be as a country if we would have truly accepted and embraced Black people as equal citizens after the Civil War. It's unfair for me to ask a large portion of a group of people to change their entire culture overnight, but what if there wasn't so much resistance? What if we were one country, under God, and indivisible in the past? Now? I digress. The early 1900s, the Black male identity was being formed and we as Black men had options with far fewer boundaries now more than ever. Don't get me wrong, there were plenty of obstacles, hate, and racism that stood in the way of many bold dreams, but some of us were achieving a different level of success. Success that was being publicized openly and in our own circles.

I am sure there were times before the 1900s where Black men showed skill, character, and personality. An interesting time as the Supreme Court ruled in the Plessy vs. Ferguson case that racially segregated public facilities were legal as long as the facilities for Blacks and whites were equal. A time in which legally we were "free" and legally we had rights, but as a people we were set up to fail. However, into the 1900s we had the opportunity of Black male teachers working in classrooms with other Black students, we had hard working fathers, brothers, and uncles pushing the next generation of Black males to take the next step in our evolution in America. We had to work because nothing was going to be given to us and, yet, there was a sense of pride in the community to come together and create the best from what we had. The Black citizen was attempting to evolve and the Black man was trying to get past the system of slavery that still had them stereotyped as animals. Even though the representation was coon work in the movies, we had Black men in motion pictures. The Black actors acting in the field of entertainment wasn't our proudest moment and it may have further cemented stereotypes of ignorance, but we were on the screen. There was enough to be proud of throughout society as we saw Black men excelling in sports. Our first Black man to win a gold medal for America in the Summer Olympics of 1908, the introduction to organized professional basketball with the Black Fives and baseball with the Negro baseball league. Jack Johnson, the first Black heavyweight boxing champion stunned white America in 1908. Johnson further shocked and angered white America as he flaunted his white women that were in relationships with him. Universities and colleges were seeing more representation of Black men and women and also we saw the birth of the Black Greek life in fraternities and sororities.

Our Enlightenment era was during these times as we had forefathers such as Sutton Elbert Griggs, Jupiter Hammon, and Frederick Douglas leading the way for future scholars, authors, speakers, and leaders such as W.E.B. DuBois, Booker T. Washington, and Marcus Garvey. I am willing to gamble that your school did not spend much time on any of these men. Perhaps, you spent a passing moment, but typically Black men are not regarded with more time in American history until we get to Martin Luther King, Jr. and half of that story is told. S.E. Griggs and Jupiter Hammon both write on concepts of freedom and equality as they give a glimpse of what we can be as a society while Douglas wrote a truth so raw that not only our nation, but European nations took notice on the inequality and inhumanity that the American Negro suffered at the hands of their white oppressors. Perhaps the emotions and truths are too real for the vast majority of our American population or more specifically, those who design the curriculum for our school system to determine the indoctrination of American values. Facts are not meant to hurt, yet we must allow the truth to disinfect our wounds of our country for us to heal.

Prior to the conflict of Martin and Malcolm during the civil rights era, Black people were choosing sides behind strong Black men with strong philosophies to move us forward as a people. The early 1900s offered leaders like Booker T. Washington that offered the strength in commerce and economic development through the skilled talents and labor of Black men and women. Yet, Washington's philosophies disconnected with W.E.B. DuBois and the Talented Tenth. The Talented Tenth philosophy rested not on the hands and work ethic of all Black men, but on lifting up 10 percent of all the Black male population as leaders with a formal and classical education. Sadly, the division caused the masses to choose a side rather than understand we could do both and have overall success as a Black community while influencing America as a country. However, it was individuals like both of these men that pushed for more education and training for Black people, that led to conversations that developed the National Association of the Advancement of Colored People (NAACP), Historically Black Colleges and Universities, and the overall layer of the social concept that Black men can be highly skilled and intelligent leaders in all facets of society. As more and more Black men saw and felt the pride that achievement brought, other brothers connected with the movement of banding together and uniting behind the cause of scholar and master craftsmen. Black men were uniting on campuses and in community locations to discuss their advancement of themselves individually and our communities. A type of "cool" was seen as brothers walked with a new truth that the Black man had the ability to excel.

Beyond formal training, athletics, and scholarship, you had Black men earning money in just about any job they could find. Some would argue it is during this time of the early 1900s that we as a people fell in love with materials and started to try to buy our respect from all who would see us. We didn't have much, but what we had was going to look good. A false sense of power and control as we would want to look clean, important, powerful, wealthy, and secure. Even if we had to work twice as hard as a white man and, in some cases, work a job a white man was too good for, to earn a dollar, we would then make sure we had the look of success. Our professional ladder was quite different in the early 1900s. The south was still rural work and labor jobs with skilled and unskilled labor. However, we also found migration routes in various directions to start a different lifestyle off of the farm. Opportunities to cities such as Miami, Florida and New Orleans in the south and several cities such as Chicago, Detroit, and Harlem in the north allowed the Black man to migrate being pulled to the American dream.

Miami was a vast opportunity for Black men prior to the Civil War as a land that was not controlled by the British colonies, but found "ownership" in the hands of Spain and France various times during the 1800s. Black men as pirates frequently harbored at the shores of Florida and into the area that became Miami in 1896. One notorious captain was a Black pirate, Black Caesar who also traveled with Black Beard, the infamous pirate. As time developed, Florida had become a dangerous locale for colonists. While slavery was legal based on the various "owners" of the land, the Indigenous peoples of the Seminole were prevalent and remained a strong partner to runaway slaves. Additionally, a strong consideration to abolishing slavery were the revolutions that were occurring. Florida was the closest territory to the country of Hispaniola where one of the most successful revolutions of Black people occurred not once, but twice. The name of the general that led the revolution in Hispaniola, Toussaint Louverture, was growing like an urban legend in the colonies. Growing through the Civil War and the Reconstruction the Negro communities within the city of Miami grew. A large part of that growth was the continued professional gains with Black people working in hotels and homes of the white citizens from various ethnicities that were able to own land

and businesses. Specifically, Black men found themselves working in businesses such as railroads and in the trains which lead to a new influx of economic growth for Black men and a different sense of pride and vision.

New Orleans was another city that witnessed a boom in development in the Black culture. As a city that also saw a collective gathering of several different types of ethnicities as a hub for trade among the French, Spanish, Indigenous peoples, and Africa through the slave, New Orleans created a flavor all of its own. One remarkable birth from our interaction as slaves was the musicality that your slave ancestors brought. Using skills and talents connected to our roots of West Africa, we sang and danced through the aches of our minds, bodies, and souls. We took those same skills and talents that were passed down through and beyond the Reconstruction period and created the sounds of blues and then to jazz. As those wonderful melodies were formed, so were the personalities of these artists. You will find that from this point, the story of Black people is closely tied to the rhythm that we produce and own. Black young men had a new connection to their identity. A new layer and reality of what it meant to be a Black man had been created.

Chasing the vision and the dream, Black men migrated north. Traveling to find a job was a gamble, but one of the most "fortunate" Black men was the Pullman Porter. Working inside the trains as a "boy" on the trains was the opportunity to make money through a low wage, but more than nothing, and show a skill in something some of our ancestors performed in some cases as slaves. Cooning, schucking and jivin', and the wearing of a mask has been an interesting slavery defense that some of us has still use to this day. This overplay to appease our white citizens in perceived power was well played to trick, hustle, and play on the emotions and egos of white people was indeed a skill. Convincing the person in front of you that could beat you or have someone do it and/or remove your livelihood and your means and access to a better life, that as a Black male you were not a threat, but nothing more than a simple creature for their approval, was a talent. A talent that was taught to us and we mastered during our oppression and dehumanization as slaves and we passed down to generations. The larger you made your eyes bulge, the more you spoke broken English, the more you figuratively and literally danced for their approval, the larger tip from the hand of white men that needed this type of reassurance in his life. The reassurance to this type of white man that he was at the top of the perceived power structure of society and he would always be better than the least of the human beings; the Negro. Black men found other jobs in the service industry, but the Pullman Porter was a "good job." Imagine the damage that would be done as you spend your days reminding others that you are less than they are. "Oh no suh, I'm just here suh to make you happy suh." "I find joy in making you smile, suh. I aims to please." We have always found a way to entertain the more dominant group of white people with our antics. Even though I have seen you walk the halls and streets in being "you," I have seen and witnessed the spirit that continues to laugh at us as we pose no real threat. We flash with our jewelry, cars, and clothes as we make sure we have the best shoes and the latest phones and attachments. You do what the mainstream tells you to do. Mainstream does what sells and we typically are not the CEO of the companies that are making the decisions or getting the profits. "I find joy in making you smile, suh. I aims to please suh." Our culture is often observed and sold. Your generation has done better than mine in rights and ownership of material. We have more Black people in positions of perceived power now more than ever in our past in America. However, with the Black population nationwide, we see the financial opportunities through selling to "all people" which is code for "I want white money." Yet, there is a fine line between "selling" and "selling out." "Go ahead boy, wear these clothes, sing that song, do that jig." You say that we are keeping it real? That's just the style? We have been subdued to think as peasants and continue to settle for far less than we should have because we don't have a strategy for the bigger picture as men, son. I am not saying we can't be "cool," whatever that is, but we have to add layers to our "cool" that coincides with our God-given freedoms and to live in a better state of peace.

Even the Pullman Porters were not always about grinnin' and cashing in their self-esteem for a dollar. The Pullman Porters that were customarily called "George" early on based on the company being owned by George Pullman also had their social status upgraded as George Pullman allowed a better servant model with clean uniforms, well-groomed Black men, that understood their role to support the white patrons with whatever they needed, which also included secrets and a great bit of trust. These Pullman Porters have been connected with the rise of the Black middle class as the men found themselves near and around various ideas, teachings, learnings, and philosophies while the Black men traveled through various states of the south and north. While earning a low wage, these men were still making more than the average Black man, dressed well, had access to and retained more knowledge than the average Black men of the early 1900s, and had more overall life experiences than most Black men of the 1900s. These Black men grew into the first labor union and paved the way to the Civil Rights Movement. Yet again, another layer of what it could be to be a Black man in the early 1900s.

As the Porters found themselves traveling throughout our country, they also moved our Black culture throughout the states. Soulful sounds and new blues, jazz, and big band from the south made their way to the north. Artists of all types collected their dollars and thoughts and made their way to starting a new life in their vision of putting their skills and talents to work. I want to point out that some of these brothers had families they left as they chased those dreams. Leaving sisters to raise kids alone in some cases. I could spend twice as much time as we will spend here on the strength of our women over the generations. However, you need to understand that as men we have been forced to leave our families one way or another to survive. In some cases, we went back for the families that we left. In other cases, we faded away into a memory leaving sisters and our children as if they didn't exist. Don't let the false narrative fool you into thinking we are "bad" husbands and fathers. However, you have to understand that there is a "lift" here that may pull you in different directions to provide for your family and be a "man." Son, don't forget to be present and offer quality time to your family. We can be selfish in the dream and the vision. We at times will want all that we are "owed" or what we have seen in the American dream and in search for those items we want to chase what calls us in the name of provision for the family or into walking into who we are as men. Remember when you make the decision that leads to possibly being a father and you indeed become a father, the child is a product of your decisions and you should hold yourself responsible for your decisions.

By the time of World War I in 1917, based on the resiliency toward a vision through supporters both Black and white, we had Black men that were working the lands, working trades, working jobs, working on their intellect through school with some becoming doctors, professors, lawyers, authors, profound public speakers, artist, athletes, and vocal and instrument masters. Legally we were no longer slaves, but we were slaves to the lender in the regards to land we "owned" or the lifestyle for which we fought. The Black family, the Black woman, and the Black man fought for survival and the opportunity to eke out the perceived security and safety in the new position of freedom. As we did so, despite the disrespect, despite the beatings, despite the undue jailings, despite the lynchings, and despite the continued efforts of oppression and lies to create a narrative where Black people were less than human, we found something. We found our "cool."

Now in the early 1900s, we were evolving the image of the Black man. As propaganda against the Black male was being used to feed the narrative of hate and ignorance through newspapers and movies from the 1900s to 1920, there was still a delicate social resistance of Black people defining themselves. Historically, the 1900s was a push forward for Black people. There were many of us fighting for the dream to own land, to provide for themselves and their families, and to have a path to pursue the same happiness our white American brothers and sisters seem to have access to "naturally." We remained diligent and hard working with our eyes on some sort of vision that was before us. This struggle for the elusive dream started to take root in literature, visual arts, and music. This passion and resistance to the oppression of centuries was now being expressed for other brothers and sisters to use as an echo chamber. We heard others were struggling and we heard others were fighting. We heard others were tired, but we also heard others were persevering and celebrating their blackness. Popular culture was now being influenced by Black culture. Sons and daughters and grandsons and granddaughters of former slave owners were now slowly listening to live bands filled with the very skin types that were once hated in their family tree. Toes tapping and attending art galleries and private gatherings, the talents and skills of the Negro of the times was slowly seeping into the conscious of America. Black pride was swelling as it was evident on the sports scene that Black athletes were a force to be reckoned with or at least really entertaining to watch.

Black people were getting vocal with their philosophical view and becoming more connected in their backroom meetings regarding government. The advancement of the Negro began to become a regular talking point with names such as Marcus Garvey, Booker T. Washington, and W.E.B. Dubois. All these men wanted to further Black lives differently, but all had the message that Black lives were important and the advancement of the people meant remaining united as a people. Many Black people identified with these efforts as more started to attend meetings whether at churches, homes, and other secret corners and as these ideals and numbers grew, Black men found a new optional identity. We could be academic types as Black men, We could write as we saw in Langston Hughes, Paul Dunbar, James Weldon Johnson, Alain Locke, Claude McKay, and Countee Cullen. You probably didn't spend much time on them in English class, huh? Sure, maybe Langston, but the others or any other Black authors? I bet you can remember the various times you spent on Shakespeare though. These Black men and others like them were the birth of the Black scholar identity in mainstream. This identification along with women counterparts in their academic efforts lead to the sororities and fraternities and of course the NAACP. Black folks were thinking and strategizing and evolving.

Your time in history class may mention the arts of the 1920s, but chances are you missed the Black leadership of the times. The slight whispers of the uprising against the American democratic system that wasn't working for the Black race? No, maybe US History classes wouldn't carve a space out to remind students that Marcus Garvey built an organization for all Black people of African descent to unite and build a better nation through the organization of all African lineage. Brother Garvey wasn't speaking for the American Negro alone, he wanted an advancement for all brothers and sisters on every continent through a unification. This concept of Pan-Africanism is a bold effort in our current day and this one man from humble beginnings of Jamaica created a buzz and a following that lead to four million followers and actually return some Black families back to Africa. Here we have a Black man, well educated, well dressed, and feared by the American government. This Black man was also connected with the overall movement of the achievement of Black people and other Black men that worked to identify strategic efforts to move our people. These leaders created an identity for Black males to follow and align themselves with as to say that these leaders were a main definition of Black masculinity.

But the hustle calls…

As powerful as the academic and scholarly men of our movements were of the early 1900s, they were visionaries for a "tomorrow" and some Black men didn't dream of their futures. Their present-day realities were about food on the table and advancing themselves in that false perception of security with regular food, shelter, and materialistic goods. The better the food, shelter, and goods, the more secure and powerful you were. The more secure and powerful you were, the better man you had become. Legally this life could be acquired. The Black man saw great opportunity in the entertainment field, but that took a specific skill, hard work, dedication, and opportunities all brothers did not have. Yet, a Black man had pride and a sense of cool and the desire to own their territory. These territorial gatherings connecting with an entrepreneurial spirit that was fostered by the hustle spirit we have had probably before our forced arrival to the Americas continued to blossom in the 1920s as we found ways to create the American dream. Illegal activities during these times involved alcohol and gambling.

The Black man. Cool. Tough. Strong. A natural enforcer. The birth of the Black gangster and the birth of an identity that we continue to wrestle with today. You see the Black man has always had with them, placed through the eyes of European perception, a threatening energy. Historically we see these in early interactions of Rome with Africa and this continued through the Black people slavery over the centuries into today's social dynamics. We know there has been growth, but cultural implicit bias seeps in regularly as we are now beginning to have more uncomfortable conversations about race and perceived power in America. The very reason why so many Black Americans have found success in a white male dominated America is the same reason why the majority of us don't and find other paths to the "American dream" or they don't. There is a language to success in America and it's the same language that was formed in the American DNA at its inception. White wealthy men with power funded the business venture that were the early colonies, white wealthy men pulled away from the other (British) white wealthy men because the white men in the colonies wanted more of the British men had. Over the centuries, wealthy, white men owned the banks, the property, the businesses, and other various access points to overall financial wellness which is a defining point to other wellness in a capitalist reality. Therefore, to have what "they" have there is a pull to be who "they" are. You see, people invest based on logic and feelings. Even when there is plenty of data for logic your feelings, your gut, can tell you otherwise. People are also more likely to be drawn to someone that is complementary to themselves. Sure there is the idea that opposites attract, but research will show that on average we engage with people who are similar as we are "pack" animals. There are those Black males who are raised in conditions of truly equal conditions of white males and with it there is a comfort in the Black man's skin interacting with the white culture because they have learned and fully accepted the culture. However, there are some Black people that need to be able to code switch, style flex, and/or wear a mask for white acceptance with the hope for financial wellness and access to the various other opportunities of wellness. Both of these types can have the largest lift subconsciously wrestling and battling between decisions and trying to read those that have their perception in their interactions with Black males. Then there are those who do not play the game. Who are willing to make their own rules and quite possibly suffer ramifications along with it or find a path that allows overall wellness while being their authentic selves unapologetically. We will talk more about that later, but it is important that you understand the path of the street hustler, the gangster, the thug, etc. isn't about crime for the sake of crime.

Being a Black man that is attempting to master the street elements is about using opportunities that may be legal and/or illegal, living by social norms that may be acceptable in their specific geographic location and not for others, and the Black man using their own God-given talents and honed skills to provide for themselves and perhaps their loved ones. We are people of survival as we have seen over the centuries. We have adapted in many ways and the street element is a representation of our adaptation to trying to grab the "American Pie" that, on average, isn't as accessible to others who aren't white, middle class males and on the higher ends of the socioeconomic scale. There are conspiracy theories that are unfounded about drugs being leaked into the Black community by the government. Specifically, cocaine made its surge into the Black community in the late '70s. We will talk more about drugs during that era later, but what you need to understand here son, is that the Black community is not the victim, but a partner in our demise. There are unfair, unjust, inequities that are occurring, but at this point, things are not happening to us as much as they are happening with us.

The 1920s Black man added a layer of identity with the "Gangster" persona. This "cool cat" wore the mask of being everything "masculine" and everything "power." This Black male identity wanted to not only survive, but to thrive even if it meant the oppression of others that were of their own community. A learned behavior from our "forefathers" as the Black people witnessed overtime that you had to use strength and perceived power to take what you needed and wanted to "make it" in life. This specific identity carried the belief that in this capitalist society, more "stuff" meant more perceived success and the ability to profess security, control, and power. The other part of this identity is that it "worked." Identity is formed after it is observed and practiced. Behavior is created based on practice and rewards received. If you receive outcomes that are not pleasurable, you tend to stop behaviors. The quicker you receive those outcomes, the quicker they are more likely to change. However, if the outcome you receive for your behavior is pleasurable, the more likely you are to continue that behavior even if there is a potential negative consequence for your behavior in the future. If I told you that I would give you $100 dollars per hour, but potentially someone could also come to you to "hurt" you, the first question for some is, "what does hurt mean?" Right there is where you have placed the sacrifice on the spectrum or scale of, "how much am I willing to give up for the pleasure?" The Black male gangster identity of the 1920s was willing to give their body in death and/or imprisonment because the risks were worth the rewards.

Running numbers and alcohol were the criminal financial avenues for the gangster of the 1920s. Ironically one of the largest gangsters of the 1920s was a Black woman, a Caribbean sister, of the name Stephanie Sr. Clair. Again, sisters are strong and they are built differently. Running numbers was a lottery system invented as urban legend goes by Black people in Harlem, New York that found its way to all of the major cities where Black people lived. The idea is probably familiar to you as the now "Lottery" system, which is government owned and legal, is rather prevalent throughout our country. The goal was to select the correct number series between 0 and 999. You would place a bet by giving your number to a "runner" and if your number "hit" you would get a return on your investment. Of course, the more you bet the larger the payout, which is different from today's lottery system. The igneous concept was actually based on the numbers offered from the New York Stock Exchange (NYSE). Daily there was a three digit number offered from the NYSE in their report and the winning number presented itself naturally which helped betters trust the selection of the winning numbers were fair. The NYSE actually stopped presenting these numbers to aid in the removal of the numbers running crime, but again we adapted.

In any event, in efforts to grab "easy money" and or the thrill of winning and having more financial opportunities to purchase happiness, Black communities thrived on the zeal to win by men and women of all ages handing their hard earned money to a "runner" who was usually a younger Black male, sometimes as young as ten and usually not exceeding sixteen. This money was ran to the Policy Bank. It is important to understand that this was organized crime. The Policy Bank was our mafia and the mafia life paid well. The reason why a runner was young was it was an entry level job opening for the older positions that usually involved enforcing the policy rules, security detail, money handling, and even territorial management. Did you hear me? You might have missed it and I want to make sure you really understand what the street identity involved and how it convinced us it was a "way of life."

The numbers game and organized crime offered a lifestyle that was identified with power and wealth which provided a level of security. Imagine seeing something you never saw before in your neighborhood, a Black man with power and money with the clothes and cars that would look like royalty and that's what they were. Black gangsters that were typically males were like the modern day elite athlete or musician of our current time. People would enjoy watching them and looking at them, in most cases they wanted to be like them or at least next to them. Sometimes a handshake, a nod, or a wink helped you feel acknowledged and validated by this power. Of course this identifiable "cool" and power was compounded by the gangster's ability to award community members with money in the form of handouts, good tips and regular purchases as customers in the Black community and also physically hurt you or kill you with little to no retribution. Living in the Black community the Black gangster wasn't exactly "good," but the Black community also knew there was a symbiotic relationship. The shop owners knew the gangster would have money to spend in their shops. The organized gangs of Black communities also provided order. It was the order of the Black gangsters, but it was still order and there were rules. As a young Black male you saw this life. You saw the community members look up to these older, well dressed Black men that were providing for themselves and others. As a young Black male you saw yourself in them, identified that this was the Black man's place, and went after it. You see, you didn't always see the W.E.B. DuBois types in your neighborhoods. Rallies were not public displays regularly. On a particularly powerful day and moment you would get a glimpse of a rally, hear and see a powerful speaker move the crowd, and become curious about that lifestyle. Yet, in the 1920s, you could see your talents and skills used as early as ten years old being put to good use to put food in front of you (as a 10-year-old, maybe candy too) and some coins in your pocket for your family. It took a strong family to tell a 10-year-old to stop bringing money home, especially when you knew you could not fully provide as a father or mother. Also, these early recruits of 10 to 16 years of age found something else, acceptance and validation instantly.

Running numbers and eventually making your way up the ranks in Black organized crime, meant you were a part of "something." This "something" had a community appeal as the Black gangster families did not let everybody in their exclusive club. Now, because I am a member of this organization, others in my community see me and respect me as a part of something bigger, "I matter." By identifying as a gangster and finding acceptance, I am using my skills and talents and someone is recognizing I have those skills and talents by offering me a role in their organization. Success in my role means more validation, more wealth, more power and more perceived control and security in my life. All of this does not occur immediately, but it occurs faster than white America is offering true equality and equity for Black people.

Therefore, the Black male gangster was a creation from adaptation based on survival in America. The desire to feel valued, respected, useful to a larger cause, loved, and many other attributes the United States never offered us, the Black male gangster identity emerged as a possible avenue for Black males that did not see themselves specifically for being the hard working, managed, blue collar type, the few entrepreneurs, the musician and/or entertainer, the athlete which wasn't always entirely lucrative, and the scholar. All identities play their part in the larger development of being "Black" in America, yet the more tangible a reality is the more likely more individuals will accept it as true. By the end of the 1920 going into the 1940s, the Black male had developed all of the various identities to higher levels. Representations of "us" were being seen in the newspapers and movies and our culture could be heard, read, and seen via the various formats of art. White America now had the dilemma of trying to create a reality for the Black race of people. Not quite broadly accepted as people on equal footing, we needed to have a "special" category and America was still trying to figure out what that was.

There was a time where the category was easier and we were just animals barely above the ox in the categories offered by America. Yet, by the 1920s, we were developing our own networks, communities, businesses, and churches. We were growing our expressiveness, and we were expressing a backbone through our ability to fight in wars, develop strategies, consider philosophies and we could be a problem physically in times of conflict. Our growth was shifting the optics of the balance of a perceived power. These concerns and unsettled feelings exploded in the early 1900s a few times with events that your history books might have missed. The late teens of the 1900s to mid-1940s had extreme violence in various times due to the unsettling effect the social development of the Black community had on the paradigm of the majority of white Americans. As Blacks migrated from the south to the north and as Black men returned from World War I, our government had no clue how to respond to the call for equity. As we returned from World War I against a Russian force and movement of Marxism and an anti-Russian sentiment, words like communism, communist, and Bolshevism were identifiers that were anti-American and essentially anti-White male. Our president of the time during 1917 identified the Negro social growth as a Bolshevist-like problem. You have lived through the power of words from a president that represents an emotionally confused lot. There is misplaced anger that still sits with a small percentage of white Americans. Leaders throughout the centuries play on emotions to garner political support and boost their own egos. You saw a similar leadership style that ushered in an attack on the White House that we will talk about later. This same spirit was even more prevalent with the 1900s and a tool in an effort toward the continued oppression of Black people was violence. While using violence against Black people over the centuries was almost common and synonymous with America since the inception of the "dream," the new twist was that Black communities were starting to fight back a little which also was new for white America. The Black community was united and began to defend their neighborhoods, their people, and themselves. While we never "won" in a riot, if there is such a thing as winning in a riot, we established that we could and would fight physically if we needed to in the spirit of Nat Turner.

During 1917 there were several riots in cities based on the fear of Black people and loss of perceived power and status of white. The early 1920s offered a high body count in one event that left several white people and of course more Black people dead based on an event that included Black children swimming to the "white-side" of the lake water line in Chicago, Illinois. Imagine believing you could separate the sharing of water in a lake with a manmade "line." Harlem, New York exploded in a riot based on the pinned up anger of 10,000 Black community members that wanted justice for police brutality of a Black child for stealing a small knife from a store. The more complete truth was the white owner and police released the young man from the back door of the store ironically to help keep the young man safe. The crowd was inconsolable for days as they looted and destroyed white owned stores despite the owner professing their employment of Black people and the stores commitment to the Black community. The Tulsa riots of 1921 was our worst riot of the time and arguably of all time. A Black male was accused of assaulting a white woman in a town just outside of Greenwood, Oklahoma and he was taken into custody. Fearing the Black man would be lynched, as another Black man was lynched a year prior by the same legal system in the town, an estimated seventy-five Black men arrived at the jail, armed and prepared for resistance.

These Black men were from Greenwood, Oklahoma which was a mecca for Black families and business owners. Labeled the "Black Wall Street," the town housed many former World War I veterans and various other Black community members striving to create the best version of Black excellence and achieving the American dream that was promised to all Americans. Prospering banks, stores, schools, theaters, nightclubs, doctor offices and churches all in a Black community and thriving. This town not only offered a version of our best selves, but also as a reminder to some whites we could do what they could and in some cases better.

Thus, as the Black man was brought to the jail for pending justice, the Black men of Greenwood appeared to remind the all-white legal party that the Black community understood the law and were ready to defend their liberties. There was a point of peaceful resolution to the initial encounter when the sheriff of the town outside of Greenwood convinced the seventy-five "defenders" that there would be fair treatment of the community member in custody. However, a white man attempted to take a rifle from one of the Black men and the white male was shot, sending an uproar on both sides. Retreating to town, white men quickly united for an opportunity for "justice" of their own and what would seem like the release of some very hostile, pinned up, feelings toward successful Black people who had the audacity to think they were equal. 24 hours of relentless attacks on the buildings and the approximately 10,000 citizen population of Greenwood. While the coroner's count was in the twenties, there was no account for the need for the mass graves that needed to be built. Most egregious accounts include an aero-assault from low flying planes that includes gun fire and glycerin bombs that ignited the streets, buildings, and residences of Greenwood. While this is considered a massacre and is now a staple in Oklahoma history, other states may not broach the subject, but you should remember what anger, jealousy, and the fear of losing a social construct of perceived power can do to people. There was an opportunity to physically put a group of Black people in their place and this opportunity was strategically performed and lasted a full twenty-four hours before a stronger governmental entity stepped in to stop the mayhem.

What is important here, son, is that these are instances when our people begin to show they are willing and able to fight back. These Black men saw that they were just as American as any other person who was a citizen of this country and they were willing to fight for their rights. There was much opposition on the path to the pursuit of happiness for Black people and they were not guaranteed liberty or their lives. The Black American was a failed experiment that white men of perceived power had to deal with and had no idea how to do so, mainly because the white men of perceived power could not adapt their paradigm of Black people. Again, not all white people, not all white men with perceived power, but enough people to guide the culture of America could not wrap their minds around the fact that the Black American people were equal human beings and should be treated as such. The Black American people had been in the country as long as white colonists and we were responsible for literally building so much of what was the backbone of the country. However, the idea of sharing perceived power that was thought of as naturally ordained to white people based on the views of specific white people of perceived power was scary and deep down some are still scared. Scared of accepting that the color of one skin does not come with a birthright to so much privilege is a deeply rooted fear based on the animalistic need for survival. It takes individuals of enlightened consciousness to progress toward the harmonious truth of ethnicity being celebrated while promoting the advancement of us all as a human race.

The late 1920s and 1930s brought in new challenges for all people as the country encountered the Great Depression. I am sure you spent time on this in history classes. I am sure you saw pictures of bread lines and faces of despair. Perhaps what you didn't see were the Black people that suffered the blow first and longest as they were first to lose their jobs and last to obtain one. Black men that were providing a living through factory work and other means were first to become unemployed as companies could not afford employees due to the financial misery of the country and these companies saw the best opportunity to save dollars was to save white jobs first. Hear me say, this was a bad time for most, but again you should know that. You should have some remembrance that this was a time when many Americans, regardless of color, saw homelessness and hunger. To many white individuals and families this was a very close glimpse of the struggles of Black America as jobs, income, food, shelter, safety, and security were not guaranteed. I would not want this type of struggle on any person. Though you should also understand that when you are the last in line as a Black person, the line just gets longer when times are hard in the country. I could say that about various other categories of race and gender, but the Black male hasn't figured a way to collectively move past the back of the line while other ethnicities and women forge ahead to empower themselves and move.

We have seen this recently with our struggles as a nation with the COVID pandemic. We spoke of employment rates as a country when we are "getting better," yet when you peel the numbers back Black people are still behind in the data. When you look at education and the country's growing concern for "our children," a point missed in so many conversations is Black people tend to enroll in schools that are far worse in basic operations, not to mention academic gains than the average primarily white school. This is because these schools are in predominantly communities of color with a high Black American percentage. Additionally, in these Black schools across America, the Black male students typically perform the worst. Do you think the academic abilities of the Black male improved during the "gap" school year of the COVID pandemic? No.

Although a miserable start in the early '30s, the mid-1930s moved America forward into a more prosperous time. As we typically do as a country, we "found" money to help create opportunities for people to earn wages in different ways. I have to pause here and make sure I help you understand that the country "finds" money when "they" find a reason for it. In my conversation with you, I told you about the Reconstruction and how we had money to help alleviate the gaps Black people had and the government suddenly could not afford it as we were making strides as a people in tandem with conscious white people of America. We know that Black people still could benefit from the government offering sizable financial interactions to civil programs to increase skills of Black people and close the gap between us and access to opportunity to wellness. We know that if the government would intervene in schools and truly had high expectations and support through financial means all students would perform better and Black people, especially Black males, would grow in their reading and math skills to influence their ability to perform better in classes and not drop out of school. These are investments in American people and not handouts to Black people. Yet, we don't have money for that.

As the 1930s progressed, Black people continued to endure as we always have. We saw some powerful leadership efforts politically with boycotts, strikes, and later a few close council type positions with Black men working "close" to the US president in the federal government to understand the "Negro problem." Yet, we also saw the continued development of Black man and the development of the various identities in the other areas as well.

During the late 1920s and throughout the 1930s, big band music continued to thrive and with it so did the Black male entertainer. Louis Armstrong, Duke Ellington, and Cab Calloway are just a few names that were leading a new American movement and increasing the awareness of the artistry of Black people. More specifically, these Black men were being increasingly idolized which in turn created more Black men to aspire to be these new stars. Whether or not you could lead a band or play an instrument did not matter. It was about being able to look the part, walk the walk, and talk the talk. This was a subculture that was being defined and taking the hearts of people of various colors and backgrounds in America. Granted these Black men could not stay at white hotels, but they were being allowed to play for all white crowds. Yet, in our communities and in the urban roots of the city, you heard the greatest music and the best dancing as Black people embraced our music and Black men continued to identify with "cool."

The Zoot suit was amazing. Don't let anyone tell you that what you wear is crazy, bad, or wrong. I mean there is professional and casual and I see those lines blurring a little these days, but each generation has some interesting style choices. The Zoot suit was not only a suit, but a statement. The Zoot suit was a belief and lifestyle in fashion form. When you wore a Zoot suit you were clearly saying you were a man with an edge and cool. The Zoot suit had directly connected to the urban, street realities. As you wore that suit as a Black man, there was specific vocabulary and even poses and walking style that needed to go with it to solidify your identity with the trend. No sir, these weren't those book reading, academic Black men. These brothers were not on the council for any government officials. Yet, these brothers were attempting to create a space of safety and security through their identification with what was gaining attention. Along with the Zoot suit was a remarkable hairstyle called the "conk." As Black women had been pressing and perming their hair to align with European hair trends as the social definition of "beauty," now the Black men would begin chemically altering their hair for the appearance of straight textured hair. Adding a variety of chemicals to their hair, Black men would sit as long as possible for their hair to "take" even though this could mean severe discomfort and a burning sensation to their scalp. This was all to be cool and look the part. Sadly, this was also us hating our own texture of hair as the goal was to have "white hair." Our image has always meant so much to us.

Movies now had sound in the 1930s and with that sound came more dancing and singing Black folks. You can always find room for Black folks singing and dancing in America. These movies offered crowds of Americans in separate seating and theaters of course, to see the artistry of the acrobatic moves of "Flash Dancers" that made their way from white crowds in the Cotton Club of Harlem to the big screen for all of America. Amazed by the sounds and skill, crowds would leave theaters aspiring to be these entertainers and Black men were no different. Still though, even in the world of arts and skill on the dance floor and with instruments, there still was the gangster who was still about securing a perceived power through illegal activities. The streets were becoming more violent and more territorial in our neighborhoods as these Black men who just wanted to own something for security were killing each other for something that didn't belong to them. A corner, a block, an ambition to "own" a city, all of it could still be taken away like Greenwood, Oklahoma.

The Black male athlete identity was being developed further as well. Even though there was a strategic agreement by the then owners to not add Black players to the teams at a later date, initially the National Football League (NFL), founded in 1920, started with a Black player that performed well. The Negro leagues in basketball was growing much attention during the late 1920s and 1930s. Top Black male fighters and boxing champions were dominating in their specific field in front of white crowds and listened to by Black audiences. The Negro League for baseball was growing serious interest from white crowds and Black boys were increasingly becoming knowledgeable and admiring these Black men excelling in their craft and status. Yet, one of the most powerful statements was those made in the Olympics of 1936. As America made a bold decision early to allow Black athletes to compete in track and field events with white athletes, the grand stage for a Black male was offered in Berlin, Germany.

Only a few Black men had earned a medal on a national track and field circuit outside of college by the time Jesse Owens and his other seventeen Black athletes stepped into the world's view in 1936. An interesting opportunity as brother Owens was representing so much during the days of these Olympic Games. Jesse Owens was now representing America as the best among us all. That was America telling the world we acknowledged that a Black man is the "best" at something superseding a white person. That statement was bold to say to America, let alone the world. Owens was of course representing Black people and specifically Black men as a representation of our finest model. Little Black boys now had a possible champion going across the world to be the "defender" of

America's claim to greatness. However, this was a special opportunity because these games were being played in Berlin, Germany during a time of racial discrimination and attempted genocide lead by Adolf Hitler. As America continued to remain strategically silent in the murder and destruction of innocent people and the growing imperialism of a dictator during the 1930s, Hitler's philosophy of a white superior race, an Aryan race, yelled and screamed. A Black man competing against a white man was not even competition to the eyes of an Aryan supremacist. Yet, in 1936 Jesse Owens showed Germany, Hitler, and the world that a Black man could be the best in the world at something. Additionally, there were other Black athletes that competed very well and even medaled during these games, but Jesse Owens walked away with the most. The details are a little unclear with the response from Hitler regarding the Jesse Owens wins. Whispers of Hitler being "annoyed" by the triumphs of Owens, to Hitler walking out on the presentation of the medals to Owens, to Hitler offering a halfhearted wave of congratulations to Owens. What is known, sadly, our government didn't acknowledge the amazing victories until 2016 with a Black president in office. Jesse Owens noted that he didn't even receive a telegram from the then US President Franklin D. Roosevelt.

A final note about this era, this was a time for a pivotal political move for Black people. We were trying to figure out the rules and we knew that we had the right to vote since the late 1800s. Now in the 1920s, Black men and Black women could vote and white politicians began to understand what the mobilization of the demographic could mean. Not being satisfied with the Republican Party forgetting the needs of Black people, Black men and women organized to offer unified support for the Democratic Party. This was again a great representation of what we can do when we strategize and mobilize. We don't have the majority of the population of

America, however, if we strategically come together we can be a force that demands attention and results.

World War II (WWII) brought yet another opportunity for Black men to prove themselves to America. Far from being accepted and still battling white supremist, hate, prejudice, and oppression, Black men and women enlisted and willfully accepted the call to join the military to fight soldiers over the ocean that were fighting for their countries desire to continue their philosophies of white supremacy, hate, prejudgment, and oppression. Even though Black men had served in every American war prior, the US government was not totally convinced on including Black men in the draft. However, our community pushed for the opportunity to fight for "our" country and the federal government could not deny the desire for the sheer numbers allowing Black men to serve would create. An approximate 1.2 million Black men served in the armed forces during WWII. Despite the glaring hypocrisy we fought and we fought hard. These Black men fought the enemy across seas, but still battled their enemies of their own country. Racism did not end with enlistment. Equality and fair treatment was not standard ordered with a uniform. Black soldiers had separate and unequal training facilities, hospitals, living quarters, and recreation areas. Additionally, as these Black men were fighting behind the symbolism of American freedoms to the continued propaganda of "life and liberty," their daily food rations were often less than white male soldiers, Black soldiers received blood from segregated supplies, wounded Black soldiers received less quality medical care when wounded as care team providers prioritized white lives over Blacks, and Black men even found themselves less equipped in weaponry and tactical equipment to perform the tasks at hand for American victory. Yes, and all this occurred with white male soldiers and higher ranking officials hurling racial slurs for insults or simply saying them as a common day speak.

Initially the Black male soldier was not a soldier at all. The Black male enlistee was put through training and then placed in position of labor and service as they cooked, dug trenches, worked as mechanics, and loaded and unloaded supply trucks because a Black man with a gun was still a threat to the US. It wasn't until the continued request from Black leaders in America and the undeniable reality of a high casualty count set in for the US government and forced them to lean on the Black men like so many times before in previous wars to step up to their American obligation and defend "our" country. Black men were deployed on ground and in air with huge success with stories such as the ones told of the 761 Tank Battalion liberating thirty towns or the Tuskegee Airman that would run air and ground cover in such a fashion that the all-Black squadron won praise from allies and adversaries for their skill and bravery. Black men were soldiers and heroes coming home to be seen by Black community members for the children, specifically Black boys, to idolize and applaud. America's victory was attempted to be shared by Black men who served as collective "our" victory, but America had a different idea upon the end of the war. The freedoms of others were now more secure thanks to the American intervention and Black soldier support, but the Black citizen was not equal and we still needed to fight our battles in the states.

The Black soldier went back to defend "democracy" and an equality they didn't share in the Korean War during 1950 to 1953. As much as America was fighting against specific actions and atrocities in WWII, there was also a very serious threat to the western (American) economic and political system. During a time of heightened American pride from the victory of WWII and the increased spending and boom in innovation and technology, our capitalism became even more deeply rooted as individuals, primarily older white male and more specifically those who historically had a level of economic achievement and political and social power, enjoyed the increase of wealth and perceived security. The American dream was being achieved by those who turned a blind eye to gender and race inequality in our country and any form of government or economy outside of the American theories was "evil." The opinion became fact as the mass media sold the news and a largely white base of those who bought the news understood that anything challenging what was tradition was challenging America at its core.

However, just as there have always been free thinkers and whites that challenged what was "right" in our nation against what was best for humanity, there were revolutionary thinkers of all colors at the onset of the 1950s. It was at this time, the courts were challenged to decide if segregated public schools were best for our growing nation. Specifically, the question was being posed, "Is separate really equal"? Led by the NAACP, America was being forced to evolve. A very distinct evolutionary moment as a team of lawyers, led by a Black man, Thurgood Marshall, was challenging what America saw as "right," "truth," and "tradition." Now in the press like magazines and newspapers, on the radio, and on the television, there was a team that was articulating the damage that having unequal schools could do to the psyche of a Black child. No one could argue that America was failing miserably in offering the same type of schooling to Black children and white children. Photos and details concerning lack of supplies, unsafe conditions, and unhealthy conditions were in ample availability. The highest court in the land, the Supreme Court, was being faced with declaring a "truth." Was the public education system truly offering equal opportunities to Black children?

Undeniably, Black schools were far worse than white schools in lack of materials, facilities, and resources. Quite often, the Black school had too many students and not enough teachers, desks, books, and finances in general for improvement in any of those conditions. However, as much as the inequality was real, our students and families remained loyal to the power of schooling and education. While Black students learned about how great America was through their books that were based on a narrative that the white male forefathers were heroes, they still pressed on in the one room school houses that were overcrowded, hot, and falling apart around them. Teachers, who were highly educated, for other professions in some cases, were teaching because it was one of the only jobs a highly educated Black person could have. These teachers taught with high expectations for their students and supported them with the understanding that the teachers loved the students enough to expect the best from them. Again, we found victory in some cases despite the additional weight on our lift to achieve an American dream that was typically far beyond our reach.

Even as I sit and type these words for you to read, the Black male is typically the lowest achieving student demographic in a school district. I didn't say all Black males do not succeed in school. Yet, you need to understand that the Black male is most likely to get suspended, get expelled, fail a course, perform poorly on a test, have poor reading and math skill, drop out, and not graduate. More disturbing is that the more Black dense a school is which means the more Black students that are enrolled in a school, the less likely a Black male will be successful. Again, all Black males are not failing, but they are more likely to do so in a school with more Black students than they would in a school with a high population of white students. Are schools equal now? Are schools that are set in zip codes that have more white people "better" than schools with more Black people? Has there been progress since 1954 and the Supreme Court integrating schools per their verdict? Yes, there has been progress. Yet, we stopped working and we started to wait. We started to wait for our government to do "right" by all citizens fairly. We have short memories. We have short memories and we have become fractionalized in our efforts while others have become seduced accomplishing a version of "freedom." An opportunity to take care of your family and maybe even generational wealth. Our protest and actions are flashes of emotion, but we don't have a strategic understanding of what matters. We know that there are schools that have a high percentage of Black students and those schools produce students that are able to compete in any academic arena and graduate with honors and scholarships to colleges. Perhaps what we don't know is how to remain consistent and focused on the desire to have all of our schools offer excellence to our students through equality and equity efforts.

We still need leaders like America witnessed in the Supreme Court in the early 1950s. We need the Thurgood Marshalls leading teams and breaking the system down from within through logic and reason. Our battles will not be won through anger and emotion. Just as the legal case of Brown vs. Board, America needs to see the determination and will of a people united to make a change and the change has not fully been achieved. We have access to funding now more than ever. We have a larger platform now more than ever with politicians in place, entertainers and athletes, and social media. We could, if we wanted to, demand better schooling and even if we had to, create our own. Have we been given just enough to pacify us? Have we earned just enough "freedom"? We have the "fighter" in us. We have a spirit in America that wants "better" for us all as a country. Yet, there is a spirit in some that have played this game since the inception of our country that hangs on to their perceived power with their use of fear and anger. We need leaders that will rally and push for change with persistence, strategy, and love for all and a desire for a better tomorrow. We need a movement.

During the 1950s, rock 'n' roll and rhythm and blues made their way through America. Various races enjoyed the sounds of the alliteration of the music and the beats that made teens tap their toes and shake more body parts to the chagrin of earlier generations. As Black voices sang on corners in neighborhoods, on records, and in concerts, more of what meant to be "Black" was defined. Segregation loomed in the 1950s, but the entertainment appeal of Black men would not be denied. The birth of "doo wop" now had offered the Black male yet another avenue for identification as the early "boy bands" gathered together and sang all over neighborhoods, talent shows, and the occasional doorstep of a young lady they were courting. Over the radio, teenagers would listen and dance to the sounds of The Cadillacs, The Drifters, Little Anthony and the Imperials, and Frankie Lymon and The Teenagers. In addition to these groups, America gave birth to rock n roll during the 1950s with Black male musicians such as Chuck Berry and Little Richard leading the way. These solo acts with others such as Nat King Cole and Harry Bella Fonte were defining the sound of a generation, leading the pulse of America's heartbeat, and creating the largest buzz of the talents, skills, and marketability of the Black man. There was accolades, fame, and perceived wealth with the Black male sounds and faces in the music industry.

As the soundtrack to the 1950s pumped through juke boxes and radios, there also came white artists that enjoyed the sounds and artistry behind the music. Artists such as Jerry Lee Lewis, Elvis Presley, and Buddy Holly set the stage for an interesting opportunity for integration. Even though Blacks and whites were separated in so many other ways, the arts were blending the races into a homogeneous culture for America. Yes, record producers were careful on how they marketed Black male singers and yes there were opportunities when Black singers were limited to sing to all white audiences because the concert hall did not allow Black patrons, but very specific seeds were being sown. There was a generation of white teenagers that were growing closer and closer to creating a bridge across the American chasm that was segregation and the views of their parents and grandparents. Listening to "Negro" music, dancing to this new rhythm, swooning over the sounds belted out by Black artist, white teens and Black teens where dancing to the same beat and finding new commonalities in the culture that was being created through music. Now with television becoming more popular, living rooms were being invaded with this new culture as well. A culture that had deep roots in the rhythm and sounds that Black people had in their DNA. Though there also was a strong anti-rock n roll movement, this music brought a strong wind of change as Black men became secret icons for their art and mass appeal was creating a new type of identity for the young Blacks of the time to emulate. We now saw another prominent avenue for us to achieve the American dream.

Sporting teams were buzzing with the athletic abilities of Black athletes on all-Black, segregated sports teams. More and more scouts and coaches were quietly respecting and secretly curious of the Black experiment in sports. The appeal of sports and entertainment with the influence of the prowess of Black males caused a direct correlation between the two and created a cultural expectancy of Black males and sports. Black and white people both were in agreement, Black men were athletic and had musical talent. However, the more important agreement was the proper marketing of either ability of Black men could mean profits. The new phenomenon of appealing through the masses using television and the radio was turning into dollars for organizations and companies. As the 1950s brought in new pride in America after being victorious in the second world war, there was increased spending for the

American dream during a time of a new birth of American culture. Now beyond just selling items to white males which was the typical type of person American business were aiming to sell their goods, products, and experiences to, new subgroups to sell and market to become hot opportunities for dollars as the market acknowledged the spending power of the woman and teenager. And while there was still a very deep racist view in America and still legal prejudice and inequality, money and the color green in large enough quantities helps organizations and companies think deeply about their efforts. Music, concerts, and records that were once "Negro" or "race" music merged into "rock and roll." Negro spirituals and slaves singing in the cotton fields, turned to the blues, swing and jazz, and now the 1950s saw a mass appeal in rhythm that flowed through the ancestry of Africans.

This new identity for the Black man was extremely seductive for the female gender across the globe and therefore, appealing to Black boys and men in their efforts to gain the same effect. The Black man now could be seen on television with crowds begging to touch them. More often we are seeing Black men perform talents that were never heard of. The Black man was being marketed as cool, entertaining, talented and gifted, and as athletes the Black man was strong, fast, a winner, and a champion. Furthermore, to the outside world, the more successful, higher achieving, and most marketed Black male entertainers and athletes were wealthy. Yes, to a degree, the Black male of America was becoming an icon for the youth and open minded. However, there were still laws of segregation. As a white teen you could listen to the music and even dance to the sounds of Negroes in the 1950s, but you couldn't dance with one. Black players were taking their mostly white teams to the championships, but Black fans still had selective seating for the "coloreds" and Black players weren't allowed in all hotels.

American culture was shifting with the demands of capitalism. Black teens and white teens spent the same dollars, which put them in the same record stores and concert halls in the more progressive areas. All-white teams saw that to compete and win and ultimately have more fans and ticket sales, the better athlete had to be on the teams regardless of the color of their skin. The 1950s introduced the "rebel" to the American dream homes. While poorer, urban neighborhoods of the city had the gangster for decades, the more suburban families of the 1950s started seeing hints of those who represented the anti-establishment through dress, style, and opposing views. As white teens search for identities, rock 'n' roll became their soundtrack to life and a new world developed around them with a major influence through television, the radio, and movie screen.

The radio and record players were humming with Black musicians and singers. This new sound playing across America could somewhat remain neutral by record companies not placing the pictures of the Black artists on the covers of the records. Yet as television and movie producers began to realize concert halls were being filled with white and Black teens wanting to watch these Black artists, the gamble of Black artists on both the small and large screen became a risky investment that white male business owners were willing to take. Profits pushed crossing the color line and as much as the laws of America attempted to separate the whites from the "coloreds," dollars of both sat comfortably in the hands of those who saw the opportunity.

As Black culture was being marketed, so was the Black man. The radio paved the way for the television and on the television there were music shows for teenagers to watch that were supported by commercials that wanted teenagers and young adults to purchase their products. Thus to have those teenagers tune in regularly, the most sought after musical talent had to be on these stages and visually delivered to homes across the country. All-white audiences were being filmed watching and at first being surprised that the vocals came from a Black man and then the audience evolved into, dancing, and idolizing Black performers which included idolizing Black men. Yes, there were Black women who performed as individuals and in groups. Yes, there were white performers who appreciated and performed what was now called "rock 'n' roll." However, further opportunities for the transition of the stereotype of the Black man was being taken into a new avenue with the new speed of technology. American Bandstand was the top rated show of the late 1950s with its twenty million viewers and 101 different stations across the states playing the one and half hour show. Early in its first season as a nationally broadcasted show in 1957, American Bandstand brought out Lee Andrews and the Hearts and in doing so pushed the narrative of the Black male sex symbol. Black men grew to identify with this new "power" and acceptance and music and entertainment became even more entrenched into the Black male identity.

Hollywood also took advantage of the Black audience and their Black dollar as well as the new culture of Black "cool" and the profits it brought. Names such as Sidney Poitier and Sammy Davis, Jr. became influencers in their acting as Americans viewed the talents of Black men on the large screen. As these young Black men evoked emotions in men and women of all colors in America acting in several types of movies in the 1950s, they further developed the identity of what it means to be a Black man in America. Further expressing the abilities of Black men and possible talents that resided in Black men, America witnessed that Black men had more depth to them that may have been thought. Black males watched role models express their abilities on a platform that was larger than life to most. These Black male actors became icons that possessed an elusive power and prestige that was desirable by America and thus desirable by Black men who wanted that same level of acceptance and perceived respect.

It was hard to see in recent times, one of the largest viewing trends in popular media is a physical altercation between two Black men in Hollywood for all to see. One of America's most renown Black male actors, widely accepted by America (specifically white America) who some would say is a role model for Black males and people in general, walked on stage and smacked another Black male who is widely accepted by America (specifically white America). This interaction was filmed for all to see and was exhibited during Hollywood's biggest night and top award show. America is having a large conversation via social media and mainstream media as they are trying to determine if this was "acceptable." While people are choosing sides and having open debates, no one is talking about the mostly white panel of politicians that yelled out of their red, white faces at a Black woman in efforts to belittle and break her to appease their voting base. Why did Will Smith slap Chris Rock? Was Will justified in defending his wife after Chris Rock joked about her outcomes of a skin condition? Where were the men that allowed the Honorable Ketanji Brown Jackson to be yelled at and ridiculed for all to see? Am I asking for brothers to make their way to senators to offer a Will Smith level of redemption? No son, I am not asking for violence. I am asking for a response that is strategic and calculated. I am asking for leadership in the states those senators represent to galvanize other Blacks, Browns, whites, and others to help them reflect on the question, "Are these the values and ethics that should be leading this country?" I am asking for you to lead. Sadly, more will remember the slap between two Black men than a panel of white men berating a sister. I need you to lead like we did when we responded to the strength of Rosa Parks in 1955 who refused to remove herself from a seat she sat in on a bus in Montgomery. A woman who was tired and fed up with the inequities and the foul treatment of Black people.

As the Black male identity was evolving in entertainment and sports, the Black male continued to grow as a leader in their communities as a change agent. Using corners, barbershops, restaurants, churches, and schoolhouses as meeting places, various leaders brought together the Black community and support from the white community to build a resistance. It was the initiation of Rosa Parks that pushed Black leaders to use the Black dollar and its power to disturb, disrupt, and attempt to destroy a historical power system. Black workers, students, and families were a key source of profit for the Montgomery bus system. As much as the Black citizens had to stand to allow white individuals to have their seats and Black people had to sit at the back of the buses, the money spent by the Black people was worth just as much as the white dollars. Thus, the decision to boycott Montgomery bus system was a strategic effort of the Black community that led to a change in the status quo. Notice, we didn't riot. This wasn't a march or people constantly asking for change. This was a calculated decision that disturbed the profits and functions of a government and their leaders. The boycott took 381 days and it was a sacrifice each day. Black citizens still had places to go in order to pay bills, to grocery shop, to attend church, and to function in general. The boycott was a staring match between the government and those who could no longer tolerate this level of unfair treatment. This was about more than the buses and the seats Black people could and could not sit in as they rode. This was about the level of fight the Black community had in it.

The state of Alabama and the city of Montgomery were willing to wait out what they thought was a futile attempt to break the position of power white citizens had. As days turned into weeks, weeks turned into months, and Black citizens were tired. They were tired of walking to work and school and to the stores. They were tired of the extra time needed to navigate the different types of transportation to get to where they had to be daily. As citizens banded together a real struggle was remaining united and strong despite the sacrifice under the vision that this was the start of something big. As the months turned into a year, the city of Montgomery would eventually break as 75 percent of their usual bus riders were Black and the court system saw fit to rule that any law or action that segregated violated the 14th Amendment that guaranteed equal rights since 1868. This victory in Montgomery catapulted new leaders to initiate what would become the Civil Rights Movement. Organizations like the NAACP and the Southern Christian Leadership Conference (SCLC) grew and became stronger in their efforts to unite Black people and supporters for equality. Leaders like Medgar Evers, Ralph Abernathy, John Lewis, A. Philip Randolf, James Farmer, Jr., and of course Martin Luther King, Jr. and Malcom X, began to build on the persona of the Black man as a leader, an orator, a fighter for equity, and a revolutionary. These Black men and others became America's number one enemy for speaking such bold sentiment as equality and, in response, the men were considered "anti-American." As much as there was an explosion of music and entertainment, the very fabric of America was being torn as Black people began to rally and fight more unified and vocal. The new nuance was that now the fight was being witnessed through the eyes of a camera to the homes of millions across the states and the globe through television. Now the more prominent leaders of the Civil Rights Movement, who were Black men, were being televised in their efforts. Black men were speaking with powerful conviction igniting emotion, stirring spirits, and engaging thoughts and the presence of these Black men were being heard via radio and observed in many living rooms.

The youth of the 1950s, still rebellious and listening to the soundtrack of rock 'n' roll, sought a new freedom and a desire to think differently than the generations before them. Whites and Black teens both female and male understood the wonder of cohabitation through music and dance. Not all white teens, but enough, saw the impact of Black artists and began to be more empathetic toward the Negro based on the white teens' personal experiences and beliefs. Moreso, the Black teenager and youth in general had a new sense of pride and strength and the rally to resist in various ways offered a deeper calling of strength. We saw a remarkable test of fortitude, tenacity, and bravery when America watched the Little Rock Nine continue their efforts to segregate schools. Yes, the Supreme Court and the federal government had agreed that segregation of public schools was unfair. Understanding that the schools for Black students were typically places that were dreadfully underfunded and in most cases was causing psychological damage as Black students saw themselves as inferior to white, America was to no longer have white public schools and Black public schools. However, the state level government saw schooling as a state government business and in some cases refused to support the Supreme Court ruling. As much as it was a right for Black students to attend formally white schools, there were white community members that were going to use everything including hate, aggression, and fear tactics to resist the action of integration in "their" schools. Nine children attempted to enter their new school daily and were met with shouting adults and the National Guard issued by the Governor of Arkansas to refuse entry. School and education was so important that armed soldiers were sent to defend it from the "dangers" of Black children. These Black children continued to remain diligent and continue to attend school daily. You can see these pictures of such a remarkable time in America. You see white youth in the picture angry and hateful based on the values they were taught in these pictures from the Little Rock Nine. You also see the strength and bravery of Black students based on the resilience and tenacity they were taught. It should be noted that this history was not that long ago. In fact, eight of the Little Rock Nine are alive in 2023 and there were plenty more white people in those pictures. White people who were taught the insecurities of their parents to use hate in their ignorance and fear. Another interesting note is that the owner of a professional football team, the Dallas Cowboys, was identified to be in one of those photos of white children mobbing during the heroic efforts of Black children. We know that all white children weren't hateful and some were curious and confused. We also know that some white people were very supportive of integrating schools, but it's the pain that America wants to hide. The pictures and images were shared throughout the nation and beyond and they showed the complete turmoil our country was going through despite being the "land of the free." It took President Johnson to send federal troops to walk students in the school and to protect them in classrooms for the enrollment to take effect.

  The federal government stepped in and made everything better and we all lived happily ever after, right? No. As much as segregation in schools is illegal, there is a de facto segregation that still occurs today. Schools are based on neighborhoods and communities. Neighborhoods and communities are based on income. Based on average, Black and brown families make less financially. Therefore, it is more likely that there are Black and brown families living together in the same community with members of other races that do not make as much money as the wealthier, majority white families. Schools are based on property taxes from houses and other land real estate. Property in these Black and brown communities are worth less than property in the wealthier, majority white communities. Thus, majority Black and brown schools do not have materials and opportunities as the wealthier, majority white schools. This is not seventy years ago I am talking about here. This type of system exists today and there are no mass movements or protests that are fighting this unfair treatment. Where are our leaders? Where is the youth that we need to stand up and demand more? Are we waiting for someone to save us? Keep waiting and you will be doing so for another seventy years.

As I think about the youth today and what it must have been like for the youth, Black youth, of 1950, I remain saddened and hurt as I empathetically try to connect to the pain of the mother of Emmett Till. This is yet another item that might have been missed in your history books and perhaps if it was mentioned, but only that. I think of you and all that you are to me. All the love I have for you and all that I want for you. I think of all that you have in front of you and I am excited for your future and prayerful for your safety. My prayers though, through all my faith, have a whisper of fear. A fear that you may not make it back home on a given day remains a small thought in the back of my mind. When I think of the pain that was caused by the murder of someone's child in such a fashion. Emmett Till was only fourteen years old and was noted to have all the cool swag of a young brother from Chicago. The same type of cool and joy I see from you at times, despite the world, and its darkness, you can light up a room when you walk into it. Emmett was in the south and hadn't experienced the world of overt racism and the dangers lurking in the land where slavery was as "American" as apple pie, guns, and the white men that carried them. The stories behind what Emmett did that day in the store has a variety of "truths" attached to it. Some would say that young Till whistled due to a stutter or speech impediment from his polio as a younger child. Another version of the "truth" is that Emmett Till flirted with a young, white lady behind the register. An extreme version of a "truth" is that Emmett went as far as to touch the young woman on the hand or waist. In any version of the "truth," what we know is that a little over 12 hours later, in the early morning, the uncle of Emmet Till had his door kicked down and several white men pulled Emmett from the home. We also know that Emmet had an eye gouged out, he was severely beaten, he was shot in the back of the head, had a large engine fan tied to his neck with barbed wire, and then thrown in the river. Till's body was found three days later by a few young boys fishing in the river.

The mother of Emmett Till was adamant that the funeral for her son would be an open casket. She wanted the world to see the truth that America was hiding. The photos of her son's funeral were published in articles seen across the nation and globe. The victory, if you can call it that, was the awareness of what the south still was in America. However, the trial against the accused murderers was in their favor and the men who brutally killed Emmett Till were never convicted.

During the 1950s, despite the continued unequal treatment, Black boys and young men responded to the call to be bold and lead. Young Black men understood this issue was a battle that needed soldiers and the young brothers were prepared to enlist. We saw there were leaders in the community and in the media across America fighting for equality and freedom. We were learning to resist as the early phases of the Civil Rights Movement were setting in and taking root. America was seeing the Black community developing for a fight or perhaps a war. Yet, there was another war looming across the globe. America was noticing a pressure that was building up on its lands while also keeping an eye on the rise of an "evil." There was a growth of politics that to some was a threat to the American capitalist based theory. America was built on ownership and profiting by individuals that "earned" it and that philosophy was being threatened by a philosophy that removed such individuality and privatization.

I am not here to talk about the positives and negatives of the various types of economic and political systems. That, like all knowledge, is for you to discover and develop your own "truth." However, there is something to be said when one system sees another as a "threat." There is something not quite right when your government teaches through fear. Much like the African was a "lost jungle child that needed to be civilized" or Indigenous people of the Americas were "savage beast that needed tamed," America's new "truth" was the Red Scare of the 1920s that continued to loom during the 1950s as communism was growing in Vietnam. I will never speak against wars because of my respect for the soldiers that lost their lives or lives or with memories. Our economy is based on each person having more because "more" is better in the eyes of our government. Our desire for "more" is not to share with each other necessarily, but to harbor and get "more." There are other governments and economies that do not support the idea of individuals having "more" and America was fighting for their identity at home and away as some of the American citizens questioned if democracy and capitalism was working. I don't oppose the concept of wealth through business and hard work. However, I think the philosophy on how we can leverage wealth for a better country should be considered.

The 1950s was a powerful time for Black people in America as it was a time to define oneself in many ways. Yes, there were the people that were concerned about their day to day life and there was an element of "the street" that resided in the larger urban cities. However, there was a calling for Black people to sign up for a "war." The war that had been waged against Black people in America since the first ship arrived with Africans before we had colonies established on the land. A war that had generals that were calling Black people to action. It is during this time Black people were identifying with "stars" who were leaders of the time. There were athletes as well as a few actors that some aspired to be like and had their level of perceived fame during these times. Yet, the other "stars" of the time were rallying in any area that could spread a message that was revolutionary. Igniting the spirits of all ages and various cities and states, there was a calling that many Black people answered to rise up and resist the inequities that America offered.

Oddly though, there was a separation in philosophies of how Black people were to achieve equality. Much like the dueling philosophies of Booker T. Washington and W.E.B. DeBois, two men during the '50s would clash in their solution to the oppression Black people were enduring. The rise of two prominent Black men began to occur in the 1950s and with their leadership there began a debate on how to solve the American Negro "problem." Attempting a peaceful approach to the efforts were the Christian ministers such as Dr. Martin Luther King, Jr. and other Christian church leaders and attendees. Along with the more peaceful movements were students, teenagers and college students poised to pose as an obstacle to the machine that was built on capitalism, racism, and classism. A different solution posed were the teachings of the Black nationalist. A separatist group that defined equality as first starting with the cornerstone of redefining the identity of the Black American. The most identified organization with this philosophy during the 1950s was Malcolm X (El-Hajj Malik Shabazz) and the Nation of Islam (NOI).

Highly disciplined, the NOI looked more like soldiers and Malcom X was their general. The NOI would march in cadence in suits and stoic faces in mostly urban areas of the northern states. Cities such as Harlem, Detroit, Chicago, and Philadelphia would see Black men and women without signing words of peace and overcoming. As the spokesperson for the NOI, Malcolm X was a master orator and spoke a bold truth into the ears of Black men and women. A bold truth then included different history that had not been taught in America regarding the ancestry of Black people of America. A truth that rested on Black people being proud of their history and who they were and to walk into that specific narrative. These men and women were not preparing to ask for equality and cooperation, it was already theirs and they were demanding that America atone for the acts against Black people. The two philosophies of X and King would clash often. Both groups wanted the same outcome of Black people being respected as human beings and offered the same respect as the white. Separate these two leaders were dangerous, united they quite possibly could have been an unstoppable force.

The end of the 1950s also brought the birth of Motown Records. Black artists have been the soundtrack for America since we were on plantations. Our emotions mixed with our talent and rhythm continue to draw all walks of life closer to our stories that we sing. Motown was different because it was the gateway to stardom and it was owned by a Black man, Berry Gordy. In a small house studio in Detroit, Michigan, Black vocal talent flocked to the studio with hopes of being asked inside for the next steps. Individuals and groups, males and females, vocalists and instrumentalists would sell all they had for their dreams and spend hours and days singing and playing in the yard of the Detroit castle of cool. This was the American Idol of their times and social media was anywhere the talent could cause a crowd to listen. The record and music industry was still a business and the artists weren't receiving the majority of the profits, but the life was still better than the one America had waiting for them and it sure did look good.

The 1960s brought a time that you do find in your history books to some degree. There was a new rock star in America and the world. Now on newspapers, on the radio, and on the television, there were protests and the rebellious act of wanting equality. Being broadcasted throughout the United States and around the globe were Black people and in many cases supportive white people that stood arm in arm to fight for the rights that were constitutionally theirs, but those who rested on oppression and built their generational empires on a perceived power, "they" were not willing to freely give their "authority" over so easily. "They" saw a shift in a perception of power. "They" saw that an oppressed group were making a run for potential wealth and control, both of which "they" wanted to keep for themselves. Meanwhile, millions were watching supporters and equal rights advocates of all colors with a spotlight on very specific Black men. Black men who were articulate and powerful in their communication. Black men that were leading organizations and movements while calling out the hypocrisy of those who were leading America at the time. A generation of children were seeing these leaders that were confronting ideals that were rooted in values that America was established on through an interwoven DNA trait of "they."

The former children of the 1950s were older now and they had learned of the various untruths that were taught to them in their younger years. Those teenagers that listened to rock 'n' roll and appreciated the art that united races through lyrics, beats, and dancing were young adults and continuing to battle the status of "they." The rebels of the '50s were now ready to force change. The young Black girls and Black boys were now young women and men who were ready to push a revolution. The Civil Rights Movement was a movement led through the actions of the youth. The leaders of this movement were in their thirties, in some cases younger than today's most famous athletes and musical artists. Your heroes, your stars, your idols that were getting the most attention were leading a cause and were Black men and women fighting against a spirit of "they." Much like the youth flock to a certain style of clothing or brand today, the youth flocked and rallied to the cause in the 1960s. More and more of the youth played their parts whether it was making sandwiches and drinks for the leaders and participants during small house and church meetings or taking to the streets to protest and being jailed, there was an identity that was established and something to believe in that brought more and more to the cause.

An interesting time because as a people, in America, we could not figure out how to love each other. By this time, our country had suffered from separatism and a specific hierarchy based on race since its inception. There were laws that defined the ownership and authority to brutally mistreat Black people for centuries by this time. There were other oppressive and, in some cases, brutal acts other ethnicities and cultures suffered all by the legal right that "they" had. To expect that this spirit would acquiesce and to just be nice and hand over access to social and financial leverage was strategic ignorance at best to this point in history. You see, even if you don't necessarily believe in what "they" represent, "they" still control the majority voter base in the majority of political races in America. Our democracy is based on representation. Theoretically, the people in office represent the beliefs of the people that put them there. As someone who is employed by the people through their votes, political candidates want to keep their jobs and thus want to stay on the good side of the majority of the voting population to continue to be their voice, their leader, and their champion of their values. Centuries in America our values rested on systemic and legal racism and oppression while turning eyes from abuse, assault, rape, and murder because of the rights legally that governed our country and the spirit of "they" that flowed through veins. This belief of the "right order of things" would not be removed overnight and any politician that aimed to do so was talking their way out of a job.

We cannot wait for politicians to lead us because they are not necessarily leaders. They are representatives of our beliefs and they should act on our behalf. It is the people that dictate the flow of the tides and if there is no change we must become a tsunami that crashes the shores of the status quo. The people took to protesting in the 1960s in small groups and eventually the waves grew. History tells us four Black students had one of the first "sit-ins" in the '60s by sitting at a "Whites Only" counter in a diner in North Carolina. These young men were never served, stayed until closing time, and came back the next day…with more people to sit in the "White Only" section. The numbers of "sit in" protests grew to thousands and involved the NAACP and a new college based organization the Student Nonviolent Coordinating Committee (SNCC). The protests were aimed at a specific store corporation across the region of America and within months the store changed its policy removing segregation. What would happen if our youth today decided collectively to challenge an issue. Teens in America spend $66 billion dollars per year in today's economy. The youth can collectively break companies and you have without knowing it. Just by trends shifting companies have struggled and some have gone out of business. Imagine a culture with a specific purpose in which your dollars spent changes who gets hired in companies, who gets raises, or how companies donate to charities and give back. You all have the power to make "them" take notice. We could also look at the "Black dollar" and remember that we spent at least $1.6 trillion dollars in 2022. Research shows that targeting marketing has decreased recently, but we still spend. Meanwhile we have politicians who boldly defy our history in schools and we do nothing.

During the 1960s, the youth were joining forces to cancel inequality. Working with Martin Luther King Jr. and the SCLC, Ella Baker works with hundreds of students to establish the SNCC. As the sit-ins were establishing themselves as viable tools, SNCC solidified itself through the beliefs of proactive, nonviolent protests from the teachings of Mahatma Gandhi. Some history would support that SNCC was formed to help move quicker and act with more "flare" than King and the SCLC. The youth were tired of waiting for orders from the elders and they were ready to fight with all the energy and passion they had.

As there were moral victories at the federal level with the passing of the Civil Rights Act of 1960 that increased the expectation of equal access to voting, the federal expectations rested on the states and jurisdictions in the states to follow through on the expectations set. A president has a higher percentage of voters that vote so, playing a numbers game, a president can lose a few percentage points with a couple of voters disagreeing with laws if they remember when it's time to vote. Governors and local politicians at the state level have closer connections with residents which makes enforcing expectations different and losing a few hundred votes could have higher consequences.

Recently, "they" decided to reverse the Roe vs. Wade decision that stated that abortion was a constitutional right. Today "they" also ruled to strike down a law in New York that required people to demonstrate a specific need to get a license to carry a gun in public. "They" doubled down on carrying a weapon for death and removed the ability for a woman to make a decision about her life. I am not asking you to think a certain way, but I am asking that you get involved so others are not thinking for you or us. There are protestors and supporters in the streets at capital buildings across the nation. There are elections that are occurring and people will return to the polls. Who is going to vote? The narrative is based on "values" and specific political strategy is making sure the voters are emotionally connected to the person running for office. Since these acts by the courts have passed, there have been rallies and social media blasts of "them" taking back our country. No talk about gas prices, inflation and costs of living, or education, but "they" remind voters this is America, we have specific views and rights, and we are winning the fight. How often do the citizens go to the media and demand answers from politicians when they do not act in our collective best interests? How often do we ask for goals from these politicians and demand they make these goals or we rally to make sure they don't win another term? We have politicians that don't talk about what matters because they don't make changes in their roles. "They" won't offer you freedom. You will need to evolve and offer "them" the life "they" will never offer you. You will need to lead and in return offer all an equitable chance to the American dream that originally was designed for the white male, but is vision still to be achieved.

The early 1960s is a time that was filled with several battles in the war for equality. Freedom Rides occurred as a protest against a law that made segregation on buses that travel through interstate highways legal. Established by the Congress of Racial Equality, buses filled with whites and Blacks traveled throughout the states as a protest to be regularly met with anger and violence that included physical attacks and bombing of the buses. Quite often these attacks were performed in the South as police stood by and observed mobs attack these riders. Angry mobs who only attacked the Freedom Riders because the mobs accepted the information that "they" provided. The information that led to racism and hate to keep Black people in their perceived place. A place that equaled paying them less and offering them less resources which was established by "them" who kept a larger profit. It was not "they" who were a part of the mob, attacking, and burning buses. It was the people who wanted to be "them" one day, but still struggled daily to have more of the American dream. Pawns being played regularly in history are those who support a narrative, but rarely benefit from it. These people look like those in "power" or control and their physical attributes connect with those who speak to the emotional connection points of crafty puppet masters, but those in the crowds are often misled. Misled by their emotions that are being used by those who are in a position of power and need the masses to support them. These are not issues of color and race, but of fear of lack of resources and control. So the pawns attack the buses, the pawns beat protestors, the pawns wave the flags, wear the shirts and hats, and have bumper stickers on cars, the pawns yell and scream and parrot the talking points of "them," and the pawns storm the capital while the leaders are in their places of comfort and safety.

  Black culture continued to permeate through America as music did its best to help some citizens forget the troubles of the days. The early 1960s brought the vocal talents of Chubby Checker along with the fun dance craze the "twist" as well as romantic ballads from groups like the Drifters and the increasing popularity of little Stevie Wonder. The early 1960s also brought an explosion of white vocalists and bands that had a very similar sound and groove that had been presented by the Black culture over the decades. The early 1960s saw chart toppers such as the Monkeys, the Beatles, the Rolling Stones, and Elvis Presley. Offering a different message was also Bob Dylan, who was bold enough to sing about the times, placing a new format of truth going into the ears of teenagers and young adults.

Athletically, there were rumbles of basketball as its popularity grew. Football also saw its share of Black athletes making a name for themselves especially in college as the first Black athlete to win a Heisman trophy occurs with Ernie Davis the running back from Syracuse University. However, the quiet strength of Wilma Rudolf in tennis and the baby faced Casius Clay dominating the Olympics gave Black people more to be proud of as representations of themselves were seen as being globally the best in their sports.

As Black people and white people were finding common ground and more and more were joining the cause, violence is the answer of those who oppose equity based on a misinterpretation of power. Now across America and the world, television and newspapers are offering insight to physical pain that is endured by those who are attempting peaceful protests. Much like social pressure that early colonists encountered, a few leaders of our nation wanted to fit in with social crowds across the globe and made decisions for the country that were mostly about money. However, a "free and democratic" nation was now being broadcast for being hypocritical as the news displayed hoses spraying on citizens and dogs ripping at the "free" people of America. Could America market itself across the world as the land of the free while violently subjugating its citizens to such trauma? More importantly could America increase trade and wealth through democracy and capitalism as other countries watch blood being shed from people in America that just want equal rights? The world was watching and America's secrets were being offered for all to view and pass judgment.

President John F. Kennedy(JFK) during the 1960s represented a bold form of progression. An icon in his own right, President Kennedy was seen as "hip" and "cool." Younger than most presidents of the time, JFK had a strong connection with the younger population and his views of unity were often seen as controversial from a strong culture that remained consistent in America. JFK offered a new era for the Democrats and as America had been through several wars of the decades and the fear of the "evil empire" of Communism was looming, Americans were looking for a strong leader nationally and internationally. JFK used his youth and swagger to his advantage. Debates were televised and in 1960, almost 90 percent of all homes had a television. JFK understood how to work the cameras and how to appeal to the viewers. The voters were looking for a change and JFK represented that change. One act in particular brought JFK closer to victory was his ability to shift Black voters from Republican to Democrat. We weren't always such a sure vote for the Democrats. As a people, we have been easily swayed by the "gifts" of the parties. Abraham Lincoln caused us to be Republicans before we could even vote. Democrats began in the 1930s to lean into the lower socioeconomic levels which included Black people. JFK once called the wife of Martin Luther King Jr., while Dr. King was in jail for protesting which solidified the Black vote as well as the progressive voter that wanted our country to advance. JFK also made phone calls that would expedite the release of Dr. King which caused Dr. King to endorse JFK. A few of the most famous leaders in America, one white man and one Black man working together for the country and the world to see.

Yet, two leaders having conversation about a vision doesn't make it so. As leadership and energy across America was pushing for equality, the force and misguided energy against love continued. Anger and hate spoken into willing and able followers continued to flame violent actions against Black people and those who fought for equality. The tolerance of hate often has unforeseen victims that the leaders of such rhetoric will not own. By not confronting a negative culture, we condone it and in some cases honor and empower it. In their own fear and weakness and their own pain and anguish, agents of hate and extremists are pieces to the chessboard that have been used historically and will continue. How many violent acts have to occur in schools today before our leaders agree we have to react? Whether or not we agree on the conditions of the Second Amendment to bear arms and what it offers, what is the countermeasure to keep our children safe at the very least? We have the most remarkable military of the planet with an extremely high budget to keep us safe and we can't figure out how to keep nine-year-olds in an elementary school safe from a nineteen-year-old shooter trained through a video game and "how to" videos? Even still, that would be a reactive and defensive measure. There is no self-reflection of the adults that are spewing hateful words on camera for the youth to see and for followers to march to. There is no public acknowledgment of wanting to do better for our collective betterment. There is only silence after the pain to grieve and mourn and then the voices pick up again.

The 1960s had images of the pain that had been shared with the world through television and printed media. I recall sitting in a few history classes and the several years I would watch slavery depictions of some sort, the atrocity of lynchings, and the brutality of the 1960s. That curriculum is being phased out and I don't know what your children will read. Future curriculum will no doubt offer the March on Washington and review the words of the "I Have A Dream" speech spoken by Dr. King. It was a peaceful representation of civilized action for desired change. It was a visual representation of white people and Black walking arm and arm asking for change.

It was America listening to its people in a moment of discourse. It was "them" allowing us to get together to talk about issues as any good leader would allow.

However, there continued to be resistance across America with issues specifically in the south, not even a month after we had the bombing of the 16th Street Baptist Church in Birmingham, Alabama. As I am writing this to you, that is sixty-two years ago. 62 years ago in America four individuals were led as they felt they were enacting the perceived orders of the narrative to blow up a church, with no regard to who was inside the building, killing four Black children and injuring many others. It wasn't until 1971 the first conviction in the case was made after being reopened.

The hate in America as a country spilled into the assassination of President John F. Kennedy. 1963 saw the commander in chief assassinated by Lee Harvey Oswald who was murdered days later by Jack Ruby. No one will really know what caused Oswald to perform the act. However, we know that JFK was incredibly progressive in his thoughts, vision, and actions in regard to equality and equity of people of color. JFK was a threat to "them" in the sense that he was attempting to offer equitable footing for countries that were in African and Latin continents and islands. By no means was JFK perfect and further research in his political and personal life will give you areas of improvement in the decisions that were made, but the brand of JFK was connected with the improvement of the lives of those who were oppressed in America and around the globe. This hateful act caused a regretful reaction from Malcolm X who was asked his thoughts on the assassination of President Kennedy. Malcolm X stated, the assassination was, "Chickens coming home to roost." The statement was later clarified by Malcolm X as attempting to offer an analogy of America's violence coming full cycle. Indeed, the hate that was and is left unchecked continues to fester and cause damage in communities of all kinds and the only opportunity to defeat it is to acknowledge it head on and collectively push toward achieving a higher understanding of being. This level of cultural change won't happen by accident, but could occur through your generation leading the charge. Using your power and influence, your financial pressure, social impact on trends, and your energy you can demand "better" from politicians, media, and talking heads. You define our reality.

A continued tugging of the best route to gain equality is ever present in America. What is also present is the complexity of the Black culture. Just as America offers different subcultures and beliefs in the pillar of "American" in this country, America continues to wrestle with the question of, "What is the Negro experience?" We continue to ask the question of what it means to be "Black." The question itself of asking what it means to "be Black" is asked in ignorance. There are experiences that Black people share and can share. Food, music, and community has become fluid over the decades as the economy has brought different cultures into the same zip codes as well as the capital gains on sales of items of the Black culture. Yet, there are experiences that cannot fully be shared by all based on the judgment and oppression that occurs in our country based on perception of others. I cannot tell you the feelings that a woman has when she walks into a room filled with men and the emotions she has to deal with in her interactions with "them." A person outside of the Black experience may be able to relate in a connection to racism and prejudice, however people outside of the specific Black experience in America may not fully understand what it means to exist in a country that has years of overt, hidden, and implicit racism and oppression since its inception. Culture of America is complex and the Black experience has a few roots and sadly the cancer of "them" is a major part of the DNA that is being a Black American.

As Black citizens continued to define their identities, they watched icons in the media to determine their allegiances. As hate is witnessed via church bombings and images of peaceful protestors being met with fire hoses and police swinging batons and vicious dogs attacking Black citizens in the south and north, the NOI and Malcom X continued to grow. Malcolm X called for more Black people to become more proactive in their resistance and prepare for war if peace was not truly an option from a select type of representation of white America. As Malcolm X had a vastly different background than Dr. King Malcolm X's message came with a resume that involves a street edge with all of the danger that intelligence and directed passion can create when united. The two men had a polarizing message and polarizing appeal. The two were so dynamically separate the relationship was often used as an analogy in other situations.

Heavyweight boxing remained an area where Black men found glory and levels of financial success and fame. Others in the Black community found idols to look up to and other communities enjoyed the entertainment and gambling opportunities on the matches. Two headlining fighters were Floyd Patterson and Sonny Liston. Both Black men, Floyd was a brother that was humble from birth, had a difficult start, but made his way through the boxing world in true form to the sport. As a Black man, Sonny Liston also found his start in life to be difficult, but had more encounters with crime than Patterson. Liston had such a connection with the elements of the "streets," he had notable perceived ties with the Mafia of the times. This type of connection and street persona was referred to as the reason why it took Liston to receive an opportunity to a championship fight based on the American champion being a "thug for the mafia." Patterson was noted as being a "good representation for his race." Those in power appreciated Patterson's ability to be "cooperative and open and polite." It was evident that the stage was set for the ignorant person to make the connection of Dr. King being Patterson and Liston being Malcolm X or at least their perception of Malcolm X.

The vast spectrum of philosophies between Dr. King and Malcolm X was further used in popular culture through the creative efforts of Marvel Comics and Stan Lee's X-Men. Sadly, you might be more familiar with the Marvel characters than the cornerstone characters so I won't offer you much detail. Just know, art models history in the comics by establishing a war against a civilization that will not accept difference and two leaders that desire equality; one through cooperative measure (Professor X/Dr. King) and the other through rebellious acts and proactive use of force (Magento/Malcolm X). There is even a reference to the use of dangerous authorized agents(Sentinels) to attack and harm mutants in the comics which is directly connected to the abuse of authority of the police.

The 1960s and Black communities rallied behind these separate leaders and American leaders were careful to watch which adversary they wanted to go to battle with in the fight for change. Will there be peaceful protest and conversation that will lead to change or will change be demanded through what could be a civil war in the streets as more Black citizens choose to take arms and grow impatient for change as they listen to a general and await their striking orders.

As Sonny Liston went on to defeat Patterson to become the World Heavyweight Champion, there was a new type of Black man that in no way quietly made his way into the boxing world. Casius Clay was known for being bold and confident. Much like the spirit of the wrestler entertainer or what you see as an "influencer" on social media, Clay was receiving plenty of attention for what was revered as "antics" and others termed him as being "cocky" and arrogant. What they may not have known was the story of a young fighter returning from the 1960 Olympics with a gold medal, but being refused service in a home town restaurant. The disrespect that day in Kentucky caused the 20-year-old Clay to throw his gold medal in the river walking home for the event. It was then Clay decided to be a "different kind of Black man" for America and the Black community. Casius Clay was witty, he was playful, he was confident, he was intelligent, he was funny, he was strong in so many ways, but he also won...a lot. Clay's victories in the boxing world and his popular appeal placed him in his first heavyweight championship fight at the age of twenty-two against Sonny Liston.

Casius Clay was an icon to many, especially to Black men. Much like the entertainers of your time seem to have it all, Clay was all of what Black men wanted to be. Clay had the opportunity to speak his mind and still make a great living. As much as others may have wanted to stop Clay from what he was saying and how he was saying it, Clay was winning. However, the larger threat to those in perceived power at the time, Casius Clay was observably building a relationship with Malcom X. Malcolm X had a few peer group members that were also in various fields in America including, but not limited to, sports and entertainment. Though the relationships with these individuals caused no notable conflict, the relationship between Casius Clay and Malcolm X was very contentious. Clay, with his iconic status aligning himself to Malcolm X and the NOI was a concern. Potentially America could have their champion, if Clay were to win, using his stage and all of his iconic status demanding the rights for Black people and publicly noting the atrocities of the "American Way" and offering historical facts that would bring a very negative light to the lack of freedoms in our nation. In 1964, Casius Clay defeated Liston as a strong, skilled, confident, articulate, and intelligent Black man. Clay caused Liston, the representation of the Black man as a street persona (which Liston was much more than the media expressed), to refuse to come out of his corner in the sixth round. Clay set out to offer America and the world a "new type of Black man" and he did just that. Two days later, Clay would double down on his defining moment for himself and so many by announcing his commitment to Islam and changing his name to Muhammad Ali.

As the relationship with Malcolm X was the gateway to the NOI for Ali, their relationship would soon suffer a break due to Malcom X publicly admonishing the leader of the NOI and separating from the organization. There had been notable stress regarding Malcolm X and the NOI and their official leader. Malcolm X had become his own identity and more than a spokesperson for the Nation. This was most apparent when Malcom X was excommunicated from the NOI for his comments regarding the presidential assassination after he was specifically directed not to comment on the situation. An interesting theme you can see in our organizations that are developed by the Black community for the Black community is our inability to remain united against the larger issue. Sadly, in several cases, our leaders fall into the seduction of power, prestige, influence, and high financial comfort. Running any organization is no easy feat. Personal bias and personal gain can get in the way of any group achieving the vision of success and our organizations are not immune to internal drama.

1964 would end on a powerful note and win against those who were fearful of losing their oppressive grip around the throats of those who historically did not have equal footing in America. President Kennedy pressed Congress to pass a bill that would offer more opportunities through equality for all Americas. Though due to the assassination of President Kennedy, JFK did not see through the vision, the vision was fully accomplished in 1964 with The Civil Right Act of 1964. The federal government needed to pass yet another law because of the 14th Amendment which stated "No state shall make or enforce any law which shall abridge the privileges or immunities of citizens of the United States...," was not clear enough or those who feared freedom just did not care. The Civil Rights Act of 1964 was established to explicitly inform those who followed the beliefs of "they" that women and all colors, cultures, and creeds were to be offered the same opportunities that were being tightly clinched by one group since the birth of our nation. This new law would remove all legal protection of segregation and Jim Crow laws as well as overt practice of racism in life opportunities such as schooling, job, housing, pleasure, and more. Please note, I said overt racism. Don't be fooled into thinking this law meant "happily ever after." Strategies would change, but the protection of a specific "power," "control," and "safety" would continue and still remain.

The hate that infiltrated the NOI eventually led to the death of Malcolm X. The death of Malcolm X came at the hands of three NOI members. There are plenty of theories of conspiracy and the influences behind the three individuals, but regardless three Black men killed one of the greatest leaders the Black community ever had. A role model in many ways, flawed in his own ways and growing as a person all the way to the end. Malcolm, before he passed, had an opportunity to express his remorse for polarization against other civil rights leaders and white leaders and participants in the fight for equality. In many ways I wonder what would have happened if Malcolm had more time to work toward equality in his new mindset and as a potential partner with those who were fighting the same battles in the war for freedom for all.

There remained a "Negro problem" in America in 1965. A problem as seen by leaders and specific scholars of the time because of the challenge to the status quo. Uncharted territories as the country wrestles with trying to force an evolution and to do so immediately. I am sure there were racists during the time who did not want to see Black people achieve any form of success. However, there were also people who were of the same race as the ones that harbored oppressive spirit, who did not have the spirit of "they" and were just confused and did not know what to do next or what needed to be done to take steps toward our collective growth toward equality as a country. I am sure some really did not understand the perils of the Black citizen and wanted us to be better as a country. However, reconciliation was not an easy request and there could be no reconciliation while there continued to be a clear and present threat against the actions toward freedom for all citizens.

The year of 1965 brought a series of explosions in the war for freedom in America. During the month of March of 1965 several marches occurred in protest of illegal voting practices. If you recall, the Civil Right Act of 1964 was supposed to end prejudice and racist acts. However, if that were the case, Civil Right members would not have needed to march from Selma, Alabama to Montgomery, Alabama. A second march was developed to continue to bring light to the situation of unfair voting practices in Alabama. The second march brought close to 25,000 participants and a high level of media presence. As yet another effort to pass laws to change hearts and spirits and force change, President Johnson works with Congress to pass the Voting Rights Act. Laws make actions illegal, but they don't always create favorable actions. Laws exist on a social contract that leans on the agreement that members of society will agree to adhere to the law. However, federal laws didn't always make it to social acceptance in all corners of our country. America's voice for peaceful resistance was beginning to lose patience in the eye of the media. One specific interview led to Dr. King stating his discontent with the Americans at war in Vietnam for democracy and the Black people of America were not receiving their democratic rights. The Negro problem had grown and the peaceful face of the Negroes of the time was tired of the waiting game and "they" were noticing the shift.

Social unrest and peaceful demonstrations in the Southwest was one example of the battles in the war for equality. On the other side of the nation during 1965, there was an example of the pressure built up in Los Angeles. During a traffic stop, a Black man was arrested by a white officer in the Watts community of Los Angeles. The reports vary on whether or not the Black motorist was resisting arrest or not. However, what we know is that over the next six days there was approximately $40 million dollars in property damages, over 1000 people injured and approximately forty dead. What has been historically termed as a gang uprising, Black Muslim insurrection, and/or a protest of generations of oppressions and prejudices, the 1965 Watts riot was a clear example of what can occur when needs are not met.

1966 brings more development in the continuous efforts for equality for Black people of America. Younger leaders are coming into their time in organizations such as Stokely Carmichael of the SNCC who took the organization into a Black Power vision. Later in the year of 1966, Bobby Seale, Huey P. Newton, and David Hillard, three college students in Oakland, California, create the Black Panther Party to help resist police brutality in the city. I hope you are somewhat familiar with the Black Panthers? Yes, I am aware of the Black Panther movies and the comic book hero. Depending on the version of the truth you decide on believing, the two concepts, the Black Panther Party and the comic book hero were introduced during the same year, but were not directly connected to each other. The Marvel character was developed to help diversify the comic book industry.

The Black Panther Party was born from the minds of three young brothers attending Merritt College in Oakland, California in the early '60s. The growth and development of these leaders led them to question the government and the use of force the authorities such as police were exhibiting in the efforts to control Black citizens. Working in a community center in their neighborhood, the three young men continued to search for an organization that matched their vision. A vision that was more proactive in protecting the Black community and advancing the people socially, economically, and politically. The three men studied gun laws and socialist and communist government and teachings in their effort to find avenues to lift the Black community. It was toward the end of 1966 when three young leaders used the logo from another proactive Black leadership group in Alabama and developed the Black Panther Party.

The Black Panther Party (BPP) was developed on the premise of self-defense and led with an almost religious methodology for the organization. Their members had strict beliefs and "truths" and even wore specific uniforms, black pants, blue shirts, leather jackets, and black berets. The organization would have several "storefront" operation stations, were equipped with weapons and understood their constitutional rights and legal allowances for their cities, and sent regular newsletters into the community. I am getting a little ahead of myself here based on the timeline that I am painting for you, but I have to make note here of the BPP and their efforts. During their peak times, the BPP offered radicalism via a sense of responsibility. Their strongest efforts to build the Black community involved leading the efforts to feed families in need of food as well as establishing an early schooling program for the youth. Additionally, the group established their vision on their goals of a Ten Point Program.

1. We want freedom. We want power to determine the destiny of our Black Community.
2. We want full employment for our people.
3. We want an end to the robbery by the Capitalists of our Black Community.
4. We want decent housing, fit for shelter of human beings.
5. We want education for our people that exposes the true nature of this decadent American society. We want education that teaches us our true history and our role in present-day society.
6. We want all Black men to be exempt from military service.
7. We want an immediate end to POLICE BRUTALITY and MURDER of Black people.
8. We want freedom for all Black men held in federal, state, county and city prisons and jails.
9. We want all Black people when brought to trial to be tried in court by a jury of their peer group or people from their Black Communities, as defined by the Constitution of the United States.
10. We want land, bread, housing, education, clothing, justice and peace.

There should not have been a need to have such a plan, but at least they had one developed and they were organized for the effort. The BPP quickly became the most dangerous organization in America. Not the mafia or the Ku Klux Klan or street gangs across the nation, but an organization that was demanding equality and were armed with weapons, the law, knowledge, and leadership were the most dangerous. Yet, depending on the "truth" you believe, it was a relatively short time before the spirit of "they" infiltrated the organization and there were steps that caused the demise of the organization. What is factual are the several police raids and murders that occurred at the hands of police during several separate situations. The BPP was a radical organization that leaned into their boundaries including sending twenty-five armed party members into the California State Assembly as politicians were discussing new law that would limit open gun carrying regulations. Other situations included the arrest of Huey Newton for his involvement of the death of a police officer that pulled him over for a traffic violation, the death of 17-year-old member Bobby Hutton that was shot twelve times after he took his clothes off to prove he was unarmed, and the raids from federal agents and police that ended in the death and injuries of several as pressures that caused the collapse of the BPP. Regarding these issues, I mentioned there are possible "truths" that negatively involve party members such as Newton being intoxicated and willfully murdering the officer and the several situations being planned that went "bad" as attempts to develop more energy for the cause. The organization also grew across the nation with several chapters with various personalities and leaders in cities. A strong run for a decade and remarkable efforts, but eventually the organization would dissolve.

The 1960s was interesting for America as it was now about half populated by individuals that were eighteen years of age or younger and they were spending approximately twenty-two billion dollars a year. That is twenty-two billion in the 1960s at a time when the average house sold for $20,000. The youth had the numbers and were a huge factor of the economy and power in this country is most often aligned with profit and finances with a false sense of security. Color televisions, movie theaters, drive-in movies, concerts, and music in general were cornerstones in the life of many of the youth of America. As there was turmoil in America that many thought was coming to a head, there were artists who portrayed the pain in acting and music, but there were also those who attempted to escape the daily drama through a new whisper sex, drugs, and rock 'n' roll. There were new expressions and trends just like with every generation. However, one of the major trends of the '60s along with Black Power movement was the concept of Black is Beautiful. A new found freedom is Black people connecting with their roots and having a new sense of pride. Much like a state having a new basketball or football team, the concept of "Blackness" and Black Nationalism was coming through artistic formats.

The 1960s saw the birth of the afro and offered our first steps into space. This particular decade offered us the push button telephone, the cassette tape, and the advancement of computers, as well as the bikini, the mini skirt and the dashiki were all prevalent in the 1960s. The youth were bringing fashion trends and pushing America into the next evolution in technology, but we remained anchored in prejudice by a very strong spirit of "they." Generations of oppression would not let go even though the new generation was pushing into a future. It would be silly of me to suggest that all 18-year-olds and younger could be accepting of Black people and wanted equal rights and opportunity. Family traditions and cultures often do lead to specific behaviors. It is also unfair for me to suggest that families that have a culture of racism and prejudice could not produce family members that do not agree with the family beliefs. We can say that there were white youth who observed the practices and actions of inequality in America and there were youth that were white that saw the injustice and fought to make change by assisting organizations. Was it an intrinsic pull to fix what was wrong in American society or was the writings of Black authors, interviews on Black-focused talk shows, lyrics of songs from Black vocalists, or media expressing the Black experience in America on the big screen in movies like *To Kill a Mockingbird* and *Guess Who's*

Coming to Dinner? Was it a cry out into popular culture that brought more than Black people to the struggle of Black people? Was the fight for equality the trend or a reason for people to be involved in something meaningful? I think you probably had a little of both in those marches and protests and in those rallies. I recall looking at the crowds for the Black Lives Matters protests across the nation and in some cases the percentage of races other than Black was more prevalent than Black faces. Was marching the sexy thing to do? Was it the trend of the times to wear a specific shirt and scream at police officers? Maybe. However, I wonder if that same energy went to making sure inner city schools were equitably funded if that would have been a better ask to prove that Black Lives Matter.

I am not saying that I did not appreciate the sentiment behind the Black Lives Matter. The amount of energy we all spent in trying to get people to say the phrase "Black Lives Matter," the social media debates, the screaming matches, the "wokeness" and our Black kids still sit in schools that are failing them at a higher rate than primarily white schools. Has there been injustice with police officers murdering Black people in the name of the "law"? Yes. Will more kids grow up to live a life that isn't "living" in a sense of equality because their schools are equal in the eyes of the law, but not equitable? Yes. Kids that don't learn will on average lead lives that do not connect with life, liberty, and the pursuit of happiness. Where is that fight? Where is the fight for our students to understand how credit works? Real estate? Taxes? For our next generation to have schools that push healthier life choices in nutrition and exercise? That allows our kids to think analytically and push them to be leaders and question the status quo? When will we stop asking and just build what we need? It is not as sensational as a police video or cell phone images, but our kids are still dying slowly each day they do not receive the opportunities that the most affluent schools receive.

Some died for the cause of equality in the 1960s. Some were so tired of the oppression that violence was all they had left. There was plenty of bloodshed in the 1960s. Riots were occurring from coast to coast. Riots are pure rage that start with a "cause," but often the damage and violence occurs in the same neighborhoods of the oppressed. As riots occur, they are a reaction or a response to the emotions of anger and helplessness. Yet, the riot is not the answer to change. Riots are not protests. Protests involve strategy with desired outcomes in mind. Riots typically have one outcome and that is to release frustration and exhibit a form of unbridled freedom. The riots that I have seen in my lifetime to the time I have written this to you have always been controlled to remain in specific zip codes. The anger is taken out on local business owners and local businesses whether they are small corner or strip mall types or larger chains. The lawlessness is an effort to display control and a short reminder that the peace that is exhibited day to day is a choice. There typically is a time period the government allows the people to believe they have a perceived power and then the government shows a stronger exhibition of force. "Let the [negroes] blow off a little steam." Slave masters would let slaves have parties to do the same. Again, it has been my experience that this increased "protection" occurs after most areas in the neighborhoods where the riots had begun are rather destroyed and the rumor begins of people venturing into more affluent communities. "Have to keep [them] in their place." As I have said before, we are not oppressed by a color, but by a specific spirit or culture that is often identified with a specific race in America. Yet, the benefits of the American dream does not rest with one type of person. However, there are more challenges to some on their journey to life, liberty, and the pursuit of happiness. Other "minority" groups have had their challenges on their road to equality and their "freedom." This is not the space to argue who had "it worse" in their generational trials in America. Though, other races don't riot...they build. They build social and economic capital and with it comes political respect. The past offers examples of oppressed people that looked within their communities and worked to remain cemented on a code of ethics of their people. These moves are not fits of rage, these moves are strategic, consistent, and persistent.

The 1960s riots were about not seeing results and continuing to see a level of aggression toward us regardless of laws being passed for our equality. Regardless of what the law said, in some cases the law was killing citizens. 1968 in South Carolina at South Carolina College, three college students were shot to their death and twenty-eight others were wounded during a conflict with authorities at a local bowling alley. Almost all victims were shot in their backs and other parts of their bodies on the back sides denoting they were not posing immediate threat or aggression toward the authorities. It was also in 1968 Dr. Martin Luther King, Jr. was assassinated.

April 3rd in Tennessee, Dr. King states in a speech to a congregation that he had "seen the promised land" and he "may not get there...." By this time, Dr. King was not the star that he once was. Much like your stars come and go and your idols may fade, Dr. King's brand of activism was losing its energy. Dr. King was not the role model that he once was to Black youth. As a younger minister in the '50s and early '60s, Dr. King was a rebel in his efforts. Yet as the youth lost their patience, the voice of progressive activists became the new trend and leaders that had an edge to their expression was the new male icon for the Black male and/or Black identity. Dr. King remained vigilant in working with leaders in government roles that would listen to reason. Dr. King still had insight and the ability to connect with high ranking, influential people. Dr.

King was the Black civil rights leader of choice in 1964 for mainstream America, but he had since turned to speaking against the Vietnam War as well as the struggles of the poor. By 1968, King was falling deeper into not only being pro civil rights for Black people, but anti-government and more specifically anti-capitalism. April 4th, 1968, Dr. Martin Luther King Jr. was murdered by James Earl Ray, and the death of Dr. King started hundreds of riots across the nation. Riots based on the lack of patience as we had seen our most peaceful representation taken out by violence.

The 1960s ends with a haze of violence, anger, and an attempt for peace being ushered in with a music festival called Woodstock. The decade was filled with assassinations of prominent Black leaders such as Brother Malcom X, Medgar Evers, Dr. Martin Luther King, Jr. and Fred Hampton just to name a few that were murdered out of fear and anger. These deaths were on top of the beatings and physical abuse that was witnessed on the nightly news. The BPP continued its growth and Black men in America had less consideration for joining the old conversation of civil rights. As Congress passes its last equal housing right legislation the civil rights era fades as well. Of course there was work to be done and there would be people who continued the efforts to strategize and mobilize as the civil rights efforts exhibited, but the youthful energy had shifted to the pro-Black movement because "asking" for equality was reaching the true impact needed. The laws were being passed at a federal level for equality, but the hearts and practices did not change as the Black community desired. Did we think the laws could be enforced? As if there was going to be a way to police the actions that lead by such a hateful and jealous spirit. Legally citizens could sue, but there weren't that many lawyers in all of America to defend the prejudiced practices in each corner of the nation that continued to oppress specific citizens of this country.

The laws passed were moral victories for America and as a people, the Black community accepted the "win" while a smaller percentage continued to demand change.

As the trend shifts, so does the social influence of what is the "Black man." By the end of the 1960s, the definition of the Black male added a layer of edge to it. The conscious voice of the Black community is no longer the balance with Baptist preachers and the overwhelming visual is the militant fist of Black Power. No greater representation of the calling to the expression of strength in the Black community as the first and third place winner of the 1969 Olympics raising black-gloved fists in the air as they received their medals in front of the world that watched.

I wish I had more history to offer you regarding major advancements in our collective American society during the 1970s, but I cannot. I cannot tell you that after about two decades of civil rights efforts and assassinations, and brutal beatings, and police dog bites, and baton beatings, and fire hose spraying, and jail sentences, and sacrifice, and bills being passed into law, that magically everything was better. We know that the laws were changed and there were many hearts and spirits that were aligned with the concept of freedom and equality, but culture can be generational and America's DNA has a thread that aligns with a need for "winners" and "losers." Our system in America limits those who haven't cracked the code or have not been able to break the generational cycles of lack. Pick yourself up and make it happen. The land of the free. If you want it, go get it. All of that, I believe in and live by. However, I also know that our weights are heavier. I know that our race can be longer. I know that we often have more hurdles than others who compete for the American dream. The argument is that immigrants do it and other historically oppressed people do it and poor white people do it and they all have "rags to riches" stories. Culture can be generational. The culture of the Black people of this country is often not in alignment with success as a people with consistency. There are various "wins" of battles that have been achieved through a united front of Black people and other cultures that have stood with us. We fought back as slaves, but it took a country war to free us. We protested and achieved legal change with the collaboration of like-minded people outside of what is called the Black "race" of people. Yet, because those enslaved are offered a level of freedom, we settle for never being able to cross the "property line" as we pacify ourselves with material goods. Ever since the emancipation proclamation we have been working to collectively free our minds and spirits. Yet we remain enslaved to the desire to want to be like our oppressors. True freedom eludes us. As soon as we think we have achieved a form of equality, "they" remind us that there still is separation from who we are as a people and the full acceptance of what it means to be "American." The hate remains that lingers from the sound of the whip and warmth of the blood. The disdain for our existence is evident as we are reminded to stay in our place with de facto laws that attempt to convince us that our life has limits that connect with the life of lack and despair. The disrespect is more prominent lately as we watch certain politicians and media personalities garner attention for votes and ratings by stepping on the throats of Black men and women with verbal lashing with no repercussions. Our champions get beat publicly and we accept it.

    The close of the civil rights era also offered the birth to gangs becoming more prevalent. Remember, gangs have been around for decades by the 1970s. The life of the streets has always had a calling to Black men, The desire to have safety and security in your physical surroundings and in the emotional sense with finances and what it can bring you attracts some to the street. There are always options, but step outside where the majority of Black people in the US live and you have instant access to illegal activity that could bring you perceived power and dollars. Historically in the late '60s, Black gangs were developed in a response to white gangs. There were times historically when the majority of the Black community's voice was about a movement for equality and becoming united against a purpose, but sometimes the movement didn't make it to the most urban elements and when there was no direction, there were plenty of leaders to step up in the street option.

Now that the Civil Rights Movement had faded, there was a void in America in what would be the new trend. That void was filled with the remains of Black Power through the Black Panthers, a hippie movement that included all races to join in an opportunity for the overabundance of love, and street gangs were on the rise. This doesn't include Black people that were just trying to live life not necessarily under any trend. There were communities of Black people that were looking forward to working toward the American dream by living out their existence as "normal" as possible which included going to work and/or attending school to grow professionally.

Another issue of the time that continued throughout the 1960s into the 1970s was the Vietnam War. Unlike prior wars, the Vietnam War did not have the "American pride" as earlier wars. Drafting young men into a fight across the globe to fight a war that many didn't believe in quickly became its own political and social issue. In acts of defiance in the 1960s going into the 1970s, Americans were burning their draft cards in protest and the most notable public defiances came from America's Heavyweight Boxing Champion, Muhammad Ali refusing to enlist, accepting a jail sentence, and having his title removed from him. During these times, even the opposing party in Vietnam America was at war with, knew of the struggle Black people were suffering in the

United States. Black soldiers were reminded that the Vietnam War was not the war of the Black people via fliers printed and offered to soldiers fighting in Vietnam. A small third world country knew Black people were not treated as equals so it wasn't hard to feel the pressure of not joining the war as Black citizen in America. Yet, it was the Black man that was often called to the war as well as the less wealthy, white men who didn't have the resources and opportunities to avoid the draft. There were very specific wealthy white families that didn't see their sons enter the draft via a legal "loophole" and some of those sons became politicians and/or are still wealthy and are perceived as powerful. I will continue to say that this isn't a race issue as much as a status issue. Those with the status of wealth and perceived power will continue to have the most opportunities. Meanwhile, those without status and wealth are used as tools in situations where the outcomes will not affect those who historically had lower status. Indeed, the ones that check the most boxes in America regarding being a male, white, and wealthy (the wealthier the better) have the most advantage. Those boxes have historically been in a position of perceived power prior to America being colonized by a European empire. This idea of pitting races against each other, cultures against each other, and politics against each other is used as an opportunity "they" use to keep the masses distracted and to keep "them" in their status. I appreciate our troops and all the military has done for my rights and protection. I just question those who have voted for the declaration of war and how we were the pawns on the chessboard in history. Now I can say there are some good opportunities to join the armed forces with good outcomes for brothers and sisters of all kinds. I am not saying it is for everybody, but enlisting was once researched as the top three opportunities for a Black man to move from empty pockets to the middle class. I wish I had thought it through a little more before college and even after graduating with my first degree. In any event, the reminder is that when the load is heavy, there are a small percentage of people that know how to step out of the way and let the "help" take care of it while they supervise or flat out ignore the struggle.

Based on the "truth" you believe, the 1970s was a different struggle for the Black community. Thinking we had made it, there was just enough comfort for us to become complacent. The art of covert prejudice, racism, and oppression was the weapon of choice for those who wanted to cling on to their control of systems and material wealth. The suburban towns and cities had taken root and despite laws against prejudice being written, there were plenty of practices to keep those who were Black, brown, and low green out of certain zip codes, certain schools, certain parks, and stores. To this day, there are cities and states that have higher populations of Black residents and this is not an accident. Black people stayed in the South despite the overt racism of the times and others moved over the decades to where they could get jobs and afford housing. Today, your more "urban" areas are where Black people live. As we talk about these "urban" areas, they are less likely to have healthy food choices, good school options, and environmental health attributes like trees. These same areas often produce citizens with poorer health outcomes, single parent homes, and lower education achievement rates. As we have done in the past, Black brothers wanted the same kind of control of their lives and in the '70s that meant defining ourselves in a "new" America.

The 1970s was bringing the "cool" to a new level of mainstream. Black Panthers remained a sense of style and high masculinity. The Black community moved from "We Shall Overcome" to "We are here and I am Black and I'm Proud!" The culture was more aggressive in the stance of what they weren't going to take anymore and the youth empowered the version of free speech and free thinking with an interesting connection to "love" and acceptance. The new freedom was pumped through music as various artists belted ballads about change, freedom, sex, and love. The spirit was rebellious and at times it was angry, but still commercialized and as always if it can be marketed and sold in America, it will be, and it was.

As a Black man, social influence pushed or pulled you into several directions. Athletics remained a popular option especially since basketball and football was becoming more and more popularized through television. As a Black man you could be a rebel against the "Man" and walk the life of the Black Panther type of activist. Black men found acceptance in the Hippy movement, but America didn't sensationalize that lifestyle because the movement was based against our form of economy and not about profit or the rich making more money. If you were born with artistic talent and fortunate enough to harness it and sharpen it, as a Black man you could aspire to be the next great actor on stage or in entertainment. There was the option of the streets that we will talk more of in a bit. And then, as a Black man, you had the option of working everyday with no regard of "being" any type, but still you found influence toward, and a society trying, to label you. Still, the list rarely offered the doctors, lawyers, architects, business entrepreneurs, bankers, and CEOs. If you made it to college, and some did, you worked middle management for someone who kept you in your place.

Even though the Hippy or Flower Child movement in America produced individuals that were, almost religiously, against capitalism, big business and profits, and materialism, there were plenty of the youth that connected freedom and success with the ability to purchase items of security such as a home, food, and clothes. Consumerism has been a cornerstone in the Black community and, as usual, the nicer of any of the items purchased the higher the status we felt we had achieved. Consistently, the Black community was a market and the community was filled with consumers. Consumers of food and drink products, clothing, transportation, and lifestyle and entertainment. More and more Black men and women were on television, in magazines, and acting in movies. The interest into the Black culture was America's new circus. Was there real equality? No. There definitely wasn't equity. Yet there was just enough space in the minds of America to offer the new narrative. Much like the narrative America could feed the world after slavery. "Look at our country, the rest of the world (mainly Europe)." "We are progressive. We are the land of the free. We are good people. We are the good guys and what we have to trade and sell is also good." Now America has fixed its "Negro problem."

America gave us the opportunity to consume equally or at least equally enough to make us feel like "them" or look like "them." We were free to buy the large cars and fancy clothes. We weren't free enough to have true equal access to education and jobs to pay for the materialistic lies. We weren't free enough to open businesses in our own communities to sell our goods because banks did not approve our loans for commercial real estate. We were equal, but unequally preyed upon through our own ignorance. One could say that "all is fair" at this point, but we miss the facts in the data that during these times there still remained a social caste system that kept established boundaries for the Black community and the Black community, at times, was too focused on their shiny pennies and small wins to establish to a movement to make sustainable change.

The 1970s were a time of activism and battles lost. The early '70s was another explosion of art in the Black community. America wanted to read, observe, and listen to the Black experience. The

Black Arts Movement offered something for the then "woke" and "cultured" people of our country to discuss as they sat and dissected our trials and tribulations. Our community was on display for all to see and America was profiting from the new trend. There was Marvin Gaye, who asked in his song, "What's Going On?" while the Jackson 5, Smokey Robinson, Stevie Wonder, The O'Jays, and Kool and The Gang offered entertainment to help lighten the mood. There was enough going on indeed to keep fighting, but America had a narrative that was fun and free that was overshadowing the voices attempting to raise awareness to the pain that continued and the oppression that remained. There are many books written leading up to and during the 1970s. Books that would be considered "controversial" in some schools now or a part of Critical Race Theory, both reasons some states would ban the books from schools. You need to get a hold of books by Nikki Giovanni, James Baldwin, Maya Angelou, Eldridge Cleaver and more to have the opportunity to open your mind and continue to question the agenda that has been prepared for the consumers of goods and information. Sadly, the majority don't read to find different versions of the "truth" to help them define their own thoughts. This same issue occurred in the 1970s as the focus for the Black community was lured away on what we looked like and resting the popular image. This meant the Black man was being defined by the masses.

The Black community was commercialized mainly through entertainment. Our souls were turned into melodies for decades by the 1970s and record companies and concert venues were profiting from it. The 1970s brought new exposure to Black actors on television, in the movies, and even on stage with standup comedians. The concept of how to sell the Black experience was created. To a degree "art" was playing out life, but in many ways "art" was also creating the social image of the Black culture. The early 1970s for Black men were filled with the images depicting what it meant to be Black, however these shows didn't always offer aspirational opportunities specifically.

The most popular television shows of the 1970s were comedies. There was the Flip Wilson Show which was a television program that included Flip Wilson a Black man, as both the main actor and one of the writers for the show. The program would offer several skits during one hour per week and Flip would play several characters. One of his most famous characters was Wilson dressed as a woman interacting in an over the top way that would send the audience into hysterical laughter. The comedian Flip Wilson would go on to be recognized by *Time* magazine as the first Black television star. The skits were "fun" and filled with jokes regarding the various types of people the audience could relate to and comfortably laugh. It was a "feel good" opportunity for Americans who wanted to watch a Black man on television. There were jokes upon jokes every hour of the Flip Wilson Show. Jokes that made fun of the Black culture, jokes that poked fun at the white culture, and jokes about America and various social and political topics. These topics weren't really controversial, but enough to laugh through pain if need be. Flip would have various guests on the show as well from the entertainment world which made his show even more appealing. Yet, what mainstream America saw was everything was "okay" and in some cases, Black men played a great role as jester.

During the early 1970s there were several Black male comedians. Artists such as Redd Foxx, Bill Cosby Dick Gregory, and Richard Pryor to name a few. These Black men were masters of standup comedy and would leave audiences face hurting from laughter. They would use their experiences as Black men and their specific struggles to offer a less aggressive view into being a Black man in their times. Most importantly, as these men become more famous for their entertainment, Black men pick up the social stigma of being "funny," "witty," and "comical." The standup routines that these comedians offered were typically harder toned than what Flip Wilson offered. Flip offered a family show mostly. These stand up comedians' material during their show was aimed at an adult audience with plenty of drinks, drugs, and sex references, with the exception of Cosby who had a brand of "clean" comedy for the most part. However, when on national television for mainstream America on programs such as the Merv Griffith Show, the Ed Sullivan Show, and the Johnny Carson Show, the material used was relatively light by even your harder comedians because during those times cursing on national television wasn't accepted and neither was making people too uncomfortable. Of course, some of these comics in all of their wit, honesty, and rawness on stage would be placed on television programs and in movies regularly if the specific comedian's brand could be sold so many comedians adjusted as needed to market their brand and skill toward the audience. As in prior times in history, the image of the Black man portrayed on the small or large screen is a reality for society to buy into and accept. Not to take away from the gift of comedy and the acting that occurred from these Black men of the decade, but there were a few more scenes and television programs in which the Black man was being laughed "at" more often than what was productive for the advancement of Black people.

As Black boy in the 1970s, you see the new superstar is the comic and being "funny" and in some cases "clownish" gains you acceptance. You see the Black man weekly faking a heart attack, or falling all over the place, or over expressing some emotion as they roll around, jump on a chair in fear, and dance in glee. Not far from the plantation in which we were pulled out into the yards for entertainment for the Master's guest. One hundred years later and we are "grinnin" and dancing for "their" approval so we can have a sliver of the life, and happiness "they" possess in search of security. We look for our identity in others and what we are offered to identify with in the times of the 1970s is not the powerful orator of the 1960s or the courageous freedom fighters of the Civil Rights Movement. The Black Panthers were offered as criminals through the media so who are the idols that are propped up for us? The cast of *Carwash* the movie, Fred Sanford of *Sanford and Son*, and JJ Walker on *Good Times*. Yes, in all of those examples and more there are strong Black male qualities that are admirable, but often it is overshadowed by bug-eyed coonery. To hear this same men of stage and off camera was a magnificent representation of Black male excellence, but they played a role on the screens and the little Black boy mainly saw what was sold.

    The 1970s in the age of movie entertainment had a specific genre of film. The genre title was offered after the '70s, but we now know how these movies can be categorized in general. These films were several stereotypes packaged in an hour and half. These movies were someone's representation of the Black males and females in the urban environment. The main characters of these films were typically over the top "cool," tough, courageous, and stylish. These may all seem like great qualities, but in many cases these main characters were street hustlers, criminals, and pimps. In some circumstances the main characters were also detectives and even vampires, but still Hollywood was sure to make these movies, that generally had mostly Black casts in the city, about a Black man that gets all the ladies, walks with a swagger and quite often theme music, interacts with drugs and violence, and probably knows a form of karate. That is even ridiculous for me to tell you, but society was soaking it up and Black men in society were living up to the hype Hollywood was selling. The big screen expressed a representation of control and security that every Black man wanted. Movies like *Superfly*, *The Mack*, and *Shaft* were hits in the early 1970s. These characters had it all figured out, all the power, all the wants a person could desire, and of course plenty of women. In most movies, there is even a time or two when a white person, including police officers, felt the wrath of the Black "Superman," and that is who our community received as their champions.

The 1970s also came with a few other trends that were not the highlights of our culture. America was becoming more familiar with drugs. The 1970s was no stranger to marijuana, but also LSD (Acid), heroin, and cocaine. The long term effects of these drugs were not known at the time. While marijuana and cocaine were in America prior to the 1970s, drug usage in general increased with a desire to enter different mind states for freedom, artistic expression, or an effort to feel a sense of joy and/or peace. Oppressed people were not free and in search of freedom and all that were denied to them, these people reached for a drug. Marijuana was the affordable drug in the 1970s, but for those who had access to the funds and the network to purchase it, the various other drugs were available and, to a degree, a status symbol. Whether you were taking the drugs or had them at your venue, drugs other than weed meant you had more money to buy drugs other than weed. Of course, selling any of these drugs was also a great way to attempt to achieve the security you never had as a Black man. Drug dealers are typically leaders, entrepreneurs, and intelligent. These are the folks that could do so much good for society given the right opportunity. However, for many brothers in the '70s, the opportunity that arises is the drug business. As with any business, there are customers and territories and street gangs and violence support the goal of both.

The concepts of gangs were around long before the 1970s and it wasn't necessarily about being Black or brown. Early gangs included mostly white people that were protecting their security from anything and anyone that was different from them or that threatened their hopes of becoming more like "them." Gangs are about protecting territory and attempting to use force to create that security we all are striving for in our lives. Gangs are connection points, networks, and relationships. Gangs take the same opportunities as politics in helping people see themselves in a larger group for a sense of control. Therefore, gangs of all kinds were around and prevalent in all areas and with all races before the 1970s. However, there was a new birth of the urban street gang. The '70s street gangs were prevalent in the urban areas which included Black and brown families that didn't have a lot of money. However, during the 1970s there was a push for commercialism and marketing to families through television programs and movies in such a way our desire to "buy" our acceptance was prevalent. As we saw the clothing on our idols and the cars that they would drive, we would desire to keep up with such trends and wear similar clothing and drive similar cars. Our desire was to have homes and all the finer things in them to prove our equality. To achieve the American dream for some would include illegal activities such as drug dealing and gang membership meant protection of your selling territory.

It was in the early 1970s major gangs like the Crips, Bloods, Gangster Disciples, and Vice Lords began to flourish. Depending on the version of the "truth" you believe, there is some report of these gangs being created with a positive community design. The Vice Lords even found themselves applying and receiving grant dollars to further organize their community. As the Black Power Movement was still providing some energy and their "role models" on the screens were taking their own control of their lives, organizing in the community was still an opportunity, but with the organizing there was also opportunity for criminal activity. Having my experiences in life, it still amazes me the minds and the skills that went into criminal activity to create and sustain a "prosperous" lifestyle in the city. Leadership is a skillset and these gang leaders established and grew organizations that would span across several states and have thousands of members. These members that join gangs have some form of code or rules that are learned through initiating rituals in some cases. There are tiers of leadership in these gangs and protocols of respect and deference. These organizations do not happen by accident. Establishing these organizations that have sustained for decades is a sign of brilliance. Organizing the various layers of workers in the community at different shifts is top tier management. However, the youth that join gangs often are not valued in school and more likely drop out of school before they graduate from high school. Yet, the values of the youth are often seen by gang and drug leaders and they invest the time and effort and build relationships with the youth. All the next generation needs is connection and a chance.

Now as a young Black male growing up you were influenced by a society that offered you images on Black men on the screens as jokesters or super suave pimps or at least over the top bravado filled with costly materialistic possessions. As a youth, you may have seen singers and athletes as well to give you aspirations and inspiration. Yet a close touch point for the youth with relatively fast results were the gangs and illegal activity. Gangs offered a pathway with the least resistance to the reality the youth desired. In addition to a "promising future" there was a fear of gangs and fear and respect are confused for the same thing. When gang members walked the streets in their typical gang fashions of the time, people moved out of the way unless you were the rival gang.

The early 1970s continued into the mid-1970s and the late 1970s. The end of the Vietnam War was marked in 1975 and continued a confusing time for America. Soldiers came home from a war to a place that was nothing like they left it. Bell bottoms, afros, flamboyant colors and suits on men and miniskirts and tighter fitting clothing on women. They kept up with the news to a degree and still had a connection with the latest trends in music, but the war spanned across two decades and with it there were several changes in society. They also came back to a country that was divided in the support for the war itself. There were no hero's welcome for these returning soldiers. These soldiers came back from witnessing gruesome warfare, The soldiers left hoping to make a difference in their lives and maybe the lives of others. The Vietnam War was fought differently in the jungle of Vietnam and in its rule of engagement. The Vietnam War included warfare with severe emotional and psychological effects on our soldiers and the use of chemical warfare. The care that was needed for the soldiers return could not have been predicted and our country never adjusted to offer the type of care that was needed to reacclimate a person from an experience like the Vietnam War. Upon their return, far too many soldiers self-medicated with weed and alcohol and in some cases harsher drugs like opium and heroin if they had access to it. There are still Vietnam veterans to this day that are fighting for our country to do right by the soldier that was never the same coming back to the states due to decisions made by our leaders.

By the mid-1970s, America had its first and only president in history resign, home video had been introduced, two major computer technologies had been founded with Bill Gates' Microsoft and then Apple by Steve Jobs, Steve Wozniak, and Ronald Wayne, abortion was legalized throughout America (now overturned in several states), video games and home computers were established, and America was considered 200 years old. 200 years since America was its own country. Approximately 300 years since the

African had been brought as a slave. By this time in our country, we had established space stations orbiting the globe, but we really had not set up a system to ensure fairness for all people. The country was advancing and Black people were still trying to find their opportunities. There were other citizens who were feeling the continued oppression from those who historically held the perception of power. Women, Hispanics, and other immigrants were not always invited to the table in America. Another group that was starting to garner more attention were those of the gay community. Men having sex with men has been historically documented for longer than America was even considered for colonization. Homosexuality has been seen as far back as the Roman and Greek empires of Europe. Regardless of your belief or practice on the subject, it remains evident that sexuality is yet another way for attempted oppression due to judgment and lack of understanding and respect. Understanding and respect does not ask for participation or even acceptance. We can all have our beliefs. Yet, when one group tries to overtly and covertly apply efforts of pain and punishment whether emotionally or physically the group applying the pain is typically acting out of fear. Fear of the unknown and fear of losing a system of control. "How dare a group of people consider themselves different from what we have identified since the beginning of time?" "Homosexuality is just immoral and unethical." "My book of religion says that this lifestyle is wrong." These are positions to take based on belief and faith as people position themselves against homosexuality. Understanding is accepting that others have different beliefs and values and we are in no position to argue correctness, but we can all have our own "truth" and exist in such. I am not telling you what your "truth" should be, but as we search for freedom, forcing our "truth" on others is not the way. Love for humanity is at the root of freedom.

A lifestyle in the 1970s, as sexuality became more free, was offered new space to grow. As a country, it wasn't illegal to have sexual contact with a same sex partner until 1961. The 1960s saw more efforts of the homosexual community for their rights and acceptance and by the 1970s there was much debate on the ethics and morals of sexuality and what was to be "allowed." Just as with civil rights, while there were laws in search of freedom and equality toward the opportunity to pursue happiness in America as a homosexual, those who refused to offer peace to those who did not fit into a specific sexual box continued to cause harm in corners of the country. This was not an issue that was larger in one region of the country. However, large urban areas were areas of growth for the homosexual communities and areas of conflict. Riots, beatings, and murders were not unfamiliar in the gay community in these urban areas. There were protests and there were conflicts in the efforts for the gay community to push for equal opportunities. It's no longer about hiding in broad daylight for members of this specific community in the larger scheme of things. These decades of the '60s and the '70s were moments of strength for the gay community and an effort to garner sustainable perceived security and power.

These urban areas were also areas of bustling business. Much like the cancel culture of today, gay communities understood the power of the dollar. Remaining as close knit as possible, the gay community supported each other in these urban areas and supported businesses that offered a level of mutual respect. Much like America found ways to respect (tolerate) Black Americans for a dollar, Americans in these urban areas found ways toward acceptance because they desired opportunities that connected with profit and perceived power as well. The difference, the gay community has, since the 1970s, owned their presence as an opportunity and remained united. Yes, our circumstances are different, but given the opportunity to review our two oppressed groups, we can see there is a dynamic of economic influence that the gay community continues to harness; the ability to flex when needed and to make those who rest on capitalism shift a little in their seats. It may not be a victory in the move toward love, but the reverence is earned.

A historical "truth" even connects with the gay community dictating the next major entertainment shift in America. The mid-'70s was a time of evolution in music in the attempt to find the next big trend. An upbeat sound of fast tempo music that allowed choreographed steps to some songs became an East Coast explosion that later made its way across the nation. The birth of "disco" was an opportunity for the freedom of the hippie or flower child movement linked directly with the embellished funk soul brother and soul sister vibes that were being sold in movies and still trending in cities. Urban environments still had issues with drugs, still remained focused on material wealth like big cars and flashy style, but now there was a new soundtrack. It was at these times nightclubs were the new spot lights in cities and in some cases they were exclusive for celebrities and those with perceived power which made their lifestyle even more seductive for the "average" person. Also, with these wealthier people in the clubs, were people who can afford the more expensive and elusive drugs such cocaine, quaaludes, and heroin. High priced drugs meant aggressive drug dealers and sales that both increased during the time in the cities. Drugs and violence became a lucrative opportunity for brothers to chase the American dream.

As America's love for disco went mainstream with top-ten hits in music and movies such as *Saturday Night Live*, America was also reminded of its ugly past. Just when brothers were content on watching images of themselves as pimps, gangsters, and "bad" soul brothers on the screen, a television miniseries brought back a hard truth America was trying to market its way out of in all of its capitalism. Based on a 1976 novel written by Alex Haley, *Roots* had Americans glued to their televisions. Records are still held based on the amount of American citizens reliving our past through episodes on a television program. *Roots* was the most historical film documentation of Black and American history of African slavery in America through the Civil War. Americans, on these evenings, watched the atrocities of slavery including representations of the abuse, rape, and graphic beatings and lynchings of slaves. There was more historical fact in a 1977 movie that is allowed in some US History courses for school students today. Based on this movie, there were shifts and some remembrance of the need for the Black community to reconnect with our ancestry of Africa or even with our community efforts of the 1960s. Not much came of it. However, perhaps one new trend possibly birthed from revisiting the African roots and the struggle. The close of the decade ended on one of the next largest trends that would lead to remarkable influence in our community and beyond; hip-hop.

It was 1979 when "Rapper's Delight" hit the airwaves. However, hip-hop was being cooked up long before the times of "Rapper's Delight." "Rapper's Delight" was the birth of commercialism and the opportunity for profit through hip-hop as record producers saw that there would be a market selling something that was gaining momentum in the Black community. Hip-hop was a culture that developed much like all the other genres of music that was created from the emotions of the oppression of people. Hip-hop was an opportunity to own a vibe as a people. Disco and the clubs had become too mainstream and in reality too expensive. The young adults of Harlem, Queens, and the Bronx of New York were tired of trying to dress a certain way to only be turned away from nightclubs. To adapt and wanting to let loose and enjoy themselves, urban youth and young adults began to host parties in their own "clubs" that were typically worn down buildings, skating rinks, and/or anything else they could run electricity to and enjoy themselves for a few hours. The style of clothing changed into a variation of disco and the urban environment and people came together to dance away their pain and struggles. It was in the 1970s that most would argue would be the birth of the skill of being a disc jockey (DJ) that did more than just keep music going. More than just playing records, the DJ became famous for blending the beats and later adding "scratching" and "breaks" to the songs. Along with the DJ was the Master of Ceremonies who officially became the MC. The MC was the hype man of the party who made announcements and even offered directions to hype the crowds up in these local clubs. Eventually a very specific skill of rhyming over the beat became a trend which opened the door for "rappin'."

The MC/rapper was an entertainer and a storyteller that caught the rhythm perfectly and would ignite the crowds. Along with the clothing and music was of course the dancing, but we will further into that in a moment. It was the close of the 1970s and the Black man was becoming something new once again. The pimp, the oversexualized, and the exploited Black man that was once the icon was slowly drifting away from the trends. The Black Panther militant type as a male role model was mostly lured away into gang social connections or quietly fighting in an opportunity to be accepted in society through employment with the aspiration of being "somebody" one day. There were athletes on the scene and entertainers, but those dreams, while a hope for children, were fleeting by their teens. Still something remained that Black community members could not point out as easily as Jim Crow and plain in sight racism. This bias was ingrained in many cases and in some circumstances the disdain for Black people was a family trait.

The message of never being good enough to be offered an equal opportunity was also a family trait. Mothers and fathers coming home from working double shifts still not bringing home enough for kids to feel the level of security they desired was continuing to cycle despair through yet another generation. Students were being sent to schools that increased the equity and opportunity gap as the suburbs flourished and a generation was being raised in entirely different versions of America. Blue collar jobs were still a good option for Black men when they could find the opportunity. Factories, manual labor, and skilled jobs if the bosses would allow offers for long, hard hours, but honest work. However, the honest work still offered an existence that was still hardly getting by and the youth were looking for opportunities for a form of success and safety.

Much as the music entertainment industry was an outlet and pathway to security for those who aspired for the dream in the 1950s into the 1960s, the 1980s opened a new viable path through the new soundtrack of the youthful generation. The Black man at this point had lived through generations of trials and tribulations. This evolutionary process had brought to the 1980s centuries of development as well as trauma. The hip-hop generation that came through the '70s was ushered through names like DJ Kool Herc, Grandmaster Flash, Afrika Bambaataa, The Sugar Hill Gang and the Furious five. All of these individuals were Black men who were looking for an opportunity to showcase their talent and their community in a positive way. The music, the dancing, and the style of clothing was a movement established by individuals under the age of twenty-five and was something that revolutionized the world.

Looking back, it was an off scene to look at, as our style of dress was radical which the term "radical" became a term to use in the '80s as a positive. It was an era born out of disco and funk so there were plenty of fashion and music connections attached to the '70s. Seeing those pictures of the time makes me laugh as our iconic men wore spikes, leather, and even eyeliner at times. I don't know if the entertainment field was running with the clothing decisions, but what is often seen on stage and in photos during the late '70s in hip-hop wasn't exactly "street" or "urban." Of course, because it was seen on television and on album covers, there were Black men that fell into the trends because their society said it was "cool" and there was a perception of success tied to the Black male entertainers. The rappers of the time were still in the story telling mode of the original or during what is appropriately called "old school" rapper and era of hip-hop. One of the classics of the time was "Rapper's Delight":

> *Now what you hear is not a test, I'm rappin' to the beat*
> *And me, the groove and my friends are gonna try to move your feet*
> *See I am Wonder Mike and I'd like to say hello*
> *To the black, to the white, the red and the brown, the purple and yellow*
> *But first I gotta bang bang the boogie to the boogie*
> *Say up jump the boogie to the bang bang boogie*
> *Let's rock, you don't stop*
> *Rock the riddle that will make your body rock*
> ("Rapper's Delight," Sugar Hill Gang, 1979)

The 1980s was yet another layer of cancer in the Black community and the urban community overall. Black and brown people have always had a higher unemployment rate than whites in this country. There are a few times in history when the highest unemployment rates were held by Hispanic citizens. However, the highest unemployment rate for our country is typically held by those of the Black community even though the Black population is lower than both the Hispanic and white population. I am not stating this to divide us by race or to increase anger due to perceived prejudices. I am stating this because data is abundantly clear there is some clear correlation to the perception held by those who hire and remove employees and those who are unemployed and the system remains ignored. It was 1980 when America slipped into recession for multiple reasons, none that had anything to do with the citizens that were hit the hardest. While 1980 to 1983 was the official recession time span, the decade of the '80s was hit by the economic and social fall out of one of America's most widespread financial downturns. America was crumbling economically and fear set in stronger than it had in years. The fear of lack of control and ability to eat was a concern for the majority of individuals and their families. Companies were forced to reduce their workforce and the majority of companies with layoffs were factories, manual labor, and specific skilled jobs like construction and carpentry. More specifically, Black men and the youth were hit the hardest in regard to employment.

The 1980s was a time for survival for most individuals and families. However, the Black male found themselves lost as job options were not what they used to be. To present oneself as worthy and as a provider was a difficult task for the Black male. No, not all Black males were unemployed, but enough to create an entirely new reality and stigma on the Black male. Yet, sitting around without much to do in order to provide, even if they wanted to, created an outstanding moment of creativity for the Black urban community. This time of expression offered the birth of hip-hop with art in the form of graffiti, music, fashion, and dancing. Residents of the urban setting in New York were just dealing with the struggles of the economic downturn, but the new hip-hop culture caught on and made its way across the nation during the 1980s. Like other times of despair, the youth banded together in gangs, but in the culture of hip-hop during the 1980s, the streets had "crews" as well as gangs. The difference between a crew and a gang was the vision. Crews had territories that were marked by graffiti artists through larger pieces of art in the public eye known as "bombs" and in smaller opportunities known as "tagging." Crews traveled in packs mostly for safety and perceived security. Crews would fight if needed. However, crews were not involved in the specific criminal element of drugs and robbery as most gangs during the 1980s. The larger victory for the crews were dance battles and the hopes to make their craft into some form of fame and fortune through the club scenes and possibly into the music and entertainment industry. Once again, we saw the youth defining a new space in America. Something created in despair and a call to expression would soon fall into the hands of the mainstream in the early '80s and America found a way to profit and oppress artists and the culture. By the mid-1980s, what was once a street rite of passage was being sold in every corner of America and people who had no idea what urban life was were rapping along to the records and picking up the dance moves. Our culture was for sale once again.

The '80s brought forth a new era of entertainment. Much as hip-hop had been building on its roots from New York and the trend of break dancin' was taking America by storm through the youth, music in general was taking a new leap with a music video station in Music Television better known as MTV. MTV, located on a cable network, would advance music into a new era with having music videos that not only offered a soundtrack to our lives, but also gave us video representation of trends and what "cool" was. During the 1970s it was the movies and sitcoms that were leading the charge in defining blackness. The '80s created a new sense of importance on entertainers. Once again, the Black man was being defined and sold through entertainment. During the '80s we could be seen as rappers and dancers. It was also during the '80s that Michael Jackson's *Thriller* was released and sparked the genre of "pop" music. Prince's movie and soundtrack *Purple Rain* further defined the coolness of Black men. Eddie Murphy was a rising star on *Saturday Night Live*, a weekly comedy show where several comedians got their big break. Also, during the 1980s, a television network took a chance to remind Black folks that Black families could live better than "below average" lives as we watched *The Cosby Show* weekly. Television and entertainment was changing slowly to connect with what America was and what it could be. Again, it's not so much about "black" or "white" in entertainment, but more about what sells. You have seen this critical line in today's world when the worst thing in America by those who reap the financial benefits from popularity is being "canceled." I have to continue to remind you that there is power in where you spend your money and focus your energy and time. The youth can determine so much by simply deciding as a generation that you will take a stand for or against someone or something. Remember, what I mentioned about the Montgomery bus boycott? The misdirection is that there is a leader in an office, but reality, you "the people" have the real power.

It was a creative time for entertainment and profitable times for the companies and investors who owned the studios and stations. Some of the Black entertainers were able to gain wealth during these times as well. However, typically those in hip-hop were used for their talent and didn't understand how they were being taken advantage of through contracts they were signing with the glitz and glamour that was being promised. It wasn't until much later when those in the hip-hop music industry understood the importance of contracts and legal workings that made them captured employees of record labels. Employees that were only getting a small percentage of the wealth that was coming through the record labels and managers.

The entertainment industry was an escape and, to a degree, propaganda in an effort to help Americans believe everything was going to be "okay." Financially our country was shaky and we were engaged in a new type of warfare with Russia and China. This warfare was just enough of a distraction to keep our minds off of the unemployment and crime rate increase. The '80s were times you could cheer for the hero in the movie to defeat the Russian villain or dance in the streets with dreams of becoming the next entertainer superstar. However, despite what was being sold in the world of entertainment, the gap between those who had security and finances and those who were slipping further and further into financial despair grew silently in the shadows of the noise of America being a "great country." Black men wanted to have the fame and fortune of the music stars and they wanted the clothing television and movies stars had, but it was also a hard reality that America did not offer Black and brown community members the equality they deserved in several areas of society.

Our country needed money which meant budget cuts. Budget cuts for the American government at the time meant removing early education options and daycare provision for those who were living in poverty. On average, more Black people were living in poverty than any other ethnicity in America in the 1980s. If we still had the spirit of unity during the early '80s that the Black Panthers had in the '70s and the Civil Rights Movement had in the '50s and '60s, we could have bound together as a community and leaned on each other call the government into action for the unequal amount of layoffs the community was receiving, we could have leaned on each to make sure we shared the resources we did have and remained united as a community, or even provided day care and schooling for our children at high levels that would have offered teachings of advancement and traditions that developed the next generation. Although some limited programs were developed and families were attempting to support each other, in the end, families were lucky if they had a babysitter and the idea of child learning and developing was secondary to survival as television did much of the teaching and our minds were not analytically being developed. This is not exactly a historical point of reference that ends here. Flash forward to our recent pandemic when the nation suffered, but Black, brown, and/or students with "low green" suffered the most.

It was also during the 1980s in which research was presented through a book to the public, *A Nation At Risk*, that America was not educating children at the level that other countries were. Which meant America was clearly losing despite all of our efforts to look like global "winners." Did America focus more on education and offer improved funding to all public schools? No. America simply increased the expectations and offered standards in education without offering support for all students to achieve the goals. Therefore, schools being identified was not about creating better schools, it was about those with more ability, wealth, and perceived power being warned to make choices in where they raised their children to have access to better schools. Meanwhile, those in certain zip codes were forced to exist in school systems that did not offer equitable access to academic achievement. If America was about equal opportunities, then we would be sure every child had an equal opportunity to top tier education. Instead, based on taxes in zip codes that pay for schools, there are better schools in wealthier neighborhoods. If our leaders cared, federal dollars would create an opportunity to fix the underperforming schools to offer students that attend these schools a chance to experience various choices in life that relate to high school graduation and post-secondary experiences. We were offered data in the '80s that our schools were failing. We knew before the '80s our schools were inequitable. Schools that have the highest suspension and expulsion rates and the lowest graduation rates, typically happen to be schools that have a Black population higher than 20 percent. These are data points and yet, our leadership does nothing.

Education is often a random question in a town hall debate or sound bite by a politician. Federal level government will offer "more accountability" under a fancy name to offer a response to the lack of action. State level governments will offer "more accountability" as a stick and dollars attached to specific desired outcomes as a "carrot." Yet, if we have seen an issue with our model of education since the integration of students in public schools with equity and we have done nothing to change the model, who are we waiting for to save the schools? If developing strong schools is a team effort between the family, student, and organization, then why are we not holding the "organization" responsible? Not the schools, but the organization that "owns" the school that has too many students in classrooms, not enough high quality teachers or paying those in the profession what they are worth, and not yielding the results of at least 90 percent of all students graduating with positive life options. Instead the government will look at the schools because they are "failing" students when the government won't offer the funding to traditional public schools to adjust per the empirical research.

Why do we wait for "them" to do anything? What exactly are we waiting for as we watch our schools year after year having more obstacles to producing pathways to success for our students. There are schools that have a high percentage of students of color that also have strong academic results. These schools are producing these results despite the trend and usually have very strong plans of action to overcome the usual oppression that has historically and currently led to children of color having fewer life choices. There are schools that have the breakout stories that one day turn into a movie because the staff, school, students, families, and communities lifted the weight despite the shift in gravity against the community. Is it fair that any community has to lean on itself and cause a movement to make change? No, but that is the only way we will have what we need. That is the way any community in America has "made it." It wasn't the government that changed the people, it was historically the people that changed their reality through action. To have the best teachers interested in our schools and to have buildings and facilities that our students feel safe in and look forward to being in for hours and days. We know that schools that have a specific mission to end the cycles of poverty and fight back against oppression are the most successful, yet "they" don't want us to teach Critical Race Theory? Meanwhile, you can carry a gun, concealed, legally in some states, but you can't read books like the Autobiography of Malcolm X or Frederick Douglass.

Meanwhile, the schools in the more affluent communities are more likely to offer the top tier teachers and staff and cutting edge materials to keep students engaged. It still amazes me how some schools in one type of community will look like a college and another school in communities of color will look like a prison from a 1950s movie. We have millions, billions, and even trillions of dollars to spend on the areas that are "needed" in the country and in other nations. We have decades of data that says that schools of color are on average not as strong as primarily white schools. So what is the answer? I don't know for sure. However, we know more schools can be built for smaller class sizes. We know scholarships can be offered for those to attend college to be educators with a commitment to teach in specific school districts. We know there are specific steps and moves that "master" teachers perform to move ALL kids in classrooms. We know we could offer a higher rate of pay to teachers in these high need schools and hold these school employees at a higher rate of accountability so we can remove the employees who aren't helping kids learn at high rates. Don't tell me we can't fix this issue. There is recent conversation about increasing the minimum salary of teachers to $60,000. This is the federal government effort to fix the issue of teacher shortage. I wonder how much push back schools will receive from "them" to control schools and continue the inequity.

As a Black boy in the 1980s, there was a high chance you were witnessing your family struggle. While the Huxtables on television had a strong family with two parents that were six figure professionals, that was not typical for the Black families in America. Black and brown communities suffering from the recession and high unemployment rates saw an increase in crime and gang activity as well as drug use. Much like the night clubs that were exclusive to "high rollers" the more popular drugs were rather expensive. The allure of cocaine faded away with the '70s because of the costs and a new drug rushed in with the 1980s. This drug used cocaine as an ingredient, but was also cooked with other elements to purify the cocaine which resulted in a stronger "high" with a smaller amount. Smoking cocaine in any fashion offers a more intense, quicker psychedelic response than snorting the drug. Hence, people who could never afford cocaine now had access to a form of it for a cheaper price.

Crack took the cities by storm. Offered the name due to the crackling sound while being cooked, the small rocks that were smoked through a pipe ran rampant through urban America. The amazing disturbance with the drug is that it is not more chemically addictive than cocaine. However, the lives lived by those who are addicted are so painful that crack offers a joy they could never believe to achieve without the drug, even briefly. Once streets that Black Panthers protected to keep safe and united, communities that once fought for equalities such as the right to vote and to integrate public spaces, these streets were infested with a highly addictive drug. Crack was the final destruction of the Black community in so many cities in America. Not that everyone in communities was using the drug, but enough were either using, selling, or protecting the territory to sell, that communities became wastelands in comparison to the dream that once was for the Black community.

The Black male youth were not finding solutions to their problems in the classrooms. Jobs were not as accessible in America and Black male youth were among the least likely to have a job or be offered one. However, there was just enough belief in our new "promise land" during the 1980s that we didn't listen to the few that would try to oppose the slow destruction in the Black community. There were a few voices trying to resist the pressures that continued infecting the Black and urban communities, but we were caught up in the propaganda of entertainment and marketing as we shook our heads at wisdom offered through Jesse Jackson and Al Sharpton. All that was shiny, flashy, and was available to anyone that had the money to afford it could be bought and sold as the key to happiness. The Black athletes and entertainers were visible, but that was a long game and require work and specific opportunities in times when safety and security of finances through illegal means was immediate and opportunities were plentiful. Crime was a risk, but one that paid off the quickest and crack sales was in huge demand due to its addictive nature. The "small time" drug dealer was still pulling in a couple of thousand per month which offered a lot of power to a young man in the city. Selling $5 to $20 vials or bags per customer would allow steady daily income for the young brother who wasn't seeing much success in doing anything else. No one "made" the Black community continue down this path of destruction, but our thirst for the perceived power and security and safety of the American dream was just the right nudge.

The drug game isn't easy and those who make a profit are typically good at a few things. A person can't simply get a loan from a bank with a business plan to become a drug dealer. One can't just pick up the drug of choice to sell on the street from their local store. To establish sales in the drug game, you have to have the finances and know the people to purchase these drugs. Working in a street social system, the savvy drug dealer knows and has a network to become a smaller dealer first. There is someone in the community that supplies larger quantities of drugs for resale. The kid that sells the $5 - $20 type doses of any drug, must get his supply from someone that has hundreds of dollars' worth of supply. The smaller dealer may not be strong enough in the kitchen to turn the cocaine into crack, but someone is purchasing the larger quantities of cocaine and making measurements and cooking the recipe to produce crack. All dealers need to establish territories, a customer base, and have a work ethic that means long hours and consistent effort. These character attributes align with CEOs, surgeons, chemists, politicians, and entrepreneurs, but those in the drug industry only see drugs as their option for success.

Cocaine was a sexier drug, A drug for the wealthy and in some cases those who were perceived as powerful. There were plenty of wealthy people who found themselves addicted to cocaine and they made bad choices and ruined their lives and some died. However, the accessibility of crack created a flood of the product in the cities. The increase of crack use in America also offered an increase in assault, murder, robbery, and hospitalization for behaviors and dangerous choices while on the drug. Cocaine was a dirty, party drug that America could ignore. Crack was the problem of the 1980s, but America turned the problem into an issue in the Black community and specifically the young, Black male.

Depending on the "truth" that you want to believe, drugs are allowed in this country to destroy specific communities. There is a theory that exists regarding the '80s and the ability for crack to make its way through the nation from city to city. Something to consider is that while there are marijuana farms that are plentiful in America now, the coca leaf which is used for cocaine is not typically farmed in America and is quite illegal. Most would say that Florida was one of the major ports for most drugs including cocaine and the skill/recipe for crack. There are some that would say that the flood of crack that flowed through America was an effort to further destroy the poor communities, specifically Black and brown communities. These are just theories and thoughts with very little evidence to them. We are a very large country. Yet, you would think, before we focus on helping other countries and fly off into the universe to new worlds, we would consider improving our efforts to keep the US secure. In any event, I know this, the United State of America was in a recession in the '80s and the best way to work a country out of financial struggle is a war. Our country in the past was able to strengthen its economy after several of the past wars such as World War I and WWII. The "war" that was occurring with leaders across the globe in the '80s was "cold" and did not produce much, but fear and gossip. There was enough Cold War narrative to help an agenda regarding America needing to be #1 and for some to remain prideful, but it wasn't war enough for a political party to run their campaign in hopes of re-election and the "war" wasn't improving the economy.

During the 1980s, America was involved in war efforts in the Middle East with a war between Russia and Afghanistan. As the enemy was Russia according to the American government, and the "enemy of my enemy is my friend" was the logic at the time, our government supplied a growing resistance in Afghanistan. Specifically, a name and leader that came from the era was an individual that would later be connected to the longest American war, almost 2 thousand American lives lost, and the largest terrorist attack on American soil decades later. We were arming the people on the other side of the globe to fight a war and we were not concerned with arming our American citizens, who were historically underserved, with job access, with education for advancement, and with hope.

Another war was established during the 1980s. To fight the destruction of the fiber of America, the president, President Ronald Reagan and his wife Nancy declared a war on drugs. The Regan administration was going to save America's families by improving schools and locking up criminals. Sounds like a great idea when you read it or hear it for the first time. However, when we dig into the "war" it was a clear attack against Black males. The jail system has a history of unethically jailing Black boys and men. The 1980s would bring an influx of Black males to prisons that would profit by having the men jailed and from the work they would perform for pennies. As a reminder, prisons are a business that is often owned by a private company that can donate to a specific candidate or political party. Something to always consider are the donors of politicians and who is profiting off of these deals and laws. Crack was a problem in the poor neighborhoods and in the urban neighborhoods. By design, it would seem, the criminal offense for being in possession of a small amount of crack was the same as having a much larger amount of cocaine. Additionally, the individuals who were arrested for the possession of cocaine typically had cocaine money and perhaps strong lawyers. The crack dealer was typically a teen or young man that was willing to take the risks of getting caught for their opportunity for "success."

The images of the war on drugs was video of Black teens and young men being thrown against cars and/or concrete, handcuffed, and put in squad cars. Images of jail cells filled with Black faces was the new poster for the Regan administration handling business and protecting American values. Meanwhile, jobs for Black males were not plentiful and schools were still failing the urban child regardless of the new standards in schools. There was no war against poverty or unemployment or low reading rates in our schools, but the war on drugs made the inner city Black male the enemy of the country. I am not condoning the actions of the individuals that were selling drugs, but if you are a leader, there are times when you have to consider what part you played in situations of failure. The drug dealer, then and now, is trying to gain access to security and control. The ability to have access to the level of security they desire is so guarded by bias, prejudice, and oppression, the drug dealer does not see favorable outcomes in taking the legal pathway to success. The drug dealer has the same aspirations as the kid that wants to be a surgeon, lawyer, entrepreneur, entertainer, and/or athlete. Most people that desire lots of material objects need wealth for self-esteem and/or security. Black men have been looking for their confidence in material objects to look like their oppressors or those that have "power" since slavery. The desire to be able to walk freely and not have to look away when their child or partner is looking to them as leaders to provide and protect. The drug hustle is a means to an end and the end is to achieve a "power" we have been denied or at most offered unequally since America was founded on our sweat, tears, and blood. If you want to go to war, go to war against what really ails America, inequity.

Though again, I am not saying that we "had" to make these choices in our community. We were not offered equal footing in the establishment of America and there remains a lack of opportunity in access due to the lack of accepting accountability and any intervention from a loving, humane effort from our country to address the issue as one people. Yet, in the movements of revolution of the past, there was a call to discipline ourselves, learn, and take ownership of the true power that we already possess. Louverture, Nat Turner, and Harriet Tubman and those of the Underground Railroad had to overcome fear and leaned on faith as a discipline. Various individual people and families looked toward their ethics and character in their paths as discipline to make change. Marcus Garvey, Martin Luther King, Malcolm X, and more all preached to lean on sacrifice and discipline to make a sustainable change. We cannot continue to fail each other, point the finger, and give away our power in apathy. We need to take care of us.

There were victories in the '80s for the Black community. There were entertainers that made it into a level of mainstream America that placed certain people into an iconic status. Yet, we had been icons before in the entertainment industry. The growth in this particular department was the artist having more control and profit in their careers due their increased abilities to read and negotiate terms. We had our first Black Miss America and for the first time the NCAA basketball championship was won by a Black coach. We had Black Entertainment Television (BET) founded by a Black man, even though the first decade BET wasn't nearly as strong as MTV. We had the youngest heavyweight champion Mike Tyson destroying competition in the ring and we had General Colin Powell representing as the first Black man in two different roles during his time at capitol hill. Yet, what you won't necessarily see in the history books is how the '80s redefined the Black man in many ways. You may not have read the reality in which there was a tale of two Black communities. There was one view of Black America in the public eye that used the athletes and some entertainers as a focus point when providing evidence that racism had been overcome and we are all happy in our middle class and above lives coexisting. America could say, "Look, there are opportunities." Yet, on the news, we saw a darker time without understanding the root of the struggle.

There was a story to be told. There was the explosion of music and dancing that defined a decade and gave birth to a culture that has gone global and is still consistent. Then there was a Black community that was deeply affected by the covert racist tactics, open and implicit bias practices, and generational systemic oppression of centuries that eroded what was left of Black pride from the 1970s despite gangs and pimps. It was what could have been the final blow in the attack against a community of people that has been fighting for true equality for half a millennia. The Black community had become the most unemployed or underemployed, the most uneducated, the most impoverished, and then a criminal campaign was established that systematically removed Black men from the community as if they had no value to offer. Society saw Black heroes running up and down courts and on the big screens, but Black children saw their Black men being arrested and killed who were closer to their reality.

There was a cycle, as always, in entertainment with what the street produced as a trend somewhere and what the streets accepted. As in the past, during the '50s, '60s, and '70s, the '80s were filled with pop culture that included fashion, art, and music. In the '80s, athletics were advancing on the airwaves and as a business. Specifically, professional football in the NFL and basketball in the NBA was profiting more from attendance, ratings on television, and sponsorships. Even professional wrestling was becoming a "thing" with wild storylines and massive men beating on each other. On any given weekend you had Black men on television at the height of their profession. In the '80s you saw Black men with charisma, strength, fame and fortune, but what you may not have known was that these athletes did not have as much control as they deserved of their own career. In many cases, there was always someone taking the higher percentage of any profit. As little boys viewed their televisions and idolized those stars, opportunities were few and dreams didn't put food in stomachs. There was still a recession that had hit the Black community the hardest and men in Black community were still getting arrested and targeted in communities.

Even with all that was going on, the Black community had a way to hurt ourselves in deeper ways. The Black community has had an issue historically with colorism. As the European definition of beauty had been marketed as pinnacle, there was a push in certain times in the Black community to also achieve a connection with the European aspects of beauty. This was true during slavery with house negros and field negros. This was true in the 1920s with the conk and the perm to straighten our hair so it mimics white textured hair types. This was true in the 1980s as there were obvious trends of defining lighter complected Black people as the version of the Black person to promote in entertainment and marketing. Not to say there wasn't diversity in those that were seen in movies, on television or in magazines. However, there was division in the Black community because of a lie that remained since slavery, that Black skin had shades of value. There were groups like Shalamar, Debarge, and the Jets that mostly landed in the "light skinned" category. Also, there were individuals like Prince, Morris Day, Lionel Richie, James Ingram and later Al B. Sure and Christopher Williams who were seen as icons in America through the music industry. Even Michael

Jackson was getting lighter by each album cover. Actors like Philip Michael Thomas, Billy Dee Williams, Adolfo Quinones from the *Breakin'* movies, and Taimak as Bruce LeRoy were being lifted up as an attractive man of the times. I think sisters had it worse in the '80s with the various lighter complected Black women that were often casted as the pretty and/or sexy co-star of a movie or television show. Both brothers and sisters also fell victim to wanting an alternative to their texture of hair and the Jheri Curl became a trend throughout America in the Black community. There still remains an argument on how a few of the Cosby kids on the show ended up so much lighter than their parents. It's amazing that with all that was going on in America, we still found ways to divide ourselves in categories as we fight to be like our oppressors. Poverty, drugs, gangs, violence, and low access to equal education and jobs and we were dividing each other over who looked "mixed" or not.

Eighties hip-hop took the lead in response to the primary struggle of violence and drug use in the Black community. There is a risk to being political in your music. As I said before, the youth control the trends in music entertainment. Highlights of the '80s included some amazing pioneers both male and female in the rap industry. I could write pages on the Roxanne Wars between fore-mothers of rap The Real Roxanne and Roxanne Shante. Later in the decade Mc Lyte and Queen Latifah both offered the nation and world strong Black women with MC skills that helped develop the culture to new levels. While all flocked to both genders in the world of "good" rappers, the Black boys gravitated to what they saw in the Right On! magazines and in the videos to define Black male masculinity. A young leader in the rap industry in the '80s was LL Cool J who was one of the first major artists of Def Jam records. Much like Motown, Def Jam was the new budding mecca for rap artists in the 1980s. The record label was established by a young

Rick Rubin at New York University and partner Russell Simmons, a young, Black brother. At the time Rick Rubin was focused on rock music when Russell Simmons brought him into hip-hop as Russell needed Rubin and his knowledge of the studio. Depending on the "truth" you believe Def Jam was not known for offering equal shares of the profits that were made with some of the largest talent in the industry over their first decade. Rubin actually left the company five years after the birth of the business and Simmons stepped away about fifteen years after the 1984 establishment of the company. The ownership and production of the album is where the money has always been. Russell Simmons had done the same thing Barry Gordy did with Motown Records in his ability to sell dreams to artists and then cash in on their talents. The artists were paid a percentage from their records, but considering the artists were the ones on tour and making promotional travels, the percentage they would receive was far from fair. Black athletes and entertainers were not known as the types that had access to lawyers to read contracts and many of the athletes and entertainers figured they were living the dream and signed on the dotted line. Both Rubin and Simmons did well with their ownership and even better when they sold their share of stock to the company. The business continues to thrive today as one of the major labels of rap music throughout the decades.

The media used the images of hip-hop giants as America's evil. It wasn't the unemployment and schooling being negatively disproportionate, and it wasn't the incarceration rate being lopsided in the favor of more Black men going to jail that caught the attention of mass media of America of the time, but it was this strange culture that was building momentum with the youth. There was huge attention from the media on the lyrics in rap songs that were the enemy of America, but we will talk about that in a moment. As much as hip-hop started with disco roots with guys in leather, head dresses, spikes and chains, and fingerless gloves, it had started to take a more street element as the new birth of hip-hop introduced the nation to a harder street type persona. Run DMC and LL Cool J in the grand scheme of things were great pioneers as they were extremely marketable to urban and suburban communities, and Blacks, browns, and whites. Also, during this time, the sound of hip-hop changed from the various funk and disco rhythms to hard bass kicks and rhythms to go with a harder walking "B-boy."

By the second half of the 1980s decade, it was clear there were two distinct leadership styles through music in America. The East Coast had often been the leader of hip-hop, but there was a new sound coming from the west. This new sound was authentically raw in the telling of their realities. All of the stories of the Black youth in the communities that were filled with the violence and crimes that America was not proud of and would not own up to creating was being pumped through speakers. The late '80s gave birth to "gangster rap" with its graphic stories and profanity that mainstream America had no idea on how to respond to. Maybe it was curiosity, for those that didn't live it and it was pride for those that did, but gangster rap grew into a phenomenon. Historically, some hip-hop heads would say that the "gangsta rap" birthplace was in the east with artist Schoolly D with lyrics and rhythms that would picked up by both East Coast and West Coast rappers in their more aggressive topics and messages citing the element from their environment and the need to make money, utilize violence as a tool, and "getting" women.

West Coast gangsta rap icon Ice T moved from the East Coast to the west and developed into becoming a godfather of the style in California which later led to some of America's largest culture clashes in regard to the image and access the more affluent kids of politicians were being drawn to and listening to in their headphones. East Coast remained with their harder hitters with names like EPMD and Eric B and Rakim, but also the east came along with artists who offered a "conscious rap" of sorts along with their street tales that were not as "bold" as the west. What started out as turf wars in New York later mended and New York in the '80s became the voice of a social movement against the American system that was failing the Black community and a call for the Black community to unite under a calling of pride and unity as well as power and a call to action. There were plenty of artists that had rap music for music's sake that sold well, but there was definitely a birthing of a variety of voices as well. The genre types could not have been more different and it caused an interesting fork in the road for Black men to decide their paths.

We live in a world in which the music you listen to can define you and place in you a specific box. Much as Malcolm X and Martin Luther King, Jr. had in the '60s, the genre of music had followers and the followers had a very specific brand of thought and philosophy. It is far from this simple, but each genre had its primary leaders. There were other individuals and groups, but a rap group of the name NWA or Niggas With Attitudes were one of the most influential hip-hop groups of the late '80s and into the '90s. This group was famous in various cities, but infamous to the government. As a group of several individuals from Compton, California they all lived a reality and were on fire in the rap industry for telling their "truth" that mainstream America wasn't ready for as America was further introduced to gangsta rap. This wasn't a white issue, but a reality that the middle class and above, across all races and color lines, were not ready to accept and allow in their homes. Lyrics of murder, assault, drugs, sex, and gangs were various topics, but also this group was one of the first in the late '80s to use profanity as an art form. Prior to this point, the most curse words you heard through an album was a comedian and if you retold the joke, you knew your audience and would adjust the words as needed. Now these words were being blared through speakers, memorized, and recited by the youth and then some. NWA and others offered a reality that those who lived in the same or similar neighborhoods would use the lyrics like anthems. Thus, when the group created a song entitled "Fuck the Police," the youth were chanting to the rhythm their refusal to accept the police as authority figures as well as singing along to another hit, "Gangsta Gangsta!" Black people, especially Black males, were drawn to the boldness, the edge, and the defiance the group had which created a trend for many young, Black people to follow. There were street elements and there were stories in the lyrics that was America's dirty secret of the urban Black community. Some were worried that the glorification of gangs, violence, and drugs in Compton and greater Los Angeles was not good for the youth across the nation. The West Coast sound was making it across America and there were plenty of people who lived similar lifestyles they heard through NWA and it became their anthem. These brothers weren't claiming to be role models, but they were. Brothers across the states once again saw the dollars, the cars, and the popularity NWA and other rap stars had and the brothers were drawn to it and wanted to walk in the same footsteps. They were drawn to the perceived power and control they always wanted for themselves and their families. Brothers who weren't gangsters tried to become one, those who were gangsters walked harder than before and with a sense of pride.

  NWA never claimed to be role models or desired to do so. However, when they were asked about their music, articulate brothers would say to the media, "We are products of our environment." These gangster rappers would note that what they rapped about was what they would see daily in the reality of their lives in the streets of Los Angeles. The brothers were not making up stories to scare America, they were describing their city blocks, their struggles, and they were using language that they used in their neighborhoods to communicate. If America did not like what they were seeing, they simply did not appreciate the fruit from the seeds they had planted over the decades.

The East Coast still remained with their giants of hip-hop that other young, Black men idolized. Groups with names like Erik B and Rahkim and EPMD offered the edge of New York and the east while other lyricists like Kool Moe Dee and later Big Daddy Kane offered influences and opened doors for some of the most popular and successful rappers of all time. Also, during the mid to late '80s, there was a civil rights revival. Hip-hop started to find its voice in pop culture and now understood that it had the attention of America. As much as there was concern for explicit lyrics in rap, there was also a trend of explicitly calling Black America to recognize the oppression that they had been under and the failure of America in working with the Black community. Specifically, artists like KRS-One and Public Enemy were pioneers in the awakening of hip-hop in the late '80s.

The leader of Public Enemy, Chuck D, was the most vocal and prominent in his conversation with the Black community. Other members of the group changed a few times, but the original core included Professor Griff, Terminator X, and Flava Flav. This group had strong connections with the NOI and their music was directly connected to Black nationalism and the Black community taking responsibility to establish our sense of power. Something different for America to see and definitely something to make "them" shift in their seats as the image of various Black brothers on stage including five soldiers that would continuously march or stand in attention as lyrics offered items such as:

"Farrakhan's a prophet and I think you ought to listen to
What he can say to you" What you ought to do
Is follow for now, power of the people, say
"Make a miracle, D, pump the lyrical"
Black is back, all in, We're gonna win
("Bring the Noise," Public Enemy 1987)

KRS-One, who led with Boogie Down Productions or BDP had a similar approach that was mainly focused on the development of the Black community and the improving of our collective unity and education. His videos and concerts were filled with images of Marcus Garvey, Bob Marly, and Malcom X as lyrics rang out such as:

Some MC's be talkin' and talkin'
Tryin' to show how Black people are walkin'
But I don't walk this way to portray
Or reinforce stereotypes of today
Like all my brothas eat chicken and watermelon
Talk broken English and drug sellin'
See I'm tellin', and teaching real facts
("My Philosophy," KRS-One, 1988)

As a Black young man, or anyone who could turn on a television or look at a newspaper or magazine, you could have several representations of the Black man. There wasn't an either/or in music as there were other artists such as Kid n Play, Biz Markie, and DJ Jazzy Jeff and the Fresh Prince. There was even the first white group to be lumped into hip-hop, The Beastie Boys. Also, there were the male vocalists of the '80s as well. The '80s were filled with artists like Michael Jackson, Prince, Stevie Wonder, Lionel Richie, and Luther Vandross and groups like New Edition whose members later had their own careers. These versions of the Black male were, on average, outside of the norm. These brothers were able to speak a specific language that could get a party going in ways rap didn't always offer. Oddly enough, it was a Prince song in eighty-five that started to form "Parent Advisory" labels that were later placed on almost all rap albums as an industry norm. What wasn't available to young Black men were representations of Black men that were CEOs, entrepreneurs, architects, accountants, and various other careers that led to the middle class and above in the 1980s. The social construct of what a Black man was once again being solidified through media and popular trends.

Movies in the 1980s were a huge opportunity to offer some relief to the stress of daily life and also tell serious messages for those in the Black community and any others who were willing to better understand the historical heavy lift. Those films that were filled with action and laughs played a similar role in the 1980s as they did for America in the '70s. You would have thought actors like Eddie Murphy and Richard Pryor didn't sleep for years at a time in as many movies as they were in helping America laugh during troubling times. Pryor was offering his laughs as usual and Murphy had become a comedian and a sex symbol at the same time. Pryor's character remained with a thread of strict comedy with relationship sentiment or wittiness of overcoming some issue with a grand scheme. This formula has worked for Hollywood for years as some main character plays a clown type role only to offer their intelligence to overcome some manager or oppressive role or situation. Murphy found himself in similar roles, but also located his position of power to determine his own roles and even created and produced films. These roles put Murphy in a more savvy, smooth role with splashes of action to further express his alpha male status. Again, similar to the '70s without over the top pimp lines and overuse of drugs and gangs, but Eddie was the pinnacle of cool and many men wanted to be him. Murphy even had an iconic laugh that young boys and men would imitate. Eddie Murphy was on television in interviews, in magazines, in movies, and he even had a few songs that landed on the top hit charts. It wasn't long before you saw various young, Black male adults doing their best to style their hair like Eddie's in each movie he was in or wear the clothing trends he would wear on stage.

Other movies of the time were all over the place as Hollywood was attempting to find what genre of film was going to cash in the most. Hip-Hop movies had several rap stars and dancers while offering the soundtracks and trends of the movement in the streets. Movies like *Breakin'* and *Breakin' 2*, *Beat Street*, and *Krush Groove* were more about the music, dancing, and artist cameos, than acting and plot. *The Last Dragon* was an iconic '80s classic with martial arts, which was still somehow an interesting connection in the Black community. The movie still had a hip-hop soundtrack with a female co-star that was at her pinnacle of popularity who brought good numbers for attendance. Prince's *Purple Rain* brought a different element to the big screen. A great soundtrack, but Prince's music landed in the category of pop. It told a darker story of the main character overcoming personal challenges in the music industry in the town. However, in all cases, young Black men were identifying with these main characters on the large screen and America was also creating more boxes to put Black men into. An entirely different decade and Black men were being glorified as funny, charismatic, musical, good dancers, cool, fighters, witty in most cases, and sexy. Still though, we didn't see many of our icons as fathers, providers, responsible, steady, and specifically skilled or intelligent in anything that was tangible on the average in the real world.

We even saw a prominent director in a newcomer, Spike Lee who brought some of the most hard-hitting social concepts to the movie screen for viewers to wrestle with during the '80s and still today. Lee's movies in the '80s dealt with freedom of sexuality, colorism, poverty, and racism in three different films. Lee's movies were the type that left theaters silent at the end because the viewers were in deep thought in reflection upon their exit. The movies were ahead of their time and remain some of the most thought provoking pieces of cinema. All the issues were real issues in communities across America and the films started good conversations in the Black community and in America overall as the mainstream became uncomfortable with the topics. *Hollywood Shuffle* by director, co-writer, and actor Robert Townsend was also a "truth-telling" film that gave us insight on the struggles of America's stereotypes on Black men and Black male actors. In all of these movies, the reality snuck up on people who thought they were just coming to be entertained and they left with more honesty than they thought they were signing up for on a given night. Along with other various movies, *Glory* was released in 1989 and told the story of a Black platoon of the Civil War that fought with pride despite continued pressure and racism from the North and South. As much as these movies would start a conversation, a movement never really occurred as we quickly got comfortable in the daily grind for material goods to grow our perceived power in the eyes of others.

On the smaller screen, in the '80s, there were a few shows that offered the Black youth guidance and offered America depictions of the Black experience. There were lighter shows that typically left the audience feeling good like *Gimmie a Break, What's Happenin', Different Strokes, Benson, Amen,* and *Family Matters.* There were others of this genre, but ultimately these shows would very rarely deal with real or challenging issues in America because the goal was to disconnect and laugh with or at Black people depending on your "truth." Not saying anything negative about these shows, but any Black person has to audit the characters they are portraying in comical roles and determine are they acting as a caricature that stems from the cooning we allowed to do early on in entertainment as we acted out stereotypes to please those who controlled the narrative of the Black identity on screen specifically, in most cases, a ridiculous Black man. A few favorite TV shows of mine of the decade were *Yo MTV Rap*, *The Cosby Show*, and *A Different World*. The other shows had their place for a kind of brain bubble gum, but the style of television these three shows offered helped usher in new generational trends and some change in narrative.

The Cosby Show was first aired in 1984. Before I get into this, I recall mentioning this in another setting and I feel like there were a few people triggered by a similar conversation. Bill Cosby was sentenced to jail in 2018 and served three years in jail before it was overturned. He was accused of sexual assault of a woman in 2004. The courts have made their decision and Cosby is free based on their decision. Regardless of all that, growing up, the character Bill Cosby played on *The Cosby Show* was my role model. Also, because the show was called The Cosby Show many, myself included, would blend fiction with reality and talk about the Cosbys and the Cosby kids, but the fact is the family on the show were the Huxtables and they had it ALL. They lived in New York, but in one of the suburban areas. Their house was large, cool, safe, and clean. The family was filled with love, laughter, and support. There was a mother and a father that lovingly cared for each other and the kids. It was a two parent income, both parents graduated from multiple schools with multiple degrees. The father Heathcliff "Cliff" Huxtable was a doctor and the mother Clair Huxtable was a lawyer. Despite the busy careers of both parents, both parents were always around and they had family dinners. There were five kids and the teenagers were iconically cool as the actors were fitted with very trendy styles in every episode, but their style was their own. There were plenty of jokes and laughs, but the show didn't shy away from social issues in a few of the airings. There wasn't a worry of bills not getting paid and no talk of unemployment. There was no violence and maybe one episode regarding drugs and one regarding alcohol as they tackled the topics and the desire for the kids to stay clear of the items. This was the Black family that made it in America.

As a kid, I would watch *The Cosby Show* and would ingest all of the teachings of the parents. I wanted to be Cliff and I wanted to marry Clair so we can have kids and live like the Huxtables because that was the "win." To some, to be the Huxtable seemed like a possibility and a viable option. You can work hard and be all that this family was. To others in the Black community, they would state, "We ain't the Cosbys." A world in which a Black person could have all the "Cosbys" had was just too unbelievable. The lifestyle offered through television once a week was a fairy tale and to some fake. Others in Black community opposed the lifestyle of the Huxtables and dismissed it as "selling out." The concept of "acting white" wasn't new in America in the 1980s. Historically, "passing" was a way of survival during slavery times through the Reconstruction. Throughout American history and the Black American journey there has been a dance of what is acting "white" and what is acting "Black." Yet, it was in the '80s when specific research shows that Black kids would on average reduce their academic efforts because to work hard in academics would be "acting white." Based on the experience of some Black Americans, the successful suburban family that eats together with parents that attended college and are well paid professionals was not Black enough for reality.

Another program of the decade, *Yo MTV Raps* might as well have been the church for the Black teens and young adults in America. It offered glimpses of all things Black and trending in hip-hop culture which was growing stronger by the minute. This opportunity was like the change of print only media to the invention of the radio or the search for information in a library to Google. Any person who had access to cable had the ability to study the young Black culture from all corners of America and hear the latest and greatest music and soak in all the teachings the hosts and guests on the show would offer. Those of us that didn't have cable, would find someone that did and hopefully be in front of their television at the same time every day. Again, hip-hop was male dominated and so were the hosts and guests. This hour of television was a window into how a Black man should act to be cool. Language, dance moves, jokes, clothing and even how we engage with each other and women was all taught overtly or as a part of the hidden curriculum. Any icon of rap had their time on *Yo MTV Raps* and received some sort of "nod" of approval as they made their way to the next level of stardom..

    The third television show was something spectacular for the Black community and for America in general. Bill Cosby saw the opportunity for a spin off from his *Cosby Show* as his on-air daughter had grown up and she was off to college. She could have gone to any college the team thought of in America, but both Cliff and Clair Huxtable went to a Historically Black College or University (HBCU). Americans in the South might have known about HBCUs and I assume Black people in the South knew about HBCUs. However, *A Different World* made one HBCU a focus in pop culture. If you were to ask some teens what they were going to do after high school in the '80s, some would say they were going to attend Hillman. It should be noted that there has never been a "Hillman" and it was created through *The Cosby Show* and a frequent talking point for the main characters at times. Now the beautiful daughter was off to college and those who believed in the reality got a glimpse of what college life was like. During a time where there was a narrative thread of "college was for white people" due to weaker school systems in America failing Black and brown kids, some of us now saw a campus filled with Black people once a week. A campus that was doing more than studying and taking tests which was all we thought college was. It was beautiful, cool, funny and trendy Black people of all shades laughing, dancing, struggling, crying, loving, and living together while they aspired for a better outcome. These actors made us believe colleges were available for Black people and we didn't have to check our culture at the door. The men and women actors were portraying characters on that show who were popular, secure in their own style, intelligent, hardworking, interested in a social life, and working hard toward a future. Even though Hillman wasn't real, the show opened a thinking path for some Black community members to connect with and aspire to be.

The mid-1980s was a huge jump for the Black male athlete in football and basketball. Both sports had made their way to major networks and additional views were bringing more attention to the new gladiators. The 1970s had great football and basketball, but it wasn't marketed like it was starting to be in the 1980s. Television was taking leaps with cable networks and new sitcoms. The very look of network television changed with the decade and even though we were in a recession, the goal for America was to push citizens to spend, spend, spend and forget about their troubles. Football and basketball became a moment that people could forget their issues personally and in society and root for a team from their town or their liking. This, in many cases, meant you were rooting for some Black male athlete and lifting him up as a champion. There was a larger push for promotional ads with athletes, as Americans wanted what their champions endorsed to somehow have a better connection. The early '80s opened with Kareen Abdul Jabar and Magic Johnson at the height of the Lakers dynasty in basketball and you had stars such Erik Dickerson and Walter Payton in the football league. By the end of the decade, names like Michael Jordan, and Bo Jackosn dominated promotions and marketing in such a way that even if you didn't like sports, you knew who they were. The Black male athlete was marketable and in promotional opportunities men, women, and the youth were drawn to them.

America in general was evolving in many areas. Materialism didn't go away as new technological advancements were being sold and all wanted the new toys. Items such as microwaves, VCRs, video cameras, video game consoles, newer homes phones, portable radios, computers, cars with advanced technology, and something called a "pager/beeper" was making its way through the communities and were all major wants. Having any or all of these wants was a status symbol, but also was an opportunity that you had more security as you could afford these types of desires and not have to hyperfocus on safety, welfare, and food concerns like many others during the time. Therefore, the Black community members would try to have these items in their lives by any means necessary to have these items and the symbol of control and security. Layaway was a credit system that allowed customers to make payments on an item that the stores held until it was fully paid off and it was a big opportunity for those Black folks who would cut into their savings just to have the next shiny thing. It's sad that we would do so much just to feel like "they" did naturally.

The '80s concluded with America in a better economic place, but on average the Black community was still considerably further behind in social, political, and economic positioning. Yes, America is one country. However, by the end of the 1980s, it was apparent by several data points, that the communities that were highly Black populated were connected with failure in the game of life. We didn't have access to home ownership like other communities, we didn't have access to business development like other communities, we didn't have access to education like other communities, but we had plenty of access to drugs and guns which connected well with poverty and the desire to have power and control in any way possible. There were those who were "making it" and there were successful icons on television, in movies, and on the radio. Yet, for the flashes of success promoted, our sons, uncles, and fathers were going to prison and dying to violence more so than any other race.

An interesting conclusion in the rap industry was brought in 1989. Connected with the social consciousness of KRS-One, a movement was attempted called the Stop the Violence Movement. This was an effort to get all of those in the Black community to attempt to reduce the growth of murder in the Black community. The effort of the movement was a song that included several rap artists offering, lyrically, the need to stop killing in the Black community. The solid attempt did raise $100,000 for the Urban League, but as much as the song had some popularity, typically these kinds of songs that have attempted to be overtly socially conscious in such a way really don't resonate with those who are purchasing the music. The youth are powerful and their purchasing power is phenomenal. To make a decision to offer a specific political and/or social message through music especially in group form has never really worked for the hip-hop genre. A single artist can get away with dropping a few lines and maybe a song or two, but the united front of many artists on one song comes across very commercial regardless of the topic and ends up being received by an older generation in their efforts to "help" the next.

The economy wasn't as bad, but it did need a boost. As I said before, war is profitable for a nation and its economy when they supply the weapons. Perhaps a financial boost is not guaranteed, but it's a great way to keep Americans focused on the importance of being the muscle of the world for democracy. It has happened several times in history and the 1990s were no different. I appreciate every soldier for what they do for our country. I am not always a fan of the commander in chief's decisions to put our soldiers in positions they need to be in as we enter these wars that are for the "greater good." We have offered rationale for our participation in wars and we make them sound like they are altruistic. Yet, the underlying theme seems to revolve around spreading capitalism and increasing profits in America.

The Gulf War was oddly televised. The war was so televised the operation name, Desert Shield, that led up to and the war operative name, Desert Storm, was public information. It seemed as if America was trying to pose the war as a reality show for us all to watch from our living rooms. It was the first time Americans were able to watch missiles being hurled from location to location as if they were watching a new movie release. This was probably the start of reality television before we knew it. Perhaps the distance was far enough from the actual deaths for us to realize that we were observing the passing of lives on a grand scale. In any event, CNN displayed the war day and night like a video game allowing a window to our "selfless" efforts as Americans. We were saving the Iranians from a vicious dictator that was recently overtaking more territory and in this specific case, the land was oil rich. September 11th, we declared war on Saddam Hussein and his followers.

There were several "truths" about this war and the events that led up to Desert Storm. A version of the "truth" you probably have been offered is that this was America stepping in to defeat a dictator that stepped on the backs of his own people in a rise to power. This version of the "truth" offers America, once again, championing freedom and rights on the other side of the globe. Another "truth" will be that this war and the events that led up to Desert

Storm was about oil, the American government's trading policies with Iraq. and potentially losing the favorable relationship to a new ruler. Regardless of the "truth" you accept, American troops did as they were instructed and removed the threat of the rule of Saddam Hussein, but his removal allowed for the growth of new radical organization Al-Qaeda to grow and strengthen and we will see them in the future.

 The early '90s also offered Americans a reminder of another war that was still occurring on our own land. The war of racism and prejudice had been a subtle war that remained brewing since the end of the Civil War. The early 1990s, in the age of enhanced news coverage of the war in the Middle East, also brought us a video that rocked America's social core. In March of '91, during a routine traffic stop, for alleged speeding in Los Angeles, Rodney King was pulled out of his vehicle and brutally beaten by members of the Los Angeles Police Department. Much as cell phones are pulled out now to record potential injustice, this violence by Los Angeles Police Department (LAPD) was recorded by a nearby witness through a camcorder that recorded as four officers repeatedly hit King with their batons, using their stun gun, and their fists and feet all to "subdue" King. There was video evidence and Rodney King had medical evidence of physical damage as the damage was clear to see just by looking at him. The all-white crew of police men were clearly using excessive force against a man who was being pulled over for an offense that should have merely required a fine. As brutal as the beating was, it wasn't the act that caused disturbance in the Black community. The four police officers that clearly performed the act of violence against King were brought to trial and the courts found no charges against the four men. Once again America exploded, specifically Los Angeles, and it was all being televised.

 A key element to the riots boiling over was the decade prior and the "war on drugs" and the desire for the LAPD and the city mayor to clean up the "town" from criminal activity. The streets of LA were tough in the '80s and early '90s at new levels for the police and their response was a harder, more aggressive style of police officer. What community members saw in the Los Angeles inner city was regular "shake downs" and arrests and often by a police force that was primarily white male. There were good police officers in LA, but just like any organization, the negative components can define a reality for others. It was a bad situation for everyone as the government laid out an expectation without thinking through the root causes and the ramification of expectations. Another major issue was the racial tension in general in LA. As much as the city was diverse at the time, there was a consistent conflict over the lack of resources and the desire to achieve a level of control and safety. Black community members, Latino community members, and Asian community members were divided and often had skirmishes or shoot outs via gangs in the area. During the same month the Rodney King video was released, a young Black girl was shot and killed by an Asian store owner. The store owner was released on community service by the end of the trial February 22nd. The trial jury was mostly white with very few minorities. April 1992, our country heard the news of a majority white jury clearing the four police officers that beat Rodney King of any charges.

As I have told you, riots have occurred on American soil a few times in regard to race and injustice. In this circumstance, as in others, people of the Black community were just tired of not receiving equal access to safety and equitable opportunity that was afforded to Americans. It is an interesting phenomenon as our people are segregated in specific areas of cities in high numbers based on income. At these times you have communities that are hanging onto a version of civilization despite several conditions that cause generational despair. People of the community receive news of what seems to be a clear statement of disregard to equity, opportunity, and safety and all they have access to use as a tool is raw emotion. Sadly, these riots move from anger to simple gratification as the looting sets in and anarchy in shopping and business districts. Your history books may not tell you of injuries and deaths and even so, I believe those numbers are only approximates. We know somewhere in the thousands were injured and at least sixty people died over the three day riots and over 1 billion dollars of property damage occurred. During these dangerous and chaotic days and nights, police were forced to fall back and not enter the city based on the massive amounts of people in the streets. Cars that attempted to drive through were attacked and drivers and passengers were pulled out and beaten. One of the most disturbing scenes, caught on news cameras as well, was the brutal attack of Reginald Denny. Denny was white, male delivery truck driver that was pulled out of his truck during a red light stop as he was driving through the areas of the riots. Denny was severely beaten by four Black men and was saved by the intervention of four other Black men that witnessed the atrocity. The four attackers would later be sentenced for the attack and Denny even reached out to the men for the ability to offer forgiveness and to move forward in all lives. The streets were chaotic war zones of people that were out of control with emotion.

The first attempt of sending in 2000 National Guard troops failed and they did not contain the event. The following day included 6000 National Guard troops and 4000 Marines which brought peace to the streets. Depending on the "truth" you want to believe, those responsible for the looting and rioting were preparing to become more mobile and shift into "other" areas of Los Angeles. The "other" areas included parts of Los Angeles that were more affluent and less Black and brown.

Despite the war and the social upheavals, Black America and American culture was evolving. Hip-Hop was about ten years old in America and the concept of the culture being a "fad" had made way for the idea of hip-hop being a way of life. The '90s opened up with the marketing of Black culture hitting another wave of opportunity. It was established in the late '80s that marketing to the Black community and offering of Black culture at a cost could have a good return on investment. Top-selling movies in the late '80s had Black actors and in some cases directors and producers. Hip-hop was hitting the top of the charts and so was "pop" and R&B music as the youth were connecting with the newest trends of music. On television, Black actors were connecting with audiences and one of the largest opportunities was Arsenio Hall and his self-titled late-night talk show. Late-night talk shows were spaces for white males for the most part and Arsenio was a trailblazer for the Black community. Hall brought all the flavor and soul of the Black community to night time television as he had some of the hottest entertainment artists visit the stage and talk show couch. His interactions with the audience became national trends and his show became must see tv for all types of races. Originally seen as Eddie Murphy's wing man, Hall soon made his own name in the entertainment industry through the talk show while also acting in a few movies and even having his hand in creating music. As much of a comedian as he was, there was sincerity in some topics and questions and it was powerful to have him be more than just a "funny guy."

Hall's tone being more than just laughs was connected with the times in the Black community and the social issues that Black Americans were facing. There was heightened social consciousness in the Black community and the entertainment world was connected with the movement. More Black directors, writers, and producers were bringing concepts of the Black community to the masses. Early movies in the '90s offered powerful movies such as *Do The Right Thing* that dealt with racism in New York to *Boyz n the Hood* and *Menace II Society* that dealt with the murders that were performed by Black males more than any white hands in Los Angeles. We also saw powerful attempts to retell history through *Posse*, a fictitious movie that informed Black people there was a thing called a Black cowboy, and *Malcolm X*, based on the *Autobiography of Malcolm X* written before his death. We had comedies in the theaters that often had the humor of the Black community in scenarios that were relatable and some with hints of cooning and shuckin' and jivin'. Meanwhile the romance movies typically had the Black man being caught up in some internal and/or external struggle as a Black man trying to make it and a woman who loved him and supported him in his struggle or him being unfaithful and breaking the woman's heart.

There was still gangsta rap, but there was room for new forms of Black culture in music that offered options for the Black community and models for Black men to identify. There was a funky groove that leaned into Afrocentric roots that emerged in hip-hop in the early '90s. These artists offered wordplay, similes, and metaphors in the lines and usually aimed for "ooooo" as a response to punchlines in their lyrics. Primarily an East Coast push, artists like De La Soul, Tribe Called Quest, Leaders of the New School, and Blackstar came onto the scene. Other hip-hop groups also emerged such as Arrested Development, Digable Planets, De La Soul, and Souls of Mischief to offer a different, jazzier sound of hip-hop while wearing louder and baggier clothing when they were interviewed. Another artist with his first album that had pro-Black overtones in the early '90s was Tupac Shakur on his first full album, *2Pacalypse Now*. The rap game was evolving with new artists on the scene and the culture going in several different directions at once. The early '90s offered various images of the Black male. By this time in hip-hop you had rap artists on the East Coast and West Coast predominantly, but there were new sounds and styles coming from Chicago, the "dirty" South which was more southeast than anything else, Miami, and various parts of Texas. During these new discoveries of rap and hip-hop, America was seeing the versatility of Black men in hip-hop, but still Black men were still seen as musically talented and not as CEOs. Additionally, even if the rhythm and sound was diverse, more often than not, the topics were mostly the same. Rap music leaned into the "truth" telling of poverty and efforts to survive or thrive in drug sales, robbery, assault, and murder and these albums sold the most. There were some artists that were able to offer hardcore sounds and rested more on lyrically engaging listeners with their phrases and words. Members of Wu-Tang excited hip-hop heads with new advancements with sampling and producing. Their various MCs from the group and new sounds continued to come from the East Coast with a very distinct style. The rappers from the region were gritty and street and were known for wearing boots, baggy clothing, and oversized coats and still very much prepared to represent their neighborhood through violence. This appealed to various Black youth members and thus some Black men navigated to the style. Mainstream America was of course confused by the style and threatened and the response to the ignorance was often fear. The Black man in this format was too edgy and street when in reality these brothers were the new creatives. Quite often these brothers were poets, visual artists, stylists and more with a connection to the street. Much like the artists of Paris and Italy in the earlier centuries, this subculture of hip-hop was misinterpreted and misunderstood, but eventually embraced with more and more mainstream society members embracing the art as it caught on globally.

West Coast rap was going through a transition as the west's most popular rap group had fallen out and all had taken their career paths solo. Each artist from NWA continued to make their mark in the early '90s, but Dr. Dre from the group would take the lead to define the west's new sound. Once Dre left NWA, he soon established Death Row Records, and soon after he produced an album that would push West Coast rap into a new era. The *G-funk* sounds and beat production offered a renaissance to the West Coast hip-hop life and soon had people across the nation wanting '64 Impalas, Daytons, and wearing Chucks and Dickies. Much as the east was a lifestyle and culture of hip-hop, the West Coast lifestyle had a specific soundtrack and many who didn't live in the specific community were drawn to it and identified with the culture in any way possible. Black teens and young adults were becoming "G"s even if they were not affiliated with any gang lifestyle. West Coast rap was still very much gang driven with a focus on both Crips and Bloods as well as heavy tones of drug use and sales, alcohol, violence, money and materialism, and even pimpin' and the disrespect of women became a staple in the music.

As all this was occurring, there was an interesting effort of Afrocentrism in hip-hop. Extremely vibrant clothing with Kente cloth and African influences had their run in the early '90s. Cross Colors was established with hopes to defy the gangs claiming a color as their own. Dreadlocks were starting to make more of an appearance and medallions with Africa on them became more prominent. Negro league jerseys as well as HBCU logos became popular as artists were creating a space to celebrate being Black in America. This type of hip-hop culture was the most uplifting and safe and hence the one you saw on television the most in sitcoms.

Television had also turned into a remarkable outlet for hip-hop and Black culture expression. I am sure producers recognized the opportunity to cash in on the Black community once again. *The Cosby Show* and *A Different World* were still going strong as well as The Arsenio Hall Show and even Soul Train. Yet there was space for new shows that would have Black folks glued to their sets on a nightly basis. One-half of the rap duo DJ Jazzy Jeff and The Fresh Prince, Will Smith, found the birth of his new level of fame through the television show *The Fresh Prince of Bel-Air*. Also in the early '90s, there was the iconic sketch comedy show *In Living Color* where several comedians found their start, *Martin* by Martin Lawrence and other various actors, which catapulted his fame into future movies, and *Def Comedy Jam* from producer Russel Simmons from the '80s Def Jam records. There were also great Black women in sitcoms like *Living Single* with Queen Latifah that brought more hip-hop to television and gave us all some visual of being Black, professional, and successful. All of these shows offered a glimpse into the Black communities style of music, dress, and clothing and further helped Black people identify with this specific brand of "Black." Each show had elements of empowerment and expression and feel of the community expressing art through comedy. These shows were heavily, if not all controlled, by Black producers, writers, and directors. In general, these opportunities gave us the space to relax and offer a glimpse of what life "could be" or what a form of Black culture was. Yet, in each instance, the shows offered just enough fuel to continue the fire of a few stereotype. There were plenty of "funny" outtakes, music, sexuality, and athletic references that I am sure overshadowed the intelligence and tenacity of many of these characters.

    The '80s and early and '90s offered America a very edgy and hardened Black man. Images of the late '80s and early '90s offered a "truth" telling of the Black community informing America at large that there was poverty, crime, and violence which left Black community members to survive conditions while looking for answers. The majority of rap in hip-hop was not Afrocentric or conscious regardless of the positive message and the power it had. Something interesting happens in the entertainment world and I can't say that I have a definitive truth, but I do have my theories. We know that "positive" or music to push to change the narrative in communities of color does not financially have the gains the deficit narrative has historically. You offer an album taking care of each other and the power of the community, you can't even expect to make the money the album about "pimping bitches" and "killin' niggaz" will bring. Depending on the "truth" you accept there seem to be more resources to market music that does not send a message of change. Perhaps it is not the case in today's world, but at one point the formula to make financial gains in rap music included a storyline of pain and terror of our own people. How is music selected to have the best chance to become popular? At some point, marketing the music is a factor and that takes investing to promote the music. Before the explosion of the internet at a later date, radio and music television was the best option to promote an album which typically meant paying a company owned and controlled by faces that didn't look like the artist creating the music. Capitalism and bias to what a few people thought was "marketable" sold the stories to be told, listened to, and accepted by America at large and was this system that helped define a reality. What if we promoted the positive? What if the narrative that was selected to be told at the time spoke a different story? Various rappers on their albums had at least one song that had more of a positive message, but that song was not promoted. Yes, it is a cycle because we ultimately choose what to buy, but marketing and media have sold us stories and we have willingly accepted a "truth" for centuries. The Black man is aggressive and angry sells and we continued to buy in the 1990s. The negative activity happening in the community had some truth to it, but what's the point of talking about it if a solution isn't the goal.

The majority of the images of hip-hop that mainstream America was displaying was intimidating to most middle class individuals and above, but not important enough to engage in any real conversation to locate solutions. There were plenty of "safe" variations" being sold on television in networks version of being "with it" or reaching out to the "urban community," however, it is important to note that there continued to be a much harder reality that mainstream America was seeing portrayed in sitcoms and perhaps socially we missed the reality while we soaked in Black representation thirty minutes at time through television. We might have missed the rising murder rates, continued lack of equity in schools, and unproportional unemployment all while laughing at our favorite Black actors nightly.

Yet, television had opened the door for a space for the Black male to smile and cause others to do so as well. Much as former Black male comedians had done before, these men were offering America to see the side of the Black male that entered our lives for a moment and lighten the mood despite the hard times. The early '90s had an eruption of comedians. Some comedians had "staying power" and found their way into regular positions on programming. Others were seen for a brief time on the television or in a movie and then perhaps they went on to tour, worked in clubs, or maybe just went back to the average job market. However, the role of comedian was a viable option for someone who had the ability and talent to command an audience. Much as the younger generation now may say they want to be an "influencer," the role of comedian was a profession that some sought. The concept of writing and telling jokes is not easy. I would say that those who are really good at it have a special talent and mind and a work ethic to really master the craft.

I have great admiration for the standup comedian and the Black men that worked the stage in such a way. I also believe that television and the genre of comedy was great for Black men, the Black community, and America overall. At times, these television shows offered good insight into the comical aspects of the Black family, being Black in America, and/or just being human in the world at the time. My concerns are and always will be those who might have hurt the social efforts of the Black community in their roles and the Black man falling into the "coon" role throughout society.

Money is seductive and the ambition to want control and security is deeply rooted in human psychology. Depending on your "truth" you choose to accept, the fact is people get into comedy and then become an actor for a level of success that comes with wealth and fame. Perhaps people only want the money part of the deal, but we may want to reflect on, at what costs will our Black men go to become successful in comedy? Comedians and actors should not have to be role models, but they are by default. Black men who are comedians and actors should not have to be father figures and heroes, but by default they are. Much as rappers created a generation that patterned themselves from the experiences and the stories the rappers would tell, young Black men would pattern their roles in society after the comedians. This would not be a problem if our young men were modeling the work ethic to become a comedian or actor in comedy genre programs on television, but instead the youth just wanted to be the class clown in class. We also see role modeling and the expectation of Black men to be "funny" in the professional venue. Laughter offers healing and comfort and enjoy it and love the expressions of joy and happiness. Yet, if a Black man doesn't smile and laugh, we are "angry" or asked "what is wrong?." The "funny" Black male students in class will offer a standup routine in a class, but also get pushed through the grades while failing subjects because he is well liked and are "good kids." Sadly, humor is a tool that is often needed in the Black man's toolbox, but for those who don't have the desire to use the tool should be just as accepted and not be considered "aggressive."

When the roles of Black men in various television programs were about over the top stereotypes or plain buffooning as the audience laughed at the character playing a role, these roles were also identifiers for Black and other races to build an image of the Black man. Not saying all of the Black comedies and comedians were connected with these issues, but there were a few shows that sold their souls for ratings. During the 1990s, and still today, there are Black men actors in comedic roles who are seen falling all over themselves, using large eyed outtakes, speaking in ways that they would not if they were being spoken to naturally, and plainly being the funny buffoon that comforts many, paying audience members and I guess that is what matters. Yes, Black people see this and laugh and yes there may even be some truth in the overreaction of comedians, but we are also training others to accept and expect the same reality.

Despite the risk of possibly not gaining a large return on an investment, the 1990s also delivered some extremely serious social commentary and wrestled with several real issues on television and in the theaters. There were options and some shows did well, but they didn't stay long for "some reason." The Black community was being portrayed from every angle and the Black man was offered from several levels of depths as well, but typically the more socially conscious shows don't last too long. On television, in the 1990s, there was no sitcom that offered better thought provoking topics than ROC. The actual actor was a former prisoner, Charles Dutton, who chased his dream to be an actor once released. The television show was developed around Dutton as the main character,

Roc, as he tried to live a decent life despite the struggle of oppression and racism in America. Roc was a hardworking garbage man that wanted the best for his family and to remain in good standings with his ethics. The show offered comedy at times, but landed into the drama genre more often than not. Roc was a visual representation to hard working brothers who continued to live by a code that refused to blame others for their daily conditions and to not cheat or break the law. The show highlighted what was most important in life such as love and family, but his life on the screen didn't call to aspire the youth if their goal was to become wealthy and have a level of security in their lives. Roc's struggle was real and his role showed character, but not the path for the young Black male teen or adult who was tired of barely making it or maybe not at all. There were other "good, average guy" shows, but none that attacked ideas in society like Roc.

Other strong identifiers for Black men, Black community, and society as a whole were found in theaters in the 1990s. The Black male masculinity had shifted in many ways over the decades, but in the '90s it seemed there was a big push in entertainment for Black male representation and the movies were key in the promotion of the image of the Black male in multiple ways. The image of a gangster was a hot market in movies. As a key genre in rap music gangster rap remained and each region had their version of the urban stories being told, the tales of drugs and violence were easily marketed. Black male and female actors were acting in multiple movies the same year in some cases as specific Black males grew in fame for their abilities and their roles. Lorenz Tate in *Menace II Society* and Morris Chestnut, Cuba Gooding, Jr., and West Coast gangster forefather Ice Cube starred in *Boyz in the Hood*. Wesley Snipes and another West Coast rapper, Ice T, became Black pop culture icons with New York–based *New Jack City*, and Tupac and

Omar Epps were rocketed to fame in *Juice*, which was also set in New York. Each movie had their elements of gangs, violence, and drugs while offering insights to the urban world. Each movie also ended with a message of some sort with hopes to grab the attention of those who were viewing the films. These movies were potential war zones for the cities because there were no Crip only theaters or specific Gangster Disciple showings on certain nights. The media had run headlines in certain cities about how these movies were going to breed violence in the streets. However, due to the value of the writing, directing, and acting portrayed in these films and messages that hit home, audiences typically left in silence.

The early '90s also had their comedies and movies that were just about the drama and even romance without the deeper messages. Movies like *White Men Can't Jump, Poetic Justice, Mo' Money, Deep Cover, House Party 1* and *2*, and *Above the Rim* all had great pull to get the audiences in and without any of the overdone stereotypes we had seen in movies with Black men in the past. Hollywood had ushered in a series of Black producers, writers, and directors that knew how to tell the story of the Black community to the Black community and beyond without covertly or overtly being stereotypical or racist. Another key to this powerful growth in entertainment was the star power behind the movies. There was a time when Black men depended solely on the investment of individuals that may have misunderstood Black culture or at worse wanted to drag Black men and women through the mud on screens and paint them in whatever racist light they felt the investors and companies felt appropriate. The '90s brought an era of Black workers on all levels of the film industry that knew their worth and had grown enough in the industry to call more shots. You won't read of the importance of the advancements of Black people through Black entertainers in the '90s in most school history books, but as

I have told you, "reality" is often created by the "truth" we see and hear. The 1990s was bringing more perceived power through the Black man in a stronger representation in America. A great rendition of Black greatness on film was romantic comedy Boomerang, directed, written, and starring Eddie Murphy, that offered Black stars from multiple generations, laughs, a solid storyline, highly successful Black people in the world of business, and something else that brought various Black movies to life in the '90s...a remarkable soundtrack!

History books may or may not continue to represent the growth in culture and art through the Black community during the Harlem Renaissance, but the era never left entirely. Black cultural expression through various avenues has occurred since Black Americans were African. Representation of that creativity has cycled up and down and desire for fame and fortune has left the Black entertainers to make some choices that weren't always favorable for the representation of Black men or women, but the African DNA in Black America has been interwoven in America since the "Black" person was brought to the Americas. Seen in a variety of pockets of large influences, the world cannot escape the impact Black American has had on various corners of the globe and the largest impact in the United States.

The '90s was a perfect storm for Black community art in various forms including, but not limited to fashion, acting, dance, and music. I have talked about a few genres of Black music and some may argue with me, but R&B had its largest gains in artistic form in the '90s. I don't have the numbers to back up the claim and it's clearly my "truth" and not a fact, but I feel like more babies were made in the '90s just because of the music that was produced. I can go on and on about the groups and individuals that made the '90s, but the most important remains the image that these brothers were portraying in their marketing of what Black masculinity was for others to accept as a reality. Such as every decade that we have spoken of already, the '90s marketed the Black male very specifically and sexual ability has been connected with Black males since they were brought from Africa. The '90s offered sex in song form as well as romance and sensuality. As Black male singers were offering their version of seduction, videos and concerts came with more grinding and hip movement and less and less clothing. Being synonymous with sex doesn't sound like a bad thing to most, until you are a twelve-year-old boy living up to social expectations and there is a generation of kids who see these actions of Black men on television. These songs were not always connected with having committed relationships with individuals and typically told one step of a storyline. Hence, the goal wasn't commitment and being a good partner and not about the act of being a "good" father if/when a child is the ultimate outcome of these actions. The goal based on the music and the videos is to be sexy and attractive and seduce people and offer pleasure. Great music of the '90s for R&B, but again Black men being marketed as sex symbols and not CEOs, good fathers, and good husbands.

 This sexuality and desire for Black men was marketed and Black men were often on the cover and in ads in magazines and commercials. Some of your most notable marketed men in the '90s came from the NBA. Not only were these men wealthy, but they were athletic, famous, in good to great shape, were competitors that people would cheer for, and in some cases, good looking. It's fair to say all those other reasons were reason enough for Americans to see these brothers as icons. The NBA started to develop stars as the organization gained popularity and offered higher salaries. An increased amount of the athletes were getting the sponsorships and getting into the popular culture and living rooms of Americans. Of course, the more you and your team won, the more endorsement came your way. The early '90s was the rise of several stars in the NBA and one star in particular led the way in ushering in the NBA to new heights in America and to the world.

In 1991, the Chicago Bulls had won their first championship and their leader, Michael Jordan, was validated as a superstar. As much as the '80s brought several names to the front and more people to the stands and television to view, the '90s with the advancement in technology, cameras, editing, and television brought in a new era of entertainment for basketball. As that new era unfolded, more and more would come to watch the gladiators of the hard court compete. I don't want to sound like the old brother at the barbershop, so I won't get too caught up in the comparison of generations in basketball, but this decade was different in comparison to today. The shorts were smaller, most athletes were playing to eat, and there were harder fouls and more blood. You were expected to make the shot regardless of the physical contact and then you could actually talk trash after you scored. This type of atmosphere brought superfans cheering on their heroes for their cities and stars were lifted up to be more than men. Eventually, fans wanted to wear the jerseys of their players. Then shoe companies like Nike started to latch onto every athlete they could which in turn caused males to want to wear those shoes to play or at least have the same style of those athletes. These athletes were soon everywhere and eventually offered platforms to speak and engage in not just sports media, but pop culture, and even a few talk shows. Teens had moved away from Adidas and Converse for the most part and most wanted to be "like Mike."

Michael Jordan had become the poster child for America's image for Black men. Not a teacher in the classroom, or a businessman, or a pastor, but a guy who ran up and down a large floor to put a ball in a round hole on one end and try to defend the other round hole on the other end. The athletes were getting paid well and acquired fame so why wouldn't that make sense for aspiration? Meanwhile, the little Black boys do not connect the need to read or perform math equations to be "like Mike." Some families were raising their kids to own the basketball teams or perhaps even be the investor or accountant or entrepreneur the athletes need and the Black community had young brothers just wanting to dunk a basketball because that was the reality and "truth" they accepted. Black men play basketball. Black men are worth more as basketball players.

A less discussed, but still a worthy topic was college basketball in the early '90s. Black male athletes have been a commodity for college sports. Much as Black male athletes dominate in percentage of athletes in professional basketball and football, brothers are also in high percentage in collegiate sports. As there remains a debate for paying college athletes today, in the '90s there was no such debate or conversation. College stadiums were filled, athletes were marketed, and merchandise representing the athletes were sold and the athlete received a full scholarship at best. Some would think it is and has always been a fair trade as the college athletes have access to a "free" education, room, and board and potentially have access to a gateway to the professional level of sports, college sports could be the answer to the prayers of many. I am not going to get into the debate of how many students graduate with degrees that can advance their lives if they don't get into professional sports. I am not going to get into the gossip of some athletes during the '90s getting into college just for sports and not having the grades or skill set for college. Overall, there is good and bad in everything and some good brothers have gone onto the pros, others have gone on to have careers with their degrees if they didn't make the pros, and some of the brothers don't graduate. However, one of the most interesting opportunities to discuss race, colorism, and classism is the debate and rivalry of Duke and Michigan in the early '90s.

You would think that marketing around two high ranking and prestigious schools would be about their traditions and history as well as their school spirit. However, the two schools were more marketed like the suburbs versus the city, the good kids versus the ghetto kids, and even house negros versus field. Both schools' teams had hard working Black men on their teams who had overcome adversity to play at the highest points in their careers. Both teams had fought and dominated to come championship caliber team status. Yet, the media and marketing portrayed Michigan as thugs and connected them with "rap" and "hip-hop" as a negative connotation that mainstream media could not comprehend. Duke had a higher expectation for grade point averages and test scores for admission than Michigan. Duke was more expensive than Michigan for enrollment. However, it was also evident that Michigan's Black players were culturally different from Duke's Black players. Were the Michigan players "real" because their shorts were longer and they had a swagger when they walked onto the court? Were the Duke players "sell outs" because they didn't celebrate after a big play and smiled more? America would have to answer that because those in Black community didn't ask the question. We took sides and the Fab 5 from Michigan were our players, who, by all means, were probably amazingly good hearted people. However, the marketing we caught were Black men were "hard," "tough," and edgy. We are the "bad guy" to America's apple pie and America doesn't need to accept us. As Black men, we are everything portrayed in the media and entertainment and anything outside of that paradigm is selling out or "acting white." Even if what we do in positions of lack is for survival, being different is a threat to that very survival as a Black man.

This is a real moment in society that we tend to miss and it is played out in college sports. Duke had Black players on their basketball team. In fact, one player of Duke's team was a Black brother and one of the best in the nation and would go onto the NBA in the future. Yet, Duke was the "white" team. Duke wasn't the school representation for the Black community because of its high expectations and rigor and socioeconomic status alignment. There was factual evidence of this specific bias as well though. A Michigan player at one point noted that Duke University, "doesn't recruit in our neighborhood." Openly, the Michigan players and fans noted, they weren't the Cosbys.

Subculture was missed in this moment and there were challenges by players on both sides of the court. The attempt to place the Black male and the Black community overall in a monolithic stereotypical box was seen for all to struggle with in college basketball and it still remains. The issue remained before the Duke vs. Michigan games and still remains today, yet we still wrestle with things Black men "don't do" or even what the Black community determines as "Black" culture identifiers.

The Black male basketball hype went global in 1992. Michael Jordan had just won the championship and there was a need for America to remind the world that America was the best in something. The Black male was the most incarcerated of all demographics in jail, the Black male had the highest unemployment rate at this time. The Black male was the most likely to be undereducated and to have dropped out of school. However, as a country, our priority was to send the most dominant basketball team to the Olympics because we had suffered an embarrassing defeat four years ago. Prior to 1992, only nonprofessional athletes could compete in the Olympics. Collegiate athletes could play, but once you became a professional basketball player you could not play in the Olympics, yet that changed in 1992. Maybe those who made the decision understood the buzz and the attendance rating would soon soar if America's professional basketball stars would attend and play in the tournament, but the vote was cast and the "Dream Team" was born. America's best was a twelve-man roster that included mostly Black men.

The professional basketball players were global stars prior to the Dream Team, but to see a professional basketball player play wasn't an easy feat in all countries. The Olympics were widely televised as they have always been highly broadcasted across the globe since the early 1900s. Olympics were a time for countries to have bragging rights and America was reminding the globe that we had the best athletes and in this sport, a dominant force. Much like our Black male troops in wars that fought for rights and democracy that weren't fully allowed to Black people, our athletes went to play and demolish other teams for America the beautiful that was still really ugly. Beating teams by 40 and 50 points, the games were highlight reels as other teams tried their best, but really could not match up to the talent and skill of these athletes. Meanwhile, this team, filled with mostly Black men, were on every channel, on the front pages of newspapers, and on shirts and cereal boxes all over America. Once again, America sees the value in these Black athletes and young Black men further identify with who society is telling Black men they are to be for value. Not the owners of the teams or not even the coach, but you, Black boy, can be like Mike too if you work hard, dribble and shoot, and of course being over 6'5 will help too. Of course in 92, America brought home the gold in basketball in the Olympics and we all were proud of the USA.

These are times when our stereotypes are intensified. These times as Black males are celebrated, more and more people look for qualities in these athletes that are lifted on a pedestal and see it as a compliment to connect these athletes with other Black males. Times such as this when there is such a spotlight on Black males, other Black males look for role models and/or father figures. While other cultures have abundant images of males that look like them in various positions, the Black male in the '90s has the image of the athlete on commercials, in print, and in mass media. Collectively, realities are formed and Black males consciously and unconsciously pick up traits of these "heroes." These traits are not necessarily "good" or "bad," but are just categories that Black men are placed in and are still closely related to the limits of what a Black man can be in society.

However, as revered as we were in sports around the globe, we still had enemies in other countries and 1993 would be the first time a terrorist attack attempt would occur in the United States. Our earlier victory in the Gulf War caused us to have enemies that were extremely passionate about their cause. Engaging in Desert Storm, the United States may have sold "hero" to some, but others believed America brought their ideals of the oppressive "west" that would destroy their religion, cultures, and traditions. These resistant people were able to flee during the war with a new passion to inflict pain on America and our principles. February 23rd was the first time a terrorist attack occurred on American soil and was the first attempt to destroy the World Trade Center in New York. Using a bomb and a moving truck, two men from the Middle East attempted to ignite the bomb in the garage of one tower with hope it would fall into the other causing mayhem, injury and death, and possible further ramifications to American infrastructure. The bomb did explode and did cause a high level of concern and response. The results were six people killed and hundreds injured, but neither of the buildings collapsed. One of the two men were arrested and jailed with some reporting the guilty man as saying, "this was only the beginning."

By the mid-'90s, there was not widespread equity for all races, ethnicities, or genders. There remained a quiet oppression, implicit bias, and still overt racism and prejudice in practice and whispers in different parts and areas of America. It was still more difficult for a Black person to receive a loan for a small business, certain neighborhoods were made less accessible to Black community members to acquire home ownership, there were far more Blacks than any other race in the jail systems in reference to the percentage of Black people in the country. Black students on average were achieving academically at equal rates and being disciplined more often and harsher than other races. Gangs and violence remained very prevalent in urban areas and crack sales were still occurring despite the "war on drugs" from the '80s. Also by the mid-'90s, there were more Black men in political positions that ever before, there were more Black male CEOs, there were more Black millionaires than in the past, more graduates from college and universities, more business owners and executives, more big time entertainers, producers, and directors, and Black male athletes continued to grow in fame and fortune.

Were things perfect in America? Far from it. What we should recognize here are the opportunities. We talk about the position we have been placed in and what has happened to us in our experience as a Black community in America from pre-colonial time to now, but the largest disadvantage the Black community has is its inability to build strength within our community and offer supports for those who haven't made it to a level of financial or even social security. We know the data as a Black community and there are glimmers of unity when specific events occur, but a true commitment as a people would require a level of ethics and character that is often aimed in the wrong direction from the Black community. Our energies tend to be on the immediate need for survival or for what seems to be the quickest return on investment. If I am hungry, I will take the meager slice of bread I can grab not knowing if I plant my own wheat, I can feed generations. However, if I don't have access to land and have never been taught to farm, is it fair?

As we look at all of the various cultures and communities in America, there is a level of disenfranchisement that occurs with those that have been historically oppressed. There is a confusion within many to how the game is played and won in America. There are efforts in all communities to build from within and the Black community has their efforts as well. There are remarkable times in the past, and currently, in which the Black community develops to build each other up as well as connect with other cultures in the effort to achieve a desired level of freedom. However, for the most part, we "chase the bag" for independent gains in the same spirit the colonies were formed over the tribes of people with no regard, slaves were chained, whipped, and murdered, and several different types of cultures in America have been targeted in an attempt to stay in a specific social position and used as tools of gain, that offers the energy people within our own communities are grasping at materialism by any means. "I gots to get mine." We can find reasons to gather and we did in the '90s. Freaknik was a social phenomenon and so was "Black Beach" that happened in the '90s. The youth were able to come together for all that action, we could have come together for other reasons as well.

It's not that we can't achieve in every field in America. The road is harder and that is unfair, but we should not look for "fair" any longer. We should look for ways to gain ground in our own lives as we continue to build up each other with love and inspiration and then find ways to develop all that we have and build for the next generation. It is how we are building a cultural capital and networks that builds community wealth and a level of respect. It is apparent that this economic and political system in America has been built on certain values and asking for "fairness" is not a good plan. The plan of "hope" has come and gone and we need to build and wait no longer.

What we saw in the '90s was opportunism and a drive for profits from the Black dollar. Crafty enough, because of our desire for materialistic goods and a false sense of acceptance and safety and security, more and more Black men were flashing their wealth and the media was very helpful. As usual, we saw the large houses, the cars, jewelry, the clothes, the boats, and yes the women of Black men that "made it" and we wanted to "make it" as well. We wanted to be cool and have it all under control which in some cases did not include traditional means of making money. Athletes and actors had their status and there is a feel of "God-given" abilities and talent needed for that. The rap game and the drug game remained accessible and achievements looked like they were in arms reach. The drug game was accessible and typically there were just enough role models in the neighborhood for an onlooker to want the lifestyle of the "hood rich" even if it came with risks. To aspire beyond what you see takes a level of faith. To aspire to be something you don't see takes a level of insanity. The pressure to do the opposite of what is comfortable feels unnatural like the first time you are in water. There is fear, there is real concern for doing anything that seems like a concept that is completely wrong to you. All of your "truth" based on what you have been told and have experienced since birth has expressed to you what a Black man is. Those around you who you call "friend" pressure you to be what they have accepted as reality. Somehow you have to find the strength to do something "different." This is not a pressure many other communities in America feel unless an individual is going against an identifiable norm in their community. To a degree, this is felt on some level when a child of a wealthy family refuses expectations of the parents to become something other than their expectations. However, the difference is that the Black man is faced with images and "truths" surrounding him that Black men fit a certain mold and doing otherwise is not being "Black."

To achieve a level of success in America for many decades in history and in many cases still, included a code switching. The '90s was before there was enough strength that your generation provided to push back and ask America to accept diversity. The "American" image when it came down to it at the time was still dictated by white males as corporate America was primarily led by older white men that weren't about changing their paradigm. The concept of being "professional" was code for speaking, walking, and talking like the "boss" who was again usually an older, white man with influences from the 1950s and 1960s. "Keeping it real" was not a secret to success and "playing the game" felt like you were losing who you were. There didn't seem to be a space to be "authentically" anything, but what America said you were if you were going to remain employed. Yet, Black community members did it then in the hopes of building a better future. There is a level of cultural sacrifice that occurs when one consciously decides to be "different" for an opportunity to advancement and those same people who choose to sacrifice their culture even momentarily are not always welcomed to return to the type of Black neighborhoods they left. However, I see a shift as old paradigms die with new generations. There is plenty of growth that needs to be had, but there has been change over the decades. However, the Black community is amazing and has the DNA of all of the ancestors to grow, but we need to take the lead to fix our communities from within and remain thoughtful of our actions and how we utilize our resources including the arts we support.

While there was a positive thread in some rap, their message soon faded by the mid-'90s. The opportunity to unite and push for positivity gave way to what seemed like increased marketing of materialism and capitalism as well as a very specific "urban" personality. The larger money was to be made in rap that involved drugs, guns, violence, and the low respect of women. It was odd to see rappers of the time make conscious shifts in their rap style and their entire personality to attempt to sell records.

Quite ridiculously, there was a coastal war in hip-hop. There were rappers from all corners of America, but the two record labels that were grabbing the most attention were Bad Boy Records and Death Row Records. Sean "Puffy" Combs (now P-Diddy, Diddy, and/or Luv) was a young brother who worked his way into establishing Bad Boy Entertainment after he lost his job as an intern with another record company in New York. It was 1993 when Bad Boy Records came out with its first artist, Craig Mack with "Flava in Ya Ear." Mack and Puffy had a new sound and style and the song and album was a hit during a time when Death Row, now with a new leader, Suge Knight partnering with Dr. Dre, claimed to own the rap and hip-hop scene. Again there were various rap artists who were offering amazing lyrical content on great beats and productions, but the image and words of the Black man with a focus on pimpin' hoes, selling crack, smoking weed, and killing people was the style that had the most attention. I am not taking anything away from Dr. Dre as the producer of the albums nor from the artists, but we have to be aware of the bigger picture and how our talents are being used for a specific outcome or at least be mindful of the energy our art produces. Mack's album was lyrical and more about entertainment and parties and so was the Bad Boy brand, at first. The Bad Boy brand with Mack remained in the East Coast hip-hop scene with larger "bubble" coats, Timberland boots, and oversized jeans while West Coast rappers had the typical West Coast vibe with various connections to both the Bloods and Crips, the drop top classic cars, and khaki colored pants and chucks. These styles and more were dictating the trends for Black men and the Black community at large.

Tupac Shakur was an artist above all things. He was raised by free thinkers who were both Black Panthers that fell to poor choices and hard times while raising Shakur. The mother was still able to offer Shakur a pretty good life despite moving several times as a youth which included a school for the arts where Tupac studied several types of music, drama, and dance. Regardless of his moves from East Coast to West Coast and back again as a teen, Tupac had adults around him that saw his talent, charisma, and intelligence and pushed his star power. Tupac's early career put him as an extra in a few videos and a few guest verses until he landed his own solo album. Tupac was blunt and clear in his raps and most dealt with social issues. On his first album, Tupac offered socially resistant songs such as "Young Black Male," "Violent," and "Brenda's Got a Baby." The majority of Tupac's songs on his first album, *2Pacalypse Now*, offered wisdom, such as the song "Trapped":

> *You know they got me trapped in this prison of seclusion*
> *Happiness, living on the streets is a delusion*
> *Even a smooth criminal, one day must get caught*
> *Shot up or shot down with the bullet that he bought*
> *Nine millimeter kickin', thinking about what the streets do to me*
> *'Cause they never talk peace in the Black community*
> *All we know is violence, do the job in silence*
> *Walk the city streets like a rat pack of tyrants*
> *Too many brothers daily heading for the big pen'*
> *Niggas comin' out worse off than when they went in*

Over the years, I done a lot of growin' up
Gettin' drunk, throwin' up
Cuffed up
Then I said I had enough
(Tupac Shakur, *2Pacalypse*, "Trapped," 1991)

Tupac became a strong voice in the East Coast, but still had strong ties in the Oakland and San Francisco areas where he spent time as a teen. Several albums over a very brief time, Tupac's music started to have stronger more street lyrical content that had more violence overtones, but still remained a few songs on each album that were reflective and progressive for the Black community. Tupac's album almost spoke with a spirit of a new era Black Panther with a foot into the daily struggle and anger of Black men in the urban setting. Tupac was telling a powerful story. A story that caught the attention of a few politicians and influential people of America that didn't approve.

Looking for an artist to offer more edge and street credit to battle the gangster mentality from the West Coast, Puffy connected with a local talent in Christopher Wallace known as the Notorious B.I.G. or Biggie Smalls or just Biggie. B.I.G. was the East Coast version of everything Death Row Records. Puffy wasn't being taken seriously with his artists and his take on hip-hop and there were enough verbal jabs being thrown from the west at his street credentials to cause Combs to look for a harder hitting artist. To retaliate against the "harder" Dr. Dre artists that seemed more like the "cool kids" of hip-hop, Puffy pulled in B.I.G. who offered his reality of streets and stories of his talent for drugs, violence, and exploiting women. The first major song from B.I.G. was "Juicy," which was a theme song for materialism and brought in a strong era that still remains in the high end fashion and lyrics about items wealth as major themes in rap.

Now, with the onset of B.I.G. and Bad Boy, Black culture depicted men with flashy style and wealth. Typically, the flashy style connected with over the top expensive items to profess luxury. This sent Black men to department stores in sections that typically weren't the Black man spaces asking for Ralph Lauren, Tommy Hilfiger, Versace, and more just to be seen by the masses and recognized as important. Expensive cars with the best rims, watches with diamonds, and even silk shirts and sweaters were the rave in various cities all because the style was being marketed by a persona creating a reality.

Tupac and B.I.G. met each other at one point and were at least associates and some would say friends. A version of the story says the two met before B.I.G. was on his upward trajectory and Tupac was a solid name with several albums and B.I.G. was looking for mentorships or marketing of some sort. The two aspired to work with each other, but it never happened and B.I.G. made his gains on his own. During the same time of their relationship growing, Tupac's character continued to harden and his fame grew which eventually led him in several courtrooms under allegations. Also by this time, Tupac had a following that saw him as more than a rapper and he was, Tupac was marketing himself infamously to America and many in the Black community was sure to buy into whatever he was a part of which included his acting in several movies. Tupac was an artist and had received training formally and he expressed his talents in several movies in a very short time. Not always the same type of character, Tupac had some depth in his acting and I wonder what would have happened if Tupac had the appropriate mentorship in his acting and how his life could have turned out differently.

In a series of events, Tupac had an attempt on his life while in New York and based on a separate court case, went to jail for several months. When he was released, he signed with Death Row and became their spokesperson for the West Coast versus East Coast conflict due to Tupac believing the city of New York was out for him through street politics. Primarily at this point in his career the majority of Tupac's music was filled violence, drugs, and women exploitation and very little about Black progression. Watching his relatively short career, he transformed into a different person. Perhaps Tupac was angry and changed over time. Perhaps Tupac realized the path to more riches and materials was a path that included less about uplifting the Black community. However, more importantly, Black men and the Black community aligned themselves with either Tupac or B.I.G. as if there were no other options. Social realities had conformed to the images of the characters being played out on the national stage, the character forgot they were both living the dream, and those in the community lived out the lives of these brother's lyrics on the streets.

By 1997, both B.I.G. and Tupac had been murdered and they were at the pinnacle of their career and had fame and fortune. Lost in a narrative that was created and marketed, the two brothers died in the way they were trying to get out of from the beginning. No one stopped to think of how wealthy and secure these brothers were and those around them and how they could use their platform and capital to change lives of others in communities of lack. We have opportunities to make better choices and offer better lives to others. We have the ability to open community centers and wellness centers and places where impoverished communities can lean into for support and development. We can back politicians and run our own campaigns, but we stay trapped in our own prisons and talk about how trapped we are. You can be better. We can do more.

Positive messages in hip-hop glimmered from Tupac and Biggie and hard-hitting artists like Nas and Jay Z had their version of positive, pro-Black communities songs that made their popular rotations on the radio. Songs like Keep Ya Head Up, I Ain't Mad at Ya, Dear Mama, Juicy, If I Ruled the World, and Hard Knock Life were songs that could be played at any given time by cars driving by in different times in the '90s. There were other artists such as Bone Thugs-N-Harmony that were a break from the norm, and hit producer Timbaland had several artists that gave us breaks with lyrics with catchy bars and punchlines and entire albums with great beats. Even with those songs that offered space for Black men to reflect and express emotions, the image that we latched onto for masculinity and safety and protection was the harder image for survival that often these same artists were rapping about the majority of their albums. Our culture demanded us to "keep it real" which meant that even the college kids and folks who didn't have to survive in the streets, still found their way to the harder songs on all aforementioned artists albums. So much so, these were the times when Black men began wearing camouflage and boots, gold teeth and all gold fronts, large rims, and jewelry became a staple in the Black culture through a hard push from the South with the No Limit Soldiers and artists from Cash Money Records that included a 12-year-old Lil' Wayne. Much like their environment, the music and the image portrayed was about being less rational and more responsive with immediate violence as needed, drug deals and wealth, and women. These were heroes to many Black boys, teens, and young men growing up in the '90s.

I wish I could offer more details about Black men in politics over history and in the '90s. We had leaders such as Jesse Jackson, Jr. and Al Sharpton, but they and almost all pro-Black community groups didn't resonate with the youth. How could these individuals have a chance when the marketed images of the worth of the Black man that came through entertainment or sports? How could I pray my way out of the hell I am in or march my way into safety? No. The way to prosperity is to take it in the streets, rap about it, or play sports. Even if I am "good" in school, I still have to keep an edge to prove I am part of the culture and protect myself from those in my community and those who have historically applied pressure to my community. Politics didn't seem to work for Black folks at the time and the closest thing we had were the Democrats because that is what we were told and accepted. "Democrats care about Black people," we were told. "Black people vote for Democrats" was the rule. We weren't told why besides "Republicans are racists." We were raised in a political gang. The validity of all the "truths" we were told was based on the few Black candidates we might have heard or seen and the Black people that stood close to the white democratic candidates. Like other things in the Black community, there is apathy when it comes to voting because we haven't seen much change regardless of the candidate or political party. Also, in the '90s, curriculum had mostly white faces and deposited facts that didn't offer the importance of voting and/or the game of politics and its ability to dictate a "reality" for so many including our community. For the most part, we were far disconnected from presidential politics in cities where we were mostly densely populated and had no clue on the importance of district, judges, school board and other highly influential positions for our daily lives. Yet, we had Bill Clinton because those that look like those in the Black community said Bill was for the people.

President William "Bill" Clinton, got the ol' Negro pass. During the 1990s Clinton ruled the political scene especially in the Black community because of swagger. Bill was cool. Bill stood next to Black men and women in commercials. Bill ate soul food including, but not limited to, fried chicken. Clinton was even a guest on the Arsenio Hall show and played the saxophone!!! That's all it took for the Black vote in the '90s. Were there people of the Black community that didn't support Clinton? Sure. Were the Black people, who didn't support Clinton, socially pressured because Bill was "Black"? Yes, indeed. Clinton won office twice to be the American president and "our" president of the Black community. Yet, we didn't understand that our prayers would not be answered and equality would not finally come rushing through all of America. We forget that the president is not our god. The president is a leader in our government and our government is not a monarchy or dictatorship. In fact, a president without Senate and House control may not be able to get very much done at all. President Clinton in his eight years brought America to more prosperous times and unemployment for all groups decreased. There was much done in health care and social work during the Clinton administration. Yet, there was one decision that became a detriment for the Black and brown community that was led by the Clinton administration.

As a Democrat that leaned on the Black vote to get into office, the Clinton administration continued to push being "tougher" on crime was the answer. I am not excusing crime or those who break the law, but something is wrong with our system if our laws and penalties are not enough to pose as a threat as a consequence. Regardless of the penalty, those who feel that have no other choice for a sense of control, security, and/or power. As the Clinton administration offered federal grants for private prisons, as penalties were set to make sure that all inmates serve 85 percent of their time before an option for parole, and as the three strike rule established a life sentence for a person that returned to prison on the third time, the percentage of Black men being jailed increased. This number increased as Black men were already making up the majority of inmates in prison prior to the increase. If we know that Americans have a better opportunity in life with a proper education and skill and/or trade why not put federal money into the schools in the '90s? Some would argue that there is no personal gain in school funding and private prison owners donate to campaigns and candidates. I would say the same companies building prisons can also build schools and profit can still be made if that is the issue. However, it's more than who builds the buildings because private companies are also paid to house inmates at a profit. Meanwhile the image on television during the news was how we were getting tough on crime as Black men were lined up in handcuffs and making their way to being removed from society, someone profits and Black generations are affected.

Later in the decade, Clinton was placed on trial for sexual harassment. While the case was brought by one woman, the details of the trial lent to another woman in which Clinton denied having "sexual relations" with during his term as president. Once the detailed truth was exposed, Clinton's larger issue was that he lied under oath during an official investigation and trial which was grounds for impeachment. It was determined, based on the impeachment trial, that Clinton would be acquitted and the charges were dropped allowing him to finish his second term. Regardless of whatever good Clinton may have done for the Black and brown communities and/or the middle and lower socioeconomic class, President Clinton's legacy was tarnished with his lapse of ethics and the Democrats took a tough loss in their efforts to remain in political position. Doesn't matter what you do in America, it matters how you are perceived, marketed, and branded through the media.

The mid-'90s brought new voices that gained strength in hip-hop. The Afrocentrism of hip-hop had faded and there weren't as many groups or individuals that rested on the specific concept of idealism, Black pride or power, or even peace for that matter. There was increased focus on street matters and becoming the top of whatever "game" you were running. Names like Jay Z and Nas were coming to the front of trends as well as new regions for hip-hop bringing in different sounds such as OutKast and the various artists with Master P and the No Limit Soldiers. All of the artists started their careers before this point, but the mid-'90s was opening up room for a new sound as hip-hop is always evolving. As 1995 and 96 came, also were strong Black entrepreneurs that were getting noticed for their creativity and business savvy. As the hip-hop genre continued with the talents of Black entertainers, Black owners of the recording companies were rare. However, both Master P and Jay Z were able to revolutionize the rap music genre by owning their own companies and producing their own music and the music of others. It wasn't until much later the men were recognized for their talents as "bosses" in the industry for leading their own destiny. The mid-'90s brought them fame for their music, but I wish more Black men and society in general should have emphasized their ability to be a CEO of multimillion-dollar companies and brands.

Creator Daymon John was another self-made man in the '90s. FUBU stood for "For Us By Us" and the concept was revolutionary. During a time when rappers and those who lived the urban culture through hip-hop by choice wore name brands, Johns created a brand that called on the connection of Black community members supporting their own community. The concept and marketing paid off but not until after Johns mortgaged his own home and found an investor in Samsung to get the company off the ground. It took a few years, but once certain rap and hip-hop icons began buying and wearing the brand in interviews and in videos, the FUBU brand became another identifier of the genre. This is a Black man who became a multimillionaire by grit and determination and using his talent while staying connected with his community. Yet, the owner and designer was promoted, it was the style of clothing and its connection to the streets that was marketed.

Two very profound events for Black men and the image of Black men in society were held in 1995. Early in 1995, in an effort to promote Black unity and the Black family values, Minister Louis Farrakhan of the NOI with several other Black community organizations attempted to rally with one million men in the nation's capital. It was a beautiful sentiment and a great vision to gather Black men under the vision of creating a better path for the Black community. Although it was led by Minister Farrakhan, the rally was calling for all Black men regardless of affiliation to be held accountable for the development of the Black community. There were even whispers of gangs across America having a truce to offer time to consider ways for the communities to advance without the pain that Black gangs bring the Black communities. Depending on the "truth" you accept anywhere from 600 thousand to approximately 900 thousands of Black men attended the rally. There were no issues of violence and no particular issues of drama. There were a few protestors and "onlookers" that could have been an issue, but the leaders of the march offered explicit instructions to avoid conflict at all opportunities possible. It was a chance for almost 1 million men to be in the presence of each other and to rally for a better tomorrow. There were speeches, there was music, and there were people selling merchandise and food. However, what there wasn't was a plan for what happens next. There was "homework" in a sense for Black men to go "home and lead," but that level of expectation without support and follow up is ridiculous. Essentially, the march was a great festival with a good message, but not the movement we needed. Centuries of disenfranchizing doesn't go away with words and chants. In actuality, the many organizations that attended had several Black male development type programs.

The problem was the clear vision of leadership of what was going to happen next. Was this going to be an annual opportunity? Should we host rallies in our cities? How and where do we start? We all went home excited and talked about the "feeling" and vision for the following weeks and then got back to our usual lives...separately.

I am not taking anything from the march as it achieved something that had never been done in the past. The leaders were able to bring the largest calling of Black men together to hold them accountable and increase the expectations for our roles in society. There are many positive and powerful practices we should take away from the experience. Yet, imagine if at the end of the march there was a commitment to the next steps. If there was a nonprofit organization that was established out of the march in which men could sign up for chapters in their own cities. If there was a charter of the larger group established with expectations of behaviors and activities. A logo or a crest that each man could stand behind in their efforts. Various men came those days and were already a part of such an organization, but what if we could have walked away with the majority of us united under one flag? That is what the Niagara Movement had. That is what Marcus Garvey established. That is what the Civil Rights Movement had and gave birth to so many other activist organizations. Black Lives Matter had a glimmer, but its leadership was bitten by the power and desire to have it all in the name of the security they desired in the form of materialistic objects that caused them to use finances for the people for themselves.

We have seen what fame and fortune and perceived power can do to our Black leaders over and over again. There are steps to becoming a culture of people with consistent and sustained acceptance to the "table" of the American game. Various cultures that remain players at the table for politicians to listen to, and in some cases fearful of, stay in this position of perceived power because of their access to wealth and their ability to mobilize as a people. Those very cultures have also been taught the value of a dollar and to remember that the dollar doesn't add value to you. Capitalism and materialism is not a DNA strand. As slaves we were taught that those with the most make the rules. We continue to want to have the most or at least look like it to pretend that we have security and power. Our first large access to money, we find the flashy items that we always wanted or others have always to "flex" or show others that you have made it. Not all of us, but the majority of us don't really know the difference between having money and building wealth. More importantly, our leaders that build our organizations and collect donations or develop funding through events, media, and merchandise find themselves with more money than they have ever had and forget who they are and their role in the possible opportunity and they set themselves us to be the "star," the icon, and the recipient of the funds for their comfort. "Gots tah have a big house like Masta." As you grow to lead, be sure to finish the job. Remain humble and thankful for your position of leadership and take care of those who follow you and support you. Live your life and enjoy yourself. Just don't forget the reason why you do what you do and I would hope it's not about stacking money and buying things you can't take with you when you die.

Yet, I have also noticed that these cultures and ethnicities that have historically overcome the "immigrant" stories and challenges, also have traditions and values that remain with them in America that come from their native countries. As much as there are second and third generations that come from original immigrant fathers and mothers, there are still traditions and practices that are sacred that connect with their success and help cornerstone their character. We, as Black people, are traditionally culturally unanchored. We don't connect with our African roots because we have lost so many connections with our ancestors and honestly, we rarely know really where we are from in Africa besides the vague "West Africa." There are vast tribes and traditions and to pick on to anchor to would be generic. Meanwhile, our history of tenacity and spirit of enduring, our strength and our fight, has been omitted from American history and the effort to bring it back causes severe fear from "them" and politicians ride on the vision of destroying any efforts to tell a different truth...and get elected. Other cultures have days of remembrance and holidays in which the stories are told to remind the next generations of who they are. Immigrants that have made room for themselves at the "American dream" table have separate religious ceremonies and have lunches and dinners to remember their communities and social network. Black folks have started brunching lately...maybe that will help.

It was quiet in a room full of people on October 3, 1995. You could hear people breathing as everyone was watching the television screen and oddly a few people were holding hands. Were you praying? Are you really that hopeful? I remember wondering for a moment what they were wanting to happen so badly. I never had a chance to find out because once the announcement was made it was too chaotic for me to observe individuals. "Not guilty" and the room erupted. OJ Simpson was a star athlete in the decade of the 1970s in the NFL. This was before there were huge multimillion-dollar payouts of today. During the career of OJ Simpson, his contract was less than a million for five years which is amazing considering the fact that athletes like him were making the NFL worth watching on television or in person. OJ had star power. He had commercials and movies and even considered himself an actor as well as a professional football player. His fame came with a perception of fortune as he also bought large houses, fancy cars, and took the trips. OJ Simpson was '70s and '80s wealthy which isn't much today, but it was a lot then, especially for a Black man. America loved OJ because he was one of the biggest superstars of the NFL with his skill and talent, his team was winning championships, and he had all the "cool" of the Black man swagger and good looks. OJ wasn't an activist and didn't talk politics, he just smiled, played football, and was popular with the ladies. His social circle was typically filled with other party types or famous individuals of New York, Miami, and/or Los Angeles and white. OJ had a brand that white America accepted and Black America felt they had a role model. OJ wasn't exactly a spokesperson for the Black community, but he was at least a poster person for what skills and abilities can do for you as a Black man.

Though June 17, 1994, OJ Simpson quickly became one of the hottest topics in America for another reason. An odd scene on every television was the white, two door Ford Bronco slowly driving down a California highway with OJ Simpson riding in the backseat with a gun as his friend and former teammate was driving. Two hours of a slow speed chase had various people across the globe holding their breath and shaking their heads as it seemed like every officer in Los Angeles cruised behind that vehicle that day. The day was supposed to be far different. OJ was supposed to be coming in to be charged for the murder of his wife and their friend. Both individuals were brutally murdered and the charges were being brought on Simpson. Past the two hour parade, OJ turned himself in and for almost the next year, OJ was to be on trial. It was a trial that quickly became about race even though Simpson had once been the darling that navigated through race and color in the '70s and '80s, his race had become the covert issue of the 1995 trial as he stood in court accused of murdering two white people in cold blood. This was only years after the turmoil of the early '90s that manifested its pain through riots in the streets.

A month went by and America was painting this case of OJ Simpson being a monster of a Black man. One example of the race dynamic in this case was the *Time* magazine color that presented OJ Simpson having darker skin than he had actually been. Early in the trial, Johnny Cochran who was on the attorney team considered the Dream Team of lawyers for Simpson, became the lead. Cochran, also a Black man, was as close to star power as you could get for a trial that was getting more coverage than the Bosnian War American soldiers were in at the same time. Cochran was smooth and well spoken and highly intelligent, which are powerhouse traits for a lawyer, but this was different. This was a Black male lawyer that was owning the courtroom to free another Black man. What many Black people missed and perhaps most of America, was the fact that the prosecuting attorney who was working to convict Simpson was also Black. This fact was truly overshadowed because Cochran leaned into the issue of race and focused on the LAPD and the officers on the scene with one in particular. Simpson never took the stand as it seemed more like the officers were on trial than Simpson on any given day. Thus, the trial became about a Black man fighting for the freedom of another Black man who was framed by racist cops. There were even bodyguards appointed to Cochran through the NOI due to death threats Cochran was receiving. Were the officers racist? There was enough evidence regarding the first officer on the scene to cast enough doubt because of his frequent use of the word nigger as a slur. There were already doubts in regard to the LAPD since the Rodney King trial earlier in the decade. Witnesses would be called to the stand on behalf of Simpson's character and the relationship he had with the two victims. Finally, Cochran leaned in on the theory of the primary officer planting evidence at the scene to frame Simpson and used the catchphrase of, "If it doesn't fit, you must acquit" to drop the mic in front of the jury and America.

"Not guilty" and America's racial tension is documented. The interviews of the public over the next few weeks were like fans of opposing teams. The issue was not about two people being brutally murdered, it was about a Black man not going to jail and the justice system "not working" in the eyes of far too many in America. The Black community cheered and danced in the streets during interviews. During that time and after the victory, Black boys were being told they could be like Johnny Cochran. Black men saw other Black men in the court system working to control a fate and not just letting the "system" happen to them. During a time in which Black men in the urban setting were three times more likely to go to prison, Black boys and girls, men and women, saw a new reality. It wasn't that Cochran was the first, we had two different Supreme Court Justices that were Black men by then. Cochran was the first attorney to be this televised and hence, the perception of fame and fortune and have a level of safety and security.

Depending on the "truth" you accept, the 1990s could be uneventful for some authors of history books. I have seen history books in schools blow right through the entire decade in less than a few days depending on who is controlling the curriculum. I have even read in a version of the "truth," that the 1990s was a decade of "peace and prosperity." I am sure to some who continued to prosper off of inequitable circumstances the '90s could be perceived as "good times." However, as "truth" has various perceptions, it's best to read for yourself of the headlines your history books in school might have "missed." As a final note on the decade, an agreeable fact of the '90s was the evolution of technology. The '90s put more satellites in space and a rover headed toward Mars. The decade also offered compact discs (CD) and CD players and digital video disks (DVD) and DVD players, new advancements in computers and the laptop, cell phones decreased in size and increased in abilities, and the internet grew and introduced us to Google. These events may be shared as mankind advances. What "history" may miss is that the digital divide was further solidified and grew during the decade.

Technology is rarely "cheap" when it is first introduced. There were various entertainment type technological advancements that had high costs attached, but lower socioeconomic families still desired the toys and in many cases found access to the devices. Eventually, the prices of entertainment products like CDs and CD players and DVDs and DVD players would decrease due to advancement in product production and increased supply. However, computers and the internet did not have value for Black and brown homes that were lower middle class to poverty economic level families. Meanwhile, wealthier homes and more often white homes typically had access to computers and the internet. Additionally, school districts and schools with more white students also have a higher number of computer labs and the internet for their students while schools with a higher percentage of Black and brown students went without technology and the internet. No state level or federal programs to level the opportunity that was clearly unfair. This was the beginning of the digital divide.

In today's world there are more families in the Black community that have computers and students, in many cases thanks to the global emergency of COVID which we will talk about later, have personal access to a computing device. Prior to the need being addressed through federal funding of the school issue, students were more likely to have cell phones or access to one than to have home access to a computer. You may not see this as a big deal as most Black families saw the internet and the computer as a luxury in the '90s. However, the utilization of technology quickly became a language and a tool for communication, advancement of intellect and information, creativity, and jobs. All these items cannot be performed on a phone, but the use of a keyboard and more advanced moves such as the various office and business software is designed for the use of a keyboard and mouse and students that practice the skill more have an advantage over students who don't in academics and in their future life options. To this day, schools and families still suffer from the lack of access to technology and the digital divide overall.

As the decade closed out, the identity of the Black male had continued to evolve. Movies such as *Soul Food* and *Love Jones* offered us great entertainment and an array of Black representations through film characters. Music continued with some of the earlier mentioned artists with whispers of new artists such as Kanye West and DMX. Professional sports continued to give us icons the country worshipped or loved to hate. A note regarding professional sports is that in football and basketball this was the time of the birth of the "different" athlete. Black men were confident in their abilities and the athletes were becoming more vocal and independent in their representations. It was evident that there was a "brand" with each star type athlete and that "brand" could be profitable regardless if it was based on fame or infamy. Those great representations of Black men, in some circles, were now being tagged as "cocky" and even "dangerous." Players in the NBA had a lock out as a protest to help express their ability to flex a muscle of freedom in their profession. The evolution of sports included a younger class that America wasn't quite ready for such as an Allen Iverson who wore cornrows in the NBA, more Black quarterbacks in the NFL, and even fist pumping Black man playing golf at high levels.

This was the first notable generation of hip-hop culture coming into other areas of America. The Black males that mainstream America wasn't quite sure about and even nervous were coming into their lives through different avenues. As an American that "didn't get" Black culture or just plain had prejudices against Black expressionism, you now had unapologetically Black males on your screens in your sports bars, living rooms, and country clubs. Eventually, you found yourself as a mainstream American that might have had prejudice, bias, and/or reservations rooting for your favorite players even if their culture didn't resonate directly with yours. As someone outside of the culture and ignorant to various facets of being "Black," you would unknowingly soak in representation through your favorite pastime much like the teenagers of the '50s and Black entertainers in rock 'n' roll. You would watch your players work in their field and later observe their speech and clothing style. The Black male athlete of the '90s further ushered in the next generation of Black culture and hip-hop into America and the Black community continued to develop what it meant to be "Black." The Black man increased their connection with sports in the eyes of society and Black male masculinity exponentially grew in the relationship with athletics.

By 1999, the gangs of urban inner city areas were known for shootings that were up close, shots into crowds, and/or drive-bys. Innocent bystanders were casualties at parties, parks, parking lots, front yards, etc. The phrase "bullets don't always have names on them" became popular as too many of the youth were slain on purpose or accidently. Not as often, but still as an issue, were shootings at school yards or near schools. In all of these areas, there was death and trauma that inner city youth had to navigate daily and parents had to pray and accept the possibility that their child may get hit with a bullet with no name on it. Students and other community members had learned what potential areas and dangers would look like and how to duck and cover at certain sounds and visual cues. These were all realities for areas that were mostly populated by Black and brown community members. However, on April 20, 1999, in Littleton, Colorado, a "safe" community, school violence occurred in such a way that the threat of gun violence and the youth became a reality for all in America. Thirteen victims died that day due to two students walking through the campus murdering individuals at will, ripping a level of safety away from all parents and families across the fifty states. Sadly, it wouldn't be the last reminder for America that safety is a perceived reality. Sadly, we still can't agree that all of our children need to be safe.

Enter the new millennium with the year 2000. The year came with much drama as many people were concerned about the end of the world occurring figuratively and literally at midnight of New Year's Eve. There were theories from banks imploding because of faulty software not being able to roll over to 2000 from 1999 to people researching Mayan calendars that pointed to 1999 being the last year of existence. There were actual pop up stores with the sole purpose of selling Y2K survival gear. Of course water and toilet paper was flying off the shelves the closer the time got to January 1st, 2000. The concept really wasn't a huge issue in the communities that were mostly populated with Black, brown, and lower middle to low socioeconomic status though. Typically on the news you saw people who were doing their best to locate a form of security through their ability to spend money. There were even some wealthier people that were establishing or purchasing Y2K bunkers. Once again, communities that have historically underserved had to focus on the day and not worry about tomorrow. January 1st, 2000 came with no issues.

The biggest issue of 2000 was America trying to figure out who the president was going to be. As much as there is conversation about elections being "rigged" in today's time by a particular party which does not like to accept a loss, there was enough drama in 2000 that caused great disbelief in the system. In a very close presidential race, the voting came down to Florida where Jeb Bush was the Governor at the time. That is an important detail because George W. Bush, Jeb Bush's brother, was running for president. Ballots were hand counted and there were ballots that were not counted because they were not fully validated by the primarily Republican voting state. Regardless of the "truth" you accept, our presidential voting that year had issues, the candidate that lost had more people in America vote for the candidate, and the electoral vote determined who would be president. Typically the electoral vote follows the popular vote, but that did not occur this year. Just enough doubt in an already untrusting system increased the apathy of the Black community voting.

Perhaps your history books that you had access to in your school didn't offer specific information about 2001 being the start of the war in Afghanistan. Or maybe it was offered without much detail. My goal here is that you know that there was a consistent presence of American soldiers in the Middle East for over 20 years in efforts to control and fix the problem that the Gulf War created in 1991 that happened after America was originally trying to control the situation in the '80s. I am not saying the Gulf War didn't have to happen or that these decisions that occurred in the Middle East were "good" or "bad," that's for you to understand the facts that you have access to and determine on your own. What I am saying is that the media and the government painted a picture as if the war in Iraq was won in 1991 when in fact there remained an elusive threat. The terrorists that were established in the Middle East were extremist. Extreme enough to attack America on American soil in 1993 and now again in 2001 which was the start of the war in Afghanistan. Our soldiers showed up as they always do as warriors and ambassadors as needed, but the war continued. This was America's longest war which lost approximately 2600 American soldiers' lives and cost roughly $2 trillion dollars in taxpayer dollars. That was taxpayer money we didn't pay on our own issues in America such as inequitable education and/or college and career readiness for all.

Why did the War of Afghanistan occur? Depends on the "truth" you will accept. Some will point to the President Bush and President Regan eras and say this was the younger President Bush in 2001 completing a legacy. Others may say that America is the defender of freedom and the terrorist cells in the Middle East were growing out of hand and were a threat to the world. What it felt like was a retaliation for what occurred September 11th, 2001.

The early reports was that there was an "explosion" or perhaps an accident in which a plane crashed into the "Twin Towers" otherwise named the World Trade Center. The destruction was something unseen and devastating as the internet allowed us to pull up news quickly on computers to see live footage and breaking news coverage. As the news anchors were speaking of the fires that were impossible to contain, a second plane came crashing into the second of the two towers. It was now evident that these incidents were not accidents or coincidences, but planned efforts against America. America was stunned as they watched live damage that was caused by the planes. The two buildings were on fire and no one watching via live news feed could really understand the pain, anguish, and suffering that was occurring inside the building and on the street. Moments later the news would be cut to yet another emergency with The Pentagon in Washington, DC, being struck with yet another plane in the same style as the World Trade Center was attacked. All planes were ordered out of the sky, but there remained a fourth in the air and it was evident that this plane had yet another American target, The White House. This plane crashed in Pennsylvania due to the passengers fighting off the terrorists causing the plane to crash in a field before it reached its primary target. Americans across the states had their security ripped from them in hours. The false vail of control was no longer and Americans felt that more was to come in some fashion.

There were no more plane crashes, but there was still injury and death occurring from the attacks at the Twin Towers and The Pentagon. Almost 3,000 victims and first responders died based on this tragic event. Americans had felt "safe" prior to these attacks as the last time and only other time America was attacked was a naval station in Hawaii, Pearl Harbor in the '50s. Now we have a new truth that our power no longer has the effect that it used to. We now realized that we were vulnerable on our land and by the end of the night, we were informed of who or what would be so bold. At 8:30 p.m. on the same Tuesday, September 11th, President Bush informed Americans and the world what had happened. We were attacked and lost many lives and the group to take credit were the Al-Qaeda and their leader Osama bin Laden. There are plenty of "truths" to research in regard to these individuals and where their origin stories originated. We know bin Laden was developed and raised in a system of revolution from the '90s connected to the Russian conflict in the '90s. We know that Al-Qaeda had a deep disdain for western interference in their lives in various ways.

A few weeks later, October 7th 2001 had started our longest war to date, the war in Afghanistan. Most of the previous information will be in the history books for mass consumption. However, what won't be in the history books is the shift of racism in America. As the terrorists were of Middle Eastern descent, it had quickly become "open season" on all of those who came from the territory or had ethnic backgrounds connected to the region. Hate and spite was apparent in various parts of America as there was an increase in violence aimed at individuals with any perceived race or ethnic ties with these terrorists. Quickly the slur came to call all individuals from the Middle East "Bin Laden" or "Al-Qaeda." Anyone who had Muslim or Islamic beliefs became targeted as well. Physical threats and attacks were happening in mob forms throughout the states. Businesses that were owned by owners of Middle Eastern descent were being damaged and terrorized under the values of patriotism. To have seen the shifts in people was like watching us revert back to animals and a reminder that the lynching gene was dormant, but not removed. This is a prime example of the fear we can all have and the irrational decisions fear can cause. Various Americans felt weak and out of control and that feeling moved them to attack innocent people who were also Americans. This fear due to lack of control is based on ignorance and the need to "set things back to normal" reverts to intimidation and violence. This issue is in the DNA of America and has not left us and can only be overcome with love. This is the same fear of the slave showing any signs of strength and getting beat, the same fear of the freedoms demanded for all that caused violent mobs to attack, blow up churches, and hang and lynch human beings that just wanted to live and be happy and safe as well, and this is the same oppressive spirit that does not want us to fully discuss issues of the country and openly reflect on our history.

Every war has a purpose. This war had a purpose that changed over the twenty years. The war in Afghanistan was about safety and security of the specific areas Al-Qaeda were influencing and occupying. The war was about keeping other parts of the globe, not limited to the United States of America, safe from terrorist acts. However, regardless of the verbal mission offered to the public, the war in Afghanistan felt like a man hunt for Osama bin Laden and his top officials throughout Asia and Europe. Much of 2001 and beyond, in regard to the war in Afghanistan, was about news blasts offering efforts and strikes that included near misses on attempts at the Al-Qaeda leaders and talks about hidden caverns and caves that bin Laden remained ever elusive.

The first decade of the millennium had a few large events. This decade brought us to social media with the creation of Myspace, Twitter, and Facebook. However, before any of these was the phenomenon of BlackPlanet. BlackPlanet was basically a community where you could create your own page and your own creative corner. What was first about expression mostly became a virtual hook up spot and a popularity race for the most engaging page. It was interesting to see how people were able to make their page pop which of course now the images would look almost childish, but then the concept of web based coding was a secret language that few had the ability to pull off effectively. Again, not all Black people had access to computers or the internet so this wasn't a huge phenomenon in every home, but it did bring some of the Black community into more of an interest into the world wide web and the effects of coding. Typically though, the page took off as a place to post photos that would attract those interested in looking at certain physical attributes. Just as sex has always sold and always will, sexy photos and pages were the ones with the most attention. This website and its pages were before their time, but ultimately the fad did pass and soon others turned to new sites with advanced opportunities for communication.

Black culture continued to develop in America through various avenues, but as a community we continued to remain segmented and not as a group united for growth in any area. Even the music felt like it was trying on new "skin" for the next large evolution of style in R&B and hip-hop. Strong rap artists were making their way through the charts and there was a new introduction of a white rapper from Detroit whose comical, shock rap was later overshadowed by his authentic, lyrical skill. As much as there were white rap artists and groups in the past, Eminem was able to establish himself past the "gimmick" phase and have a story that connected him with the culture when he was questioned about his authenticity. Thus, during this decade, you could look at hip-hop and see the face of a white person as a representation. Not taking away from the talent of this individual, but it is an interesting point that should be made as we consider the role models Black males had for a reference in their search for role models.

Our Dream Teams in basketball, sports serving as another area that historically offered heroic icons, was losing. USA lost in the 2002 world basketball tournament with a different set of professional NBA players playing, but still our "best representation." The United States then lost in the Olympics with more of our "top talent" from the NBA in 2004. Our Black men were losing on a global level. Could this have been due to a missed moment of role modeling for the next generation? There was much talent on the court floors and much swagger, but there was a missing element that didn't translate to wins. There was a lack of respect from other teams we played from other countries. The men on the court were strong players in their own right, but maybe they didn't have the "x" factor that comes with a level of mentorship and character building yet because they were raised as athletes and stars and forgot they were Black men and removed the chip on their shoulder that remains as we remember that we can take nothing for granted. Should we have to live that way? No. However, we are far from a time to relax and not remember that we work for a greater purpose and to a greater calling in all that we do.

As if having our usual role model spaces being challenged wasn't enough, there was another interesting challenge with the

Black community and the raising of young Black men of the 1990s and 2000. Our OGs, Big Homies, Uncles, and fathers and father figures had been removed. Another missed affect to the mass incarceration of the 1990s under the Clinton administration was that removing Black men from communities left a void. Yes there were righteous, hard working men in the Black community that young Black boys could pattern their lives after, but consistent points of culture build relationships and identity. As we were finding things to do in communities as young men, a community standard has always been the "wise old sage" that would offer you wisdom without us asking. Periodically, the wise old sage is an older gentleman that fits the part, but mostly he was an older brother, sometimes less than a decade older, but far more mature in experience of the world. The brothers were the neighborhood heroes that were good natured for the most part, typically intelligent and physically strong enough to have won their fair share of battle. The reputations of these men could have been urban legend, but those in the streets respected them and these "sages" had a code of ethics. Ironically, it was these alpha males of the streets that would remind younger brothers to stay in school and treat their mothers with respect. It was these street kings that would remind younger brothers to think analytically in their actions and to see their lives as chess boards. It was also the brothers that would tailor the level of crime and violence to control the level of police involvement to assist with the "business" that was needed for financial purposes. These leaders of the streets would recruit as needed because the young brothers were destined for that life, but there were also plenty of opportunities for life coaching and guidance for a different path for a better tomorrow.

It wasn't always jail that separated us from would be role models. Opportunities for gentrification and the viable solution of displacing families of Black communities was and continues to be a tool for "community improvement." The sprawling to the suburbs and pivoting back to the city remains a constant for those that can afford the mobility. Areas of the inner cities that were crime riddled and locations where you "shouldn't be at night" eventually become trendy hot spots to access "energizing venues." Upgrading a few warehouses, apartment buildings, and/or poorly maintained single family homes or duplexes with coats of paint, landscaping and the right tile and countertops, investors were taking properties at their points possible, flipping the homes with the newest design trends, and raising the mortgages and rents to levels that the original community members couldn't live. In return, "affordable housing" through the government would displace families to the suburbs or even further out to less developed, "up and coming" neighborhoods. Other times, families would just have to figure it out on their own and uproot their living and often transfer students to different schools. In some cases from the Black community, the move sounded like a good idea with allure of "better schools" and a "better neighborhood" if housing allowed. Yet, the move wasn't always a "win" for shifting Black families. What occurred at time was community disenfranchisement and loss of connection, increased costs and/or job loss due to commuting, and any time a student transfers even to a "better school" there is a trauma point that may cause an interruption in learning. It's funny, all that "hard" talk and gangsta swagger, holding down the blocks and the government and real estate agents taking out entire city blocks, who has the power?

Regarding schools, as we see Black families move to the suburbs or even areas that are not familiar with working with students of different cultures of their own, there is an obstacle. We often think "American" is "American" in relation to student transfers, but in reality the move causes a need to create space for culture integration. This is yet another space for love and acceptance while still offering the support and high expectations needed for learning. Receiving students from the "urban environments" placed a strain on teachers and districts that were used students who are typically enrolled with certain supports at home, family traditions and expectations, and even student mannerism. All of these areas needed to be considered as well as potential areas of learning gaps if the student is coming from a school without the teaching practice and resources of the current, possibly, more affluent school. In some cases regarding the Black male student, there remains a need to acclimate to the safe space and to understand the cultural capital of intelligence and academic prowess. Remember, on average, in certain social circles in primarily Black schools, intelligence and good grades is a "white" thing to do and a new transfer Black student may be worried about how to navigate the social expectations of the new school. There is also enough evidence that in primarily "white" schools, there is a social expectation for Black male students to fall into a specific paradigm or mental category for the students and staff. Black male students may play into being the "jock," cool kids with swagger, and jokester and some may even start rappin' just because their new white friends see that as a natural "Black" attribute. That's a lot of pressure for anyone, especially a kid that is going through biologically and mental changes in general.

    Our government is notorious for either not fully thinking through the implications of decisions or perhaps just not caring. As much as there have been federal responses to lapse in equity in education for schools that have a high percentage of Black and brown students, there has been relatively little success in a government "answer" to the issues that create opportunity gaps for students. Every so many years there is some large plan to fix the system, but moving the needle in regard to the Black male having the lowest graduation rate and the highest dropout rate is rare. When the urban communities were scattered into the suburbs, there was no magic the schools were offering for support. Typically, students leaving the inner city schools to attend schools in the suburbs meant that the transfer students were about to hit a rough reality. These moves and sudden shifts in "truths" meant that students that did well in the city at times struggled in the suburban schools with higher expectations. Academic challenges apparent, Black students would adapt by trying on personalities for social acceptance. Yet, all of these "skins" were, at times, masks from the academic struggles that were occurring due to being raised in a less academically rigorous school system. As much as I said we need to consider the struggles of students transferring, there is also a need to be aware of overcompensating for students of the Black community and hurting them in the long run. The Black male in some school systems became a project and a sad case that needed "saving" by those who we could be seen as saviors. During the '90s, and even currently, there is nowhere near an equal representation of Black male role models in the school system in comparison to white male or female.

I appreciate the efforts of those who truly love and desire the best for all students. Essentially, these young Black men in suburban schools during the 2000s were an exercise of understanding. Many of these educators saved the lives of students of all walks of life including Black males, but still, a connection with a Black male role model was needed and rare while the young men would continue to see few images that connected their image in the mirror with excellence besides the usual stereotypes of athletics and entertainment or the more accessible avenues of the street elements.

History classes offered the men and women of color from the civil rights era, but that was a piece of history class that was carved out and never was it the development of our collective America and *all* of the history that brought us to that then current time in the 2000s. Based on recent events, even how we teach civil rights in classrooms may change. During the decade, Black boys and young men continued to look toward sports and entertainment to find our north star and few were talking about how to remain men of high character, how to make sure the bills are paid, how to be in a relationship with another person, and/or how to apply for a job or advance ourselves. There were and always have been these kinds of conversations in other homes and this cultural capital continued to be missed in the first decade of the 2000s with Black males unless he was fortunate enough to have a specific person in his life to care on that level. In some cases, Black males found strong connections and role models through religion.

Religion still remained an option for Black males as well. Traditionally, the Black culture has been connected to religion and the following of a god since as far back as one could search. Mapping back to African roots, worship in some sort of fashion has been a part of the Black culture. The centuries have offered Black people a variety of paths for possible belief, but the consistency with the culture and the concept of a superior being remains. I guess you can say that for most ethnic groups, but the Black community, experience with religion has defined us culturally in our past. The various religions and the various denominations also come with various cultures and connection points. In the Black community, these religious cultural connections were dominant points of unity.

The NOI has always been a force of order and discipline with eye opening teachings, but to most young brothers just too much of a commitment based on the rules and expectations. Growing up in an urban community, it was customary to see young brothers in suits and bow ties, including in the summer heat, offering moments of teachings, but primarily selling items in streets and offering invitations to the mosque. Black churches offered places for grandmothers, mothers, aunties, and sisters and men who were interested in those women, a joyous noise and loud worship, just enough teaching to make you consider changing your ways or at least acknowledge you could do better, and ask God, "Why?" If you were lucky, all of the activities that were just mentioned offered food in some form or fashion.

In any consideration of religion, the leaders of the organizations didn't have the star power Malcolm X and Martin Luther King Jr. had. Even with the strong spoken words of Minister Louis Farrakhan and Jesse Jackson, Jr. the streets still remained the streets and the world still remained the world. Life has been more about the day to day than our eternal soul and people would constantly ask why life was so hard if we had a caring God. The lifestyle outcomes were not there to entice long term commitment from young brothers. Ultimately, we come back to our spiritual journey whether it's Muhammad, Jesus, or some other path once the seed has been sown, but it takes a while for us to figure out the level of commitment that would offer true peace and enlightenment. The world is distracting and our people look at shiny objects as a position of peace and power. As long as we hear we have to "suffer through it for better," we figure we might as well fix it now any way we can. Additionally, sadly, in some of these cases, Black male leaders in perceived positions of power in religion find themselves publicly being ridiculed for a scandal they had fallen to or even the extravagant lifestyle that is "too prosperous" for a man of God. We had plenty to pray for in the 2000s, but we didn't see value in building a movement through religion and fighting for an afterlife in heaven if the current reality was hell.

The Black community has always been in the very core of America and much of Black culture is in a thread of much of America. A smaller, quieter percentage in America during slavery was curious about the traditions and culture that was shared on the plantations and that percentage grew and became louder by the 2000s. There have been those who want to "try on" the culture as much as possible only to remove it as needed for their own purposes, there are those who want to profit off of the Black community and culture, and there are those who have been raised in it. I honestly feel there are plenty of poor, white rural people who may not know how close they are to being official Black people. "They" still use color to their advantage, but if we look sub-culturally, most Americans struggle the same despite color. Typically "they" have to lean on the common denominator of color because "they" know lifestyle will not separate the masses from each other, but it will get votes from the ignorant. Of course politicians won't say they are working for a certain demographic, but there is a playbook of sorts and when you look out see you are speaking to a crowd that is "less diverse," and you believe that demographic holds enough votes nationally to get you in office, that is the play to use for some.

August 23rd, 2005 was the initial sighting of a tropical storm off the West Coast of Florida. Tropical storms and hurricanes come and go in the south and southeast. Residents accept them or they eventually move and the rest of the country shakes their head asking why someone would live there and then others remember all the sun and beaches. However, the tropical storm that came through the southeast tip of Florida increased speed as it came around the southern tip of Florida into the Gulf of Mexico and headed toward Louisiana shook up the nation. Hurricane Katrina was a category five hurricane at the center of the Gulf of Mexico and a category three when it hit land in Louisiana. Louisiana, Mississippi, and

Alabama have all had their fair share of hurricanes, but a category three was rare as most hurricanes come off the south East Coast and lose speed by the time they reach the three specific states. Though the issue wasn't the hurricane as much as the levees in Louisiana as over 50 of the walls designed to keep the rushing waters out of New Orleans failed allowing over 80 percent of the city to become flooded. Many people were left stranded on roof tops and more had no home to return to as the flood water remained. The situation caused President Bush to declare a national emergency, but many felt the government's actions were slow and inefficient. America's larger population was introduced to Ye, then Kanye West, as he said on live television during a telethon to help secure donations that, "George Bush doesn't care about Black people."

The sentiment of Ye wasn't his alone as the nation saw the atrocity of the cities with little response. Several areas were flooded, but the city of New Orleans was hit the hardest. New Orleans at the time was a majority Black city with close to 67 percent of their residents identifying as Black. However, for a president to ignore a city in need because of race would lead to political failure and, again, there were more than Black community members in New Orleans. New Orleans has had high pockets of severe poverty and with that high crime including murder, drug charges, and theft. The majority of the Black community members of New Orleans rented their residences while most homes in New Orleans were owned by white citizens. Again, it wouldn't make sense for a president to ignore the residents based on color because all were affected. What could be said is that the situation overwhelmed the administration and although federal support was offered, it was not enough or fast enough for one of the wealthiest countries in the world with arguably the best armed forces. Katrina was a war zone and we needed a response that would lead to a victory. Regarding those that had the ability to rebuild due to owning a home, having insurance, and/or the finances available to rebuild, they did. However, in the rebuilding process, low property values increased the opportunity to purchase property that caused a 5 percent increase in white residents and approximately a 2 percent growth in the "other" demographic post Katrina. Home building companies, private businesses, and charter schools made their way to New Orleans to jump on the rebuild. Meanwhile, thousands of families were displaced including families of poverty that didn't have much to start and now they were being relocated across the nation with little support, lots of waiting and reporting and waiting again, and, in most cases, no familiar ties in their new living areas. The trauma this caused families was cataclysmic and while there was outrage, not much changed.

Life continues based on the status quo of leadership making decisions and we are left to accept it unless we cause consistent and sustained disruption until our solutions are accepted. Yet, we continued to offer distractions from our pain through entertainment. I will continue to say that we have to be mindful of what is produced and how we are presented to the masses. If Americans were portrayed in a negative light, I am sure there would be concerns. Hell, there is a form of protection of telling identified facts in schools of all of the events of America due to the concern of affecting patriotism. Its obvious images and narratives matter and those who can control those understand and protect those areas of perception. No other genre of music in America segregates an entire category of people like hip-hop mostly leans into. America is reminded of our moral compass and the identities of the Black community is cemented in the minds of many when our lyrics offer ethical and character challenges. How is celebrating our culture connected with drugs and murder and sexuality? Entertainment is offered to all to listen to and watch and perceptions are formed. Yet, when there are songs or performances that speak negatively about other cultures in any way, there is a challenge and threats of careers being destroyed. How many albums are there filled with "niggas" and bitches and murder and drugs and they sell with no outrage? Do you think any other culture will do that to themselves? Do you think it would be allowed to attack any other culture in such a way in America?

Several television shows and movies in the 2000s made it to mass appeal that were not always providing the best image of our people which means more than those in the Black community were laughing and learning. There has always been an appeal to "urban" culture to the masses and in 2005, one of the movies depicted the realities experienced by those who typically live in southern urban settings. Driven by a hard-hitting, southern hip-hop soundtrack, actor Terrance Howard plays a drug-dealing pimp that tries to create a new path for himself through rapping, *Hustle & Flow* offered a glimpse to one reality. The movie was a huge financial success considering the cost to complete, but more importantly Terrance Howard won an Academy Award as well as hip-hop artist group Three Six Mafia, for the song "It's Hard Out Here for a Pimp." The talent in the movie and the movie itself was strong. Yes, there was a story being told that was real and one that the Black community and those who struggle in the same cities lived through daily. However, this was yet another opportunity for mass media to highlight a lifestyle that is not congruent with social mobility and security that we seek. At best, the movie received accolades for being so "raw" and becoming a pop culture darling. At worst, the movie was used to further identify Black men and for Black men to glorify. During the year of 2005, there weren't many blockbuster movies that included Black men as the main character, however, *Hustle & Flow* the movie and its actors won the attention of the entertainment world. Black boys aren't celebrating the actor they celebrate the lifestyle on the screen. Meanwhile, there is a new anthem for Black men in 2005 as we sing and rap along with how hard it is to be a pimp.

The artistic representation of the Black community has been lucrative since before Black people could participate in a program let alone get paid for it. However, if there is an angle to market and make money on the programming to a specific community or mass appeal, there will be investors in Hollywood and elsewhere. By 2005, a few Black men had earned their success into the opportunity to produce their own shows and programming. These shows were authentic in their creation and offered to all in the spirit of the art. Yet, we have to consider what is being offered to all and even what the Black community benefits from it. Two major programs were running hard in 2005.

Dave Chappelle, a comedian that worked tirelessly as a Black man to create his own show for Comedy Central, had established the first season of the Chappelle Show. Sketch shows for Black men had worked historically and Chappelle and his writers were the next big thing. Good comedy is good comedy and Chappelle has offered some highly analytical satire in his career. Yet, in the 2000s, Chappelle was at his peak and the show had huge mass appeal. Were Black people watching the show? Of course. Were there white people watching the Dave Chappelle Show? Yes. Yes, a diverse community watched Chappelle use the word "nigga" freely and laughed. All communities watched Chappelle offer sketches about "crackheads," "player haters" dressed as pimps, and restate the phrase, "I'm Rick James Bitch!" My truth is that I had several young men in classrooms and hallways who would restate these phrases and talk of tales of the various characters on the show throughout the week. I was trying to convince them to be scholars while they all wanted to re-enact the show that was previously aired and offer phrases to the young ladies like, "Does Wayne Brady have to choke a bitch?"

The concept of a Black man dressed as a woman for a sketch had happened a few times in entertainment by 2005. The idea of a Black cast expressing the culture of Black traditions to a heightened degree for entertainment and a dollar was not new either by 2005. However, *Diary of a Mad Black Woman*, *Madea*, and creator, director, producer, and actor Tyler Perry were taking America by storm. Originally, the Madea character and her representation of the culture was performed in live theaters and Black church goers would flock to laugh at the culture connections and extreme outtakes of characters in play, a good soundtrack, and a good message.

Black church plays were almost its own genre in some cities across America. Though as Madea went to the masses, more than Black church goers were in attendance in the theaters and at home watching. And while the Madea movies all had good messages in there somewhere, the movies are still considered comedies. My own concerns were who was laughing and were we being laughed with or laughed at in the viewing of the Black culture by the broader viewers. Did all see the love that was shared by Madea for her circle of friends and family or was the take away the over the top reaction she offered in response to issues in all her blackness? As we are represented in America across the states in all that we do, there is a need to recognize how all other communities protect how they are represented in television, music, and movies.

Should we care though? Or should we represent who we are authentically in every way? Yes and yes. I remember a time when no other race could use the word "nigga." The use of the word from anyone that wasn't Black was sure to cause a problem immediately. Though, over the decades of the late '90s into the 2000s, there was an allowance offered to "certain" people who were given a "pass" from a specific group of friends. We no longer own the word and the word has been offered to all walks of life to use as long as it's used in a way that's not to be negative, but did we become comfortable. Did we become comfortable with other races laughing at the antics of a Black man pretending to be a "crackhead" or a pimp? Did we get too comfortable with other races singing along with Three Six Mafia using all the lyrics including words that used to mean something? Did we get too comfortable with all races laughing at the man dressed like a woman as he portrayed the matriarch of a family and a community? We as a Black community desire perceived power, but we also give what we have away to the masses for their consumption and control. Though, in 2007, we had our savior who was going to fix it all.

Something was about to happen that Black America and, in some cases, all of America was ready to see. The idea that America had evolved enough to see someone other than a white male become our commander in chief offered an opportunity of an awakening for America in optics if nothing. A new proud moment was upon us to sit back and say, "look how far we have come." It wasn't the Black community that voted in our first Black president. Always keep in mind that the percentage of Black people in this country isn't above 15 percent. Additionally, all of the under 15 percent of Black people in the country according to a census aren't old enough to vote. Finally, a census records those who are in jail and all prisoners have not always had access to vote. However, in this case, all of the Black community who were eligible to vote didn't even vote in 2007. A candidate who wants to win a political office at the national level and even in most states, will need voting support from outside the Black community.

Fresh politically and relatively younger than his opponent, Barack Obama was a marketing dream candidate in his efforts to become the 44th president of the United States of America. Obama was up against various other Democrats to win the primary election to be the party's candidate and he beat others out with his "cool" and swag as much as his intellect. Barack Obama checked a lot of boxes fully including his ivy league education and his ability to speak and debate. In running, candidates would make mention of lack of experience in politics while leaning a little into his age. Yet, Obama was amazing under pressure as he remained collected in interviews and on talk shows. What Barack Obama was doing and what he brought was similar to what JFK had that brought him victory in the '60s and Clinton in the '90s. Obama had flare and he was "that guy." As we look at the voting data, Barrack beat his Republican competitor in 2008 in almost every voting category except for southern, white, male, Republican, over 65 years of age, and conservative in individual categories. Yet, Obama gained the majority votes of all other races, gender, region, and most socioeconomic levels. Obama was the choice of the people and he won as the rally cry for "hope" was there.

Though a notable challenge for President Obama before he took office was an age-old phrase that had become more infamous during the campaign for his first presidency, "He ain't really Black." There were challenges regarding President Obama's background being raised in Hawaii and Indonesia at different times in his life. There were challenges because President Obama's father was Nigerian and not a Black man from America. There were challenges in some circles because President Obama's mother was white and therefore Barack Obama wasn't *all* Black. And yes, there was push back against President Obama because he attended an ivy league school and he sounded "white." Did Obama convince the people in the Black community that he was "one of us"? There were plenty of Black community members that voted for President Obama, but it was amazing to hear that, to some, Obama wasn't the brother for the job and this is one of the struggles we have been talking about in this very conversation.

Again, our own people wrestle with our own identity. That in centuries of being in this country and all of the work through the oppression and struggle, we find ways to trip ourselves up in our efforts. Are there Black people that will run for political office or any job that is not about the betterment of the Black community? Yes. Are there people who are "real" based on some specific reasoning of their own that isn't doing much for the Black community? Yes. What we need to review are the hearts of individuals and if available their track records in their efforts. You will have plenty of people who will use the Black community for that individual to grow in popularity, status, and/or finance. Though it should not be how a person is dressed, where they went to school, or how they speak to determine if they are a good representation of "blackness." As we look for representations of the Black culture, let us look for strengths that will move the community in addition to comfortable similarities such as other subcultural connection points like preference to play basketball and debates on favorite soul food dishes.

2008 came and with it a new president and he was our first Black president in office. This was the day all of the Black folks of America were waiting for their entire lives and the lives before theirs had prayed for, but had not seen it in their lifetime. Tears were falling across America and they were the tears of joy that America had finally made it. Everything was going to be better now...different. Just like that, racism had ended and the Black man in charge was going to "right" every wrong. All of those who had ever been oppressed or prejudiced against in this country were going to get their equal footing now. Even during one of President Obama's ceremonial prayers, the pastor asked that we remember that the president was "only a man." Yet, we thought we had it all. We thought we had elected a savior and were reminded over the time together that President Obama was a good man, but not an all-powerful man.

We thought we had "won." A representation of equality and spokesperson for America was in office and we could say, "You can be anything." Black boys saw themselves in Obama and young Black men in elementary through high school would hear from their teachers that they could be president one day just like Obama or that the student could be the next Obama. Obama still offered a level of "cool" in his presentations and interviews that allowed him "street cred" at times. Also, Obama continued to have connections with several entertainers, actors, and athletes that would endorse Obama's level of "blackness" with the Black community. Michelle, his wife and first lady, was also a huge "win" for President Obama because she represented the strength of a Black woman and the Black family. Yet, opposing forces would remind us that the president wasn't going to force change.

The perception of power remains because of specific structures remaining in place for control. 2010 brought clear communication that one group of people knew the game better than Black people and various other demographics that originally voted for Obama. We misunderstood the title that President Obama had as the opportunity to make change. Meanwhile, there was an entire "spirit" that was still very prominent in America that understood the game of control through our government. Emotionally, President Obama was voted in, the celebration occurred, and we sat back and waited for the skies to open and blessings to rain down upon the masses. Yet, our government is set on a system of checks and balances and the midterm election of 2010 was used to check and tilt the balance in "their" favor. That same "they" and "them" in which the spirit of oppression and control was manifested since the colonialism of the new land spoke freely since President Obama was voted into office. Whispers in the grand scheme of things, but enough was being said about President Obama on certain stations that had roots in prejudice and racism. Those people spouting off their opinions would say it was politics in play and journalism and media work. However, there was an increased level of anger and frustration behind those words. There was a rally cry to take back control of "our" country and in 2010 with midterm elections, the Democrats lost sixty-three seats in the House of Representative.

You may not know much about politics and that's my fault. I find it amazing that in all the things that we do teach our collective children in this country, we don't teach how to operate in it in the development of laws and the leadership of the country. I am not saying that every student should go into politics and/or government, but information is ownership of control in our country and there has to be some reasoning why we are not very specific in our efforts for all citizens to understand how we are being led. "They" learn it and perhaps they see it in action. Perhaps there are conversations at dinner tables and robust interactions in the families to help the next generation of the spirit of oppression to claim control and hold on to their perception of power and sense of safety. In any event, we don't pass that knowledge down typically in Black or brown households or homes that are middle class and below socio-economically.

The short version is that there are three branches of government and the president is a part of the executive branch. The other two branches include the legislative (House of Representative and Senate) and judicial (Supreme Court). Presidents can rarely make decisions on their own and need the agreement of the House and Senate. Imagine owning a business and needing to ask your partners for their permission before you made changes. Now imagine you have hundreds of partners. You probably couldn't order pizza without hours of debate with this type of leadership structure. Therefore, in the case of the American government, your president has a considerable obstacle to pass laws if members of the House and Senate do not share the president's views. Thus, it's not about the president alone, it's about voting continuously and remaining a consistent voice of influence. We are not consistent as a Black community, we are emotionally reactive and responsive. Then also remember, we are not a majority percentage in America and our dollar would speak louder than our votes. Much of the negative talk occurred on a specific news station that also had access to sports. What if the Black community boycotted viewing sports on this specific station? Would sponsors pull off of the station? Would the sports program take their presentation of sports to a different station? Would the message be clear that the language of hate will not be tolerated? There is the power.

The constant bickering and fighting and consistent push back was a badge of honor in our country. Politicians that represented a specific belief system were the champions of their voters and gained more support from their voters the more aggressive and rebellious they were against the president. I wish it was politics, but there was a clear racial divide. It was evident that there were citizens that didn't care what President Obama said, but if he said it, he was wrong. The media offered cartoons and caricatures that looked more "monkey-like" than man and the very DNA of America had come to the surface. All of the peace and calm of the decades since the Civil Rights Movement had made us believe racism and prejudice was not as prominent in America than in the "old days." The past fifty years were about silent systems in place to suppress people, but the angry faces in the mob were back and the same games were being played. The faces and the crowds were back. Celebrations built on hate were being broadcast on the news with rallies "against Obama," but it looked like a rally for a lynching of a Black man from our history in this country being played out in the new millennium. In these crowds you had teenagers and younger as well being celebrated for their cultural connection with the adults. Again, like our past, there was division in the masses of people and those who historically controlled this country used fear to move the majority. The faces, the angry faces, in the crowds against President Obama had the bites of information to use for the cameras that were based on the propaganda of one political party, but what they were saying was, "The Black man was going to steal their freedom."

As much as the hate of the idea of a Black man in office might have been the point of misdirection needed to galvanize a group of voters to attempt to bring an oppressive spirit back as the head of the country was the goal, a key talking point remained President Obama's country of birth. "He is not an American" was the cry of many in the anti-Obama camps. "Who is his family and where was he born?" "He can't be an American with a name like Barack Hussein Obama!" "He was born in another country!!" The pressure mounted against President Obama for him to show his birth certificate even though no other former president needed to prove their citizenship by birth in history. Attempting to end issues in 2008, President Obama had already offered the short version of his birth certificate which is the version offered by the state of Hawaii, Obama's birth state, when a copy is requested. Furthermore, several people of the department went on record to state that they had seen all of the formal documentation and could guarantee that President Obama was born in Hawaii and is a natural born citizen. President Obama's critics would continue to present the false narrative of his birth nation and conversation was seen as a distraction to larger issues at hand for the president. President Obama would eventually present his long version of his birth certificate to create better focus on the needs at hand.

Even when the country celebrated the death of Osama bin Laden with President Obama giving the order in an attack strike led by Marines, President Obama couldn't be celebrated by his opponents. Regardless of the growth of the country and decline of unemployment and no matter if President Obama was trying to build ways to care for those with life challenges and offer health care options for all, President Obama was "bad" business for a certain type of spirit that still permeated through America. Socialism became the new hate word as specific opposition fought to make President Obama's ideas "anti-American" speech. Rallies against President Obama were popping up and shirts were being worn with borderline racist statements. The American icon of "hope" was becoming the punching bag of an angry mindset that remained unchecked. Where were those who cried when President Obama won? Where were those who voted for President Obama when he was being attacked on specific media outlets and the misaligned hatred grew? President Obama had a technique and his image remained a leader that was calm and thoughtful and rarely "angry."

Could President Obama have an emotion aligned with anger? He fist bumped his wife early in his career and that became a visualization of "aggression" to those who opposed his presidency. Could he get loud or stern? Could President Obama demand respect in any form or fashion besides being a class act and prevail with a cooler head? Did President Obama have to keep a certain demeanor because America wasn't ready for a Black man laying down the line? We know First Lady Michelle Obama did her best to gauge the temperature of America and how much "blackness" she could offer. There were several times the media tried to test the waters by speaking negatively of Mrs. Obama's facial expressions and/or tone. However, Blacks and whites quickly came to her defense and so did President Obama as he once looked into the camera and stated, "Leave my wife and kids out of this." It wasn't called "cancel culture" then, but there definitely was a force behind Michelle Obama that was intimidating to those who were also coming after President Obama. Though Mrs. Obama was seen as a smart, strong woman, loving her husband and kids as she put her career to the side to lift up her man. The first lady also walked with the spirit of a lioness and remained in a tight circle with media tours such as Oprah and Ellen DeGeneres. A strong group of followers connected with both television personalities and that group had the ability to boycott a brand and ruin it.

President Obama though, wasn't doing as many tours. He still had star status, but he was also running the country and being a global leader. People expected a level of awe in his leadership and greatness and leaders carry the weight when visions don't come true. President Obama had more weight on him than any other President. He was a Black man that people either wanted him to miraculously change the world over night while his opponents continued to press him for failure. Meanwhile, President Obama had to bear the weight of his race and his "blackness." The Black community looked for President Obama to be their champion even though many might not have known what was needed to have an "equal" footing in America. The Black community just knew there was representation in the Oval Office and because the world as the Black community knew it hadn't changed, perhaps President Obama wasn't keeping it "real" enough.

Sadly, in 2012, President Obama had to speak to the Black community and the rest of America during a time of great fear and concern in our country. February 26th was the night that opened a spotlight on the deaths of Black community members by the hands of those outside of the Black community. The death of Black youth wasn't new by 2012. Young Black people had been dying for a variety of reasons since Black people had been brought to the states in bondage. We had moved on from the sole threat of death from white hands to adding Black hands to the mix in the efforts to create a veil of power and control. Gangster types and gangs have been killing Black youth since the early 1900s and weapon access in urban neighborhoods brought an increase in deaths. On the 26th of February, seventeen-year-old Treyvon Martin was murdered by his assailant by gunshot wounds in Sanford, Florida while walking to his residence for the evening after coming back from a local gas station store. His death was by the hands of someone who identified as a "white" male who was protecting his community.

There are several "truths" to what happened that night on the 26th. There are only two that would really know the facts clearly, one was murdered and the other had the gun. What we know is that 17-year-old Treyvon Martin was in the Sanford neighborhood visiting with family and returning from the store while walking through the gated community. We also know that the gated community had over 400 calls the year prior to the 26th and George Zimmerman was a long time renter in the community and had recently become the head of the neighborhood watch. The neighborhood had recently called the police regarding suspicious characters in the community who were all identified as Black and in one case actually was involved in having stolen merchandise from a burglarized home. Zimmerman had aspirations to be a judge per an interview, he was seeking a criminal justice associates degree, and he was working in an insurance company in February 2012 as a fraud investigator. Zimmerman was licensed to carry a firearm and was 5'7 and 185 pounds. Treyvon Martin was 5'11 and approximately 160 pounds.

Treyvon Martin was an athlete that had a level of popularity at the two schools he attended. Martin had a strong showing of his academic abilities and prowess at times and was enrolled in pilot training through high school at a very early age. To most, in the public eye, Martin was a "good kid" and was the type to carry an elderly lady's groceries and he wasn't afraid of hard work. Martin also had a few documented truancy infractions and behavior issues at his school that led to multiple day suspensions. As Martin's social media account and digital footprint became public record, we learned that Martin was working through a duality as a young Black brother. Martin, a young man who volunteered at football concession stands his freshman year at his former high school, was now a junior and transfer student at new high school with his alias "slimm" on social media posting about weed and street life. You can easily be both people and more, but perception is reality in many cases.

It was evident that Zimmerman was involved in a scuffle on that night and based on the medical report, Zimmerman was losing the fight if he was battling Treyvon Martin that night. Martin would have had a better reach and being an athlete probably was superior in physical strength even though Zimmerman outweighed Treyvon. Also, if Zimmerman confronted Treyvon that night in an aggressive manner, Treyvon could have had heightened strength based on his need to survive the attack. Zimmerman, in his own mind and a title regarding the neighborhood watch, was defending the community and could have aggressively confronted Treyvon who could have been listening to headphones with his hoodie on when approached initially by Zimmerman. This could have been a misunderstanding by all parties, but we know one made a decision he couldn't take back.

A young Black teen was fatally shot and the person who pulled the trigger would not have any consequences. There were no charges for 2nd degree murder and there were no charges for manslaughter that George Zimerman was found guilty of and he walked away from the courtroom a free man. America held its breath the day Zimmerman walked away free because we had seen the justice system offer a decision and the urban community responded in the past for not receiving favorable news. Although Zimmerman has Latin blood, he represented an entitlement that Black and brown community members are not afforded in America. This was a spirit of power that has often allowed others to smile and walk away after permanently changing the lives of people who have been valued less in America. Zimmerman represented a level of comfort and level of "white" privilege that most in the "urban" community didn't have and this verdict could have set off another riot. There were already protests in the city streets calling for justice before the verdict and now the answer was not favorable for community members.

Yet, it was President Obama and his call for peace that calmed the rumblings of a storm. It was the person who the Black community and all of those who fought against the spirit of oppression saw as the leader of their cause looking into cameras calling for calm. It was Barrack, not President Obama, looking in the cameras and expressing his pain as a Black man in America that caused the country to inhale and lean in its emotional distress and continue to wait and pray for a better day tomorrow. It was Barack Obama who mentioned that Trayvon could have been his son and Trayvon could have been him thirty-five years ago as President Obama addressed the nation. President Obama also acknowledged that the Black community could be doing overall as more deaths of Black men were coming by Black hands than this case with Zimmerman.

President Obama offered the nation some powerful points to reflect on and grow as a nation in our hope to heal. Some, though, started to make a clear mention that Black lives didn't matter in America.

I wish I could tell you that this was it and there were no more deaths announced in the media in regard to Black people dying while in a specific interaction with people who identify as "white" and a conflict of perceived power. I also wish I could tell you that the Black community rallied together and committed to end gang violence and Black on Black crimes as a result of the public killings of Black community members, but I can't. I can tell you that 2014 brought the murders of Eric Garner, Michael Brown, Tamir Rice, Akai Gurley. I can tell you that the death of Treyvon Martin there were other deaths and sadly they were at the hands of police officers during active duty or otherwise retired. I can tell you that the victims were not always innocent in their behaviors and their actions that led to the arrest or other interactions that led to a confrontation, but I can also tell you that none of the victims deserved to die. Something was happening in our country that no one would notice. Our country was shifting in morals and ethics and the concept of life was less valued. It was beginning to be more about being "right" than it was about listening and less about being seen and more about being viewed.

Treyvon Martin
Eric Garner
Michael Brown
Tamir Rice
Akai Gurley
Freddie Gray
Philando Castile
Walter Scott

Alton Sterling
Stephon Clark
Botham Jean
Atatiana Jefferson
Breanna Taylor
Ahmaud Arbery

There was a need for anger and reform, but it wasn't a police issue alone.

Murder Capitals of the Nation
2012 - Chicago
2013 - Detroit
2014 - Chicago
2015 - St. Louis
2016 - St. Louis
2017 - Baltimore
2018 - Chicago
2019 - St. Louis

The murder rates of the cities are not all Black-on-Black crimes, but the majority of murders of Black people that occur in America are caused by Black hands. However, during these times, Blacks, browns, whites and walks of life ran to the streets with signs and t-shirts. We rallied behind the mottos of "Black Lives Matter" and chanted "I can't breathe," but the killing continued in the same cities by the hands of Black people against Black people. Urban community members in cities remained unsafe and insecure of their tomorrow and their basic needs utilizing strong arm robbery as a resource. Rural community members were still living in third world conditions and leaning on drug sales for income and a sense of happiness and provision. There was plenty of video footage from cell phones and police cameras. Then there were more videos on social media and mainstream of those carrying signs and inhaling tear gas. The crowds in the protest eventually looked more white than Black as the chanting of what mattered continued. Athletes took knees during the national anthem from the professional divisions down to the high school levels to bring more attention to police brutality. A professional quarterback in the NFL lost his job and career for his protest, but many officers in the cases kept theirs.

After all the tear gas cleared, police reform became a topic and more police cameras in certain cities were purchased, and those who led the executive offices of the Black Lives Matter movement faded away among the whispers of not handling finances well at the very least. Guns are still available in the inner cities, drugs are still a resource as a pathway to security for those who have been historically underserved, schools with a higher percentage of Black students fail at a higher rate, and Black people still die by homicide more than any other race in America. Black Lives Matter. The peak of all these issues came during a time in which a Black man stood as president, yet those that opposed him based on a political party had control of the Senate and the House of Representatives. While the columns of the country were shaking, the status quo remained and the spirit that built this country on oppression remained consistent and waited out the storm and resisted change.

This was nothing new to those who held onto the spirit that used the tool of control and suppression of people for the growth of their own false sense of security and power. This like many times in history is a waiting game to pacify the emotions of the masses. Throw your tantrum and stomp your feet, this too shall pass. Those in perceived power are rarely made uncomfortable as they sit in their historical and current roles in society. Though during this time, we are reminded of the impact of the youth and the voice the younger generation has in the development of this nation.

As I mentioned before, the youth can cause a billion dollar company to collapse in a matter of weeks. Based on a whim if the youth synergized around the idea of ceasing the support of almost any individual, brand, organization, and/or company there would be a large shift in status. If at any time, those under the age of twenty-five decided to create a mass movement in any direction, they would hold the fate of any entity. The "call out" culture or what was later noted as the "cancel" culture was a glimmer of that ability to shift perceived power and control in our country. The fear of being canceled by the youth or any major purchaser was dictating the choices of individuals and businesses by the end of the decade. Past issues from the history of individuals were coming up and the second half of the 2010 decade became several moments of holding people accountable for their past. Men who took advantage of their positions of perceived power decades ago were losing their career, finances, and freedom as victims found courage to speak up and out to the public about encounters that haunted them. Companies were retracting ads and statements if something "slipped" past editing eyes and the job title of diversity, equity, and inclusion director became the norm as a badge of being progressive and understanding the "struggles."

However, those canceling were not typically the youth of the Black community. The same community that somehow spends billions of dollars on the clothing and entertainment industry. This group wasn't holding individuals and companies accountable. There was some representation in crowds requesting for change, but for the most part the Black community could not see a reason to develop a movement for sustainable change by galvanizing behind the need to improve many social issues. The youth continued to focus on lyrics such as Lil Uzi Vert:

She say I'm insane, yeah, I might blow my brain out
(Hey) Xanny help the pain, yeah, please, Xanny make it go away
I'm committed, not addicted, but it keep control of me
All the pain, now I can't feel it, I swear that it's slowin' me, yuh
I don't really care if you cry
On the real, you should've never lied
Saw the way she looked me in my eyes
She said, "I am not afraid to die" (go)
All my friends are dead, push me to the edge
All my friends are dead, yuh, push me to the edge
All my friends are dead, yuh, all my friends are dead, yuh
That is not your swag, I swear you fake hard
Now these niggas wanna take my cadence
Rain on 'em, thunderstorm, rain on 'em, yuh
Medicine, lil' nigga take some
Fast car, Nascar, race on 'em
In the club, ain't got no ones, then we would become
Clothes from overseas, got the racks and they all C-Notes
You is not a G, though
Lookin' at you stackin' all your money, it all green though
I was countin' that and these all twenties, that's a G-roll
Lil Uzi Vert XO Tour Llif3, 2017

Another hit of the time was brought to us through Future and Mask Off:

Percocets (ya), molly, Percocets (Percocets)
Percocets (ya), molly, Percocets (Percocets)
Rep the set (yee), gotta rep the set (gang, gang)
Chase a check (chase it), never chase a bitch
(Don't chase no bitches)

Mask on, fuck it, mask off (mask)
Mask on, fuck it, mask off (mask)
Percocets ('cets), molly, Percocets (Percocets)
Chase a check (chase it), never chase a bitch (don't chase no bitches)
Two cups (cup), toast up with the gang (gang, gang)
From food stamps to a whole 'nother domain, ya
Out the bottom (ye), I'm the livin' proof (super)
Ain't compromisin', half a million on the coupe (gang, gang)
Drug houses (where), lookin' like Peru (woah, woah, woah)
Graduated, I was overdue (I'm on due)
Pink molly (molly), I can barely move (barely move)
Ask about me ('bout me), I'm gon' bust a move
Rick James (James), 33 chains (33)
Ocean air (air), cruisin' Biscayne
Top off (ya), that's a liability (big foreigns)
Hit the gas (gas), boostin' my adrenaline (big foreigns)
Future, "Mask Off," 2017

Our youth wasn't worrying about holding anyone accountable and you didn't have the leadership to offer you a movement to do so. Your heroes remained in hip-hop and now social media as Boonk Gang was exploding with followers and views as he visibly steals from stores and plays the fool and runs during pranks. These are the new Black men of influence as they rap about taking prescription drugs to "cope" with stress and still find time to rob, sell drugs, and murder. Images on videos in social media show the yachts, the mansions, the cars, the women, and the other perceivable images of power and security. Not even the athlete is seen as a specific aspiration as they used to because that takes work even if you are miraculously blessed with talent and physical advantages. It is easier to be a nigga with a gun or a fool with a grin than a brother with desire and a vision. You can take out student loans if you are fortunate to have the right opportunities for college, but even with a degree there is no one lining up to offer you loans for your own business. Even if there were viable funding sources for dreams, our school curriculum isn't designed for you to operate with the freedom to be your own boss as it is rare to see projects as assessments in classrooms. There are many challenges to your success and there are obvious flaws in society that pose obstacles to your life success. We need to align our energy to the lifting acquired for growth. We need to use our voice for true change and support other individuals and companies that do not hinder our opportunities.

Black youth in between 2010 and 2020 see that you can become secure and safe in the path of popularity and that is often solidified through "likes." By the second half of the decade, social media has become an outlet for the youth and even older generations. Television shows become less important than individuals watching clip after clip of various "artists." The idea of the "influencer" is born and becomes the job desire of many who perform all types of acts on camera for the views and increase of followers. "Anything" includes would also include illegal acts, acts that may not be at the highest points of ethics, shock value opportunities, pranks at the expense of others, tricks and acts that are life threatening, and sexually suggestive at the least. Clips that hopefully go viral to gain payment of some sort from social media platforms that rotate in popularity, but all are public for all to see if that is your goal and even if it's not.

Why should you care about school when you have "reality" stars that are becoming millionaires simply by being "entertaining." Especially when those reality stars become social media famous before becoming mainstream famous and you can do that with your phone and some time. Each "hit," "like," subscription, and/or view is a validation for your talent and potential stardom, fame, and security. By this time in history, aspiring artists can create their own music and videos and upload them for the opportunity to "make it big." Record labels were even losing their appeal as artists in music were uploading their music straight to fans to build their fan base. This was the new drug to deal with and this was the new game.

There is nothing wrong with aspirations to be bigger and better. There is nothing wrong with taking what you have been gifted and using it to build your brand and finding a way to profit in those efforts. There isn't anything necessarily wrong with how someone chooses to spend time staring at their phone and viewing short videos and photos of people that keep you entertained. To a degree, how some stare at their phones is no different than how other generations sat around the radio for their favorite programs, sat in front of their television for their favorite shows, and sat on game consoles. Yet, as much as social media was first posed as "real," it is important to understand that we have grown into a new era of people using effects to enhance and lie to their audience and the ability to purchase marketing and branding to increase the perceived popularity of a specific account or person. At one point, we would look at cars and clothes of the people we see in neighborhoods and wrongfully compare our self-worth and desire to want what they had. Some that view their own self-worth on social media may be comparing themselves to several lies. Social media is entertainment and it is not always the "reality" you may think it is. The people that may or may not see your posts and "like" your material or not are not a worthy holder of your happiness. Enjoy yourself, but remember, there are many layers to you and you are amazing in various ways. If you are not receiving a good return on your time investment, start to offer other interests some time to see the positive growth in your life in other areas.

There was no time to care about politics as it was evident it was a game that was rigged and we were destined to lose. Even with "our" president in office "nothing" was getting accomplished. There was no sweeping change in the status of every Black and brown person in America. The "have nots" still had "not" and it would seem the wealthy were living in heaven on Earth. The system lost its credibility in the eyes of the youthful voters and there was still ignorance to the larger "win" needed with local government to assist in the wins needed on a federal level. Generations covering those in their 30s and younger and in some cases older, were focused once again on self-preservation and security and safety through wealth and material. There was widespread apathy in the government throughout the younger generations and more and in some cases the concept of politics was a joke. The response to a political game that is a circus during a time when nothing is being taken seriously through the "entertainment" and desensitizing of social media was to not vote or vote for the most unlikely of candidates.

Hillary Clinton was a likely candidate for the Democrats hoping it was time for our first woman president and easy victory. America had seen Hilary Clinton through former president Bill Clinton which offered her weight. As a senator herself, Hilary was not new to the political world, but her mass appeal came from President Clinton. Yet, she didn't have what most former Democrat potential presidents and winners had which was relatability. Hilary didn't have the "buy in" from the people of color or those considered progressive or liberal. Hilary was the option we had, but in the times of social media and shifting of pop culture, politicians needed to be entertainers who were sensational and buzz worthy.

Donald Trump had always been his best hype man. Historically, Trump had all the appeal of an arch nemesis in a superhero movie. His name was known throughout America and in various parts of the world and that was before he was the star of his own reality television show. Trump had it all which included all that people wanted such as money, material, and fame that all provided the perception of power and security. Trump at the very least offered the optics of a crafty business man that would make America rich...again. Everyone who was wealthy knew Trump had the secret because they all spoke a similar language and those who weren't wealthy sat on the edge of their seats in hopes he would offer the secret sauce to all Americans in his leadership of the country. Beyond all of those concepts, Trump was the great white hope. Trump was the leader of choice for all those who wanted to say what they wanted whenever they wanted and have no consequences. Trump was an image and ideals of the dormant DNA of hate in America. Whether or not Trump was naturally that person, he was smart enough to cash in on it.

The Trump campaign wasn't about "white" or Black or specific racism. The Trump campaign was about rallying people behind an emotion. Trump used anger. Trump used frustration. Trump used those exhausted people across the states that had been lied to over the decades and accepted a "truth" about various types of "boogeyman" in the form of illegal aliens from Mexico and south of the border, Obama and the Democrats, and foreign countries. Trump rested on the idea of taking back what belongs to our country by bold and tough and even intimidating tactics. President Obama was a diplomat and politician. Trump created an entire campaign on being the "anti-politician" and quickly became the hero for some "common" man voters. Donald Trump was a sound bite waiting to happen in his debates and interviews. People were shocked, amazed, and entertained by his statements that were at times racist, sexist, and highly offensive. Other times his statements were false and in some cases just plain dangerously ignorant or incorrect.

Many expected him to implode and destroy his own career, but he continued to become the sole candidate for his party and on the night of election many went to bed laughing at the idea of President Donald Trump. We woke up the morning after election night in 2015 to a new world. Donald Trump would be our 45th president of the United States of America. Months of campaigning with negativity and anger. Commercials and media clips of a person saying many things that we never thought would be tolerated by a person in this position only led to our new commander in chief. America had come far we thought. The United States of America had evolved from the spirit of hate and we were a country of love because enough of our country voted in a Black man. The perfect storm occurred with apathy and the fact that America isn't all loving and progressive and the idea of keeping a level of perceivable power and false sense of security and safety overcame all other rational thought and we had President Trump.

It wasn't a set of specific laws that took America into a spiral of moral despair as President Trump took office. America suffered from a vacuum with the removal of the concept of love. Cultures are set by leadership. Trump as president was the leader of America and was one that never shied away from offering his statements regardless of any offense that might be taken. Whether it is meant to be hurtful or not when it is said, does not supersede the fact that the words are hurtful. A specific population of America was free to say whatever and have whatever printed on t-shirts, hats, and bumper stickers and boldly walk with a level of little accountability like no other time. Much as the Black community were wearing their President Obama merchandise, the Trump supporters quickly posted their American flags on their TRUMP wrapped trucks and specific media became bolder in their comments about other communities. This time was the introduction and rebirth of the bold persons yelling in the faces of people of color while the entitled yeller spouts off about the country being "theirs" and begins to call the police because an appetizer didn't come to the table. Valuable conversations were not meeting ears of understanding and we were beginning to speak or yell at each other opposed to working with each other. You would have thought a large concern that threatened the entire planet would have unified us all, but it only caused a deeper split.

It was right after New Years in the first week of 2020 when the news was starting to receive more attention. We didn't know much about it, but we could only trust what the media was offering and any details we could dig out from the internet. There was a communicable disease spreading across the globe and countries were beginning to shut down as the infections became more numerous. We would later learn that the disease was a respiratory disease that was transmitted through air and water particles transferred from human breathing. By the spring of 2020, COVID-19, otherwise known as the coronavirus, had caused America to shut down and revert to mitigated social interaction as much as possible which left us depending on technology for everything from date night and school work to day to day jobs if possible. While America suffered from the economic blow that sheltering in place would cause businesses, we had a government fighting with itself as President Trump blamed what he called the China virus on a conspiracy blown out of proportion and his cabinet offering press releases on the sincerity of it all.

While doctors and otherwise professionals were offering the need to stay "masked up" and washing your hands, President Trump led the narrative that the world was overreacting. The new MAGA hat to represent Make America Great Again, the President Trump slogan, was not wearing a mask. Not only did the specific followers of President Trump not want to wear masks, but they also wanted to establish legal obstacles to request that they do so. Stores, businesses, locations, and schools were all proponents for wearing masks and while many locations remained closed per the government, the reopening of the country was contingent on mask wearing until we found a vaccine or cure.

Imagine a country that determines your freedoms based on what they believe is best for you. Imagine a government that controls your access to resources based on the needs of the many. Imagine a system that removes your perceived privilege and vail of safety and security overnight. All of the money couldn't purchase guaranteed safety and in some cases could even purchase protection via highly rated masks that were quickly sold out across the states. Grocery stores quickly were selling out of needed items as people began to horde for the worst. Lines for gas were starting to get out of control when the lockdown first was announced. All of the history and centuries of perceived control and protection gone literally with a breath of air and some just didn't want to believe it. To date, white males over the age of fifty-five years old were the most likely to die from the disease. Similar to a demographic that supported the theory of not wearing a mask.

It was such an interesting time to see that level of anger from people. There remnants are still there, but to a degree the well of Trump style shock popularity has nearly transitioned out from politics. The rally of the "mob" that supports Trump openly has weakened in elections and the votes to come with a politician aligning themselves with the brand of "telling it like it is" while also offering a level of hateful venom are not what they used to be. We will perhaps forget the emotion that was offered by those who wore the hats and waved the MAGA flags. It may all retreat back into a dormant state and those who have these issues will use an approach with more stealth to offer their misplaced anger. Meanwhile, those who used the emotions of people who waved the flags and saw no real change in their lives will pivot to do what is necessary to stay in office and protect their wealth, their perceived power, and their false sense of security and safety. The spirit of oppression is not about color it's about position and it uses all it needs to remain.

A virus that had no respect for any culture, creed, color, or gender wasn't enough to unite us in a common cause. As if the COVID virus wasn't enough during 2020, we had another explosive case of abuse of authority as we watched the death of George Floyd by a Minneapolis Police Officer Derek Chauvin and his use of excessive force. COVID was a respiratory disease that caused issues with lungs at times, George Floyd had COVID and was also suffocated in an arrest attempt by Chauvin. This senseless act caused an explosion of people in the streets in multiple cities. The emotions of Americans were at dangerous levels and the leader of the country did not lead us in the fashion that calmed us as when Treyvon was murdered. What America saw on television was more division. Our country was being attacked by a virus and what had been ailing us since our inception of the American dream and there seemed to be very little clear, calm guidance about our future.

What COVID did was shine a greater line on specific areas. The physical and mental wellness of people were highlighted as there were great concerns for those who had previous health complications while contracting the virus. Mental health was a reflection point as the country shifted to a form of isolation, but also many took some space to reflect on their personal happiness which wasn't often afforded to us because we were all hustling for the dollar for that false sense of security. Another key issue was the inequity of education.

There has always been inequities in education and regardless of "exposing" the continuous data, nothing has been formed as a movement. We knew going into the pandemic that schools with higher percentages of Black students were less likely to produce graduates and specifically the Black male was most unlikely to graduate from these schools. Additionally, we knew that on average students of poverty, which Black and brown students are unproportionally to their percentage in America, were behind in their abilities to read and perform mathematical functions. Finally, we knew going into the pandemic that schools of high color and middle to low poverty on average had less technology access, lower level facilities, and fewer high quality and experienced teachers than primarily white schools. We now also know that the pandemic set all students in America anywhere from one to two years behind in their schooling and learning development and that would be on top of the learning loss average that already existed for the students of color.

When a student is required to stay at home and learn, on average, the white student has more support and increased access to individuals who are familiar with and proficiency in the skills needed for the student to learn needed material. As much as technology offered cameras and video conferences the learning support in white homes continued in different ways and more advanced ways than in homes of color. There are typically more books in white homes than in homes of families of color. White families on average have more family members that have graduated from high school and post-secondary schools. Sadly in the beginning of the pandemic many schools of color didn't have laptops to offer students and there were no computers at the students' homes. Additionally, another issue was the digital divide as students of color on average had internet at home at a lower rate than white families. The American government did provide, to the best of their ability, during these times and additional funding was offered to schools, families, and individuals. The concern remains that there is a deeper hole for people of color to crawl out of based on the start of the pandemic and the starting point from the specific Black community and centuries of the hole deepening.

All these factors have come about since the pandemic and all data can be offered to support these issues. However, there are no large crowds of people chanting "Black Lives Matter." There are no outraged news casters on programs discussing the need for change. There are no hard questions being asked of politicians asking what can be done to close an even larger gap than what we had before the pandemic regarding students who lack the ability to show sufficient skills in reading and math based on their grade level in school. To add more concern, there is a teacher shortage like never before and it feels as if we have just accepted it and/or allowed the issue to be the schools' responsibility. Trillions of dollars in a budget and billions to a war involving other nations and we can't pay teachers more and expect a higher level of skill set from teachers based on their new increased salaries? Can we offer a payoff for student loans for anyone that agrees to enter in education and successfully moves students academically? Couldn't we finance better paths for students to have careers when they graduate which would give them more hope and possibly more drive and tenacity to achieve in school? There are so many possibilities that we don't engage in because there is no pressure from the people.

2020 ended and the nation had elected a new leader and with president elect Joe Biden also came vice president elect Kamala Harris. Our country voted in with the president our first Black woman to be vice president. There was quite the buzz during the race as Joe Biden and President Trump campaigned. Biden was the former vice president of President Obama and everyone appreciated Biden for being "cool" Joe. Biden carried himself like a man of the people and that went a long way in the campaign. Biden also had some star power and street cred with President Obama and Joe also has a little swagger to him. Yet, when Biden announced Harris as his running mate, the Black community lit up to see another one of our firsts to occur during this lifetime. Most folks don't even know what the vice president is responsible for except they are the next person up if the president passes away and I think that's all Black folks had to know. Harris in her own right had a strong background as an intelligent attorney and the Attorney General and later a senator of California. Harris can be seen with a fierce presence in the courtroom and in debates as she represents women of all kinds well in her ability to work against the oppression that has been placed on women and doubled down on women of color. As President Trump wasn't the ideal president for a progressive America and he continued to rest on the brand that elected him, America rallied behind the Democratic nominee Joe Biden and Kamala Harris no doubt caused a few more voters to get engaged with the election in Biden's favor. November, 2020 Joe Biden became the 46th president of the United States of America and President Trump began his narrative of the election being rigged and refused to concede.

There are a few times when I stared at the screen and watched a video in disbelief. January 6th, 2021 was a confusing time for America as we watched something we have only witnessed in other countries. We have watched other governments wrestle with their citizens in their attempt to overthrow their government, but that would never happen in the United States. As President Trump spoke at a rally that same day, he offered the direction to have his supporters march to the capital as the legislative members were gathered to officially place president elect Biden as the official 46th president in defeat of President Trump. President Trump may not have known how powerful his voice was to his followers and the lengths they would go to "take back the country." By the 6th of January, there were several pipe bombs placed and 8000 American citizens and Trump supporters forcing their way into the capital overcoming and injuring security and police, causing the building to go into lockdown as best as possible, and forcing all of the government officials including the vice president at the time, Mike Pence, to go into protection. Approximately 1200 individuals made their way into the capital that day, some carrying the confederate flag, the flag of the slave states of the Civil War that some Americans still pledge their allegiance to. Some of the 1200 also were screaming death cheers as they stormed the areas looking for Vice President Pence specifically calling for his hanging. 138 police officers were injured and there were several deaths connected with the day. President Trump did not concede to the election results until the following week and it was then he also condemned the January 6th attack.

Oddly, I sat and stared at the screen on that date and I was saddened and disappointed. I was saddened that our country had come to this and our morality had decayed to this under our collective watch. I was saddened that this was where we were and of course over the years we saw this play out and no one will be held accountable. I was saddened that new media and politicians had been playing with this emotional grenade to get views and votes over the past twelve years and there wasn't a moment of reflection based on the Frankenstein monster that was created and unleashed through the years and on this day.

I was disappointed that collectively we haven't had this type of passion and fire for what we know is needed in our country for true equality and equity. Please don't read that as if I was agreeing with the insanity and loss of rationale and reason of the mob that pushed into the capital. I also am fully aware that this group's behavior was a manifestation of entitlement and a level of privilege the Black community doesn't have. I am not talking about a physical uprising. I am saying that we continue to accept our current status as a people who were brought to this country in subjugation and have yet to free our own minds and selves from the historical position of being underserved. We spend over $1 trillion dollars annually as a Black community per year which is more money spent in Spain or Mexico by their entire population. The inequity is broader than the Black community and it would make sense to align our efforts with others who have been historically oppressed by the spirit of "they." "They" who have always protected their perceived power and have controlled as much as "they" can to perpetuate social construct and create "truths" to keep us all separate and from uniting as one people. The Black community needs to find its strength, its truth, and its leadership to then unite with others to build this country to its potential dream for all.

    It's obvious there is a threat to America being free to know its entire history. To protect something with this much energy that various candidates have been running on stopping an equal voice of history to be told to all students would only mean the secret is valued. Or perhaps the fear is the pain of the truth that will be exposed and the questions that have to be answered at the dinner tables. Perhaps it's a fear of offering the building on the consciousness of American citizens and there may be an opportunity in which we can be better and better may mean losing the ability to control valuable resources to hoard a perceived power. Things are changing in increments, but perhaps your generation can speed things up by realizing the true power in your leadership.

And as I sit here in what is the present time for me, in the past thirty days, there has been a six-year-old that brought a gun to school and shot his teacher and a few mass shootings in various locations. "They" have bought the souls of politicians that refuse to have a conversation about what needs to occur to help aid this country slip further into its own grave. A country established on freedoms should also help citizens understand those freedoms. The argument of gun control goes nowhere and innocent people continue to die. Even those who are extremely fond of the Second Amendment have noted that "guns don't kill people," yet we do nothing proactive or strategic to help those "people" that do. We have people killing people and politicians want to remove socioemotional curriculum from schools because "it's not what we need."

As I write these words we have politicians that openly run on platforms that openly attack the opportunities for equity. We have a politician that bans curriculum for Black students in their state and we have a politician that still uses President Trump's name like he is a god to worship. We also have citizens and voters who approve of these actions and media that promotes it all like it something in which we should have pride.

And as I write these words, America continues to deal with murders at the hands of police. It's easy to have outrage when the police officers are white, but now we have six Black men that brutally beat another Black man to death in the streets. These Black police officers were brothers who probably wanted to make a difference in their community. A few were reported Black Greek fraternity members where they would have mentioned they were interested in being a positive social influence. Yet, somewhere, the spirit of "they" grabbed each of them. The six Black men were sucked in by a perceived power through their shields and blue uniforms. The group was even in a select unit to help clean the streets up which the title would have offered an increase in status and perception of power. This same spirit that ran through slave masters and Klan members, the same that bombed churches, the same that beat a Black boy and tried to sink him under water with barbed wire, the same spirit of the fire hose and the dogs, the same as the same that hordes jobs and refuses to hire those that don't look like them, the same that pushes a narrative of hate in the news, and the spirit that holds children back from freely learning, is the same spirit that beat this Black man through six pairs of Black hands and feet. As I said, this isn't a color thing or a Black or white thing. This oppressive spirit is built in the DNA of various peoples and is brought to life by fostering and allowing it to grow without a conscious response. It's in me and it's in you, and if we all are not mindful and remain as keepers at the gate, the spirit takes over and leads our minds, hearts, and actions. Remain vigilant and keep your balance. Stay driven and stay passionate, but also remain selfless and humble. There is enough...there is always enough...you are enough...and you can always give more...to others and in your efforts for your gains.

I have nothing more to give you. I know you and I have not always seen eye to eye and we have fought and you have walked away before we finished talking at times and I have walked away from you in frustration, shaking my head. I know I haven't always said it and perhaps not have shown it, but I love you and I need you. I need you to be the best you. I don't need you to be Martin, Malcolm, or Barrak. I don't need you to move thousands, hundreds of thousands, or millions. If you are destined to lead a revolution then that is your journey, but I will ask that your revolution starts with you. I know you have free will and a free mind. I know you will believe that you are your own man and nothing and no one can control you. You may not believe all that I have told you and strike it all off as an old man talking at you. I don't offer you conspiracy theories and I don't offer this as "the" truth, but my "truth." You have all you need to find details that I couldn't provide or dig deeper into what I said. Just remember that as much as who you are, you have been influenced. You have been taught a language and you have been taught belief systems. You have been taught morals and ethics and you have learned various social and otherwise street codes. You are a Black man defined in America since its inception and you are ever evolving. As much as we have advanced as a people collectively, fear is ingrained in us all to protect us as a primal instinct. What we choose to fear in society is taught. You have been and will be feared by the status quo. Limitations have been placed on you and you have been placed in positions of lack in hopes that the "haves" continue to have based on a spirit of conquest, suppression, and oppression.

There can be equality and there can be a society in which we love and care for each other. It will take your strength and your will to refuse the spirit of "they" that remains in the DNA of America dormant in all of us. This beautiful country offers so much, but it was established on bloodshed and born from rape. The dreams of colonizing immigrants and nightmares of slaves and Indigenous people, our country stands as still one of the most free and beautiful today. We are far from perfect as a country and no history book in your schools should hide the facts of our establishment and management of our growth over the centuries. You have the freedom to know your history and determine your future. You should be fully informed. Informed not for you to be angry or for others to feel guilt, but for all us to face the mirror and then grow forward and become better.

I believe this country has a chance, but it will take the next generations to move us forward as a people. As we move forward as a people, don't forget your history because it is important. Continue to read and learn more about your history and it will help guide your future. Our country will continue to grow as I see your generation already merging through music as we did in the '50s. I can already see country music dipping into hip-hop with certain beats and rhythms and more of our rap artists are singing and some of their tunes have a close to country melody. The '90s rap artist Nelly started something with his duet with country singer Tim McGraw, Beyoncé crossed culture lines in her *Lemonade* album and even performed on the Country Music Awards, and today you can hear a solid "urban" influence in popular country music and our rap stars sure do sing a lot. Most of us are more similar than we are different.

However, your life will be harder for you and that is unfair. There are biases in this country and the world based on the color of your skin. There are images that are stained in the minds of people, all people, that create a "truth." As a Black man, you will be pushed into an identity when they encounter you. You will be someone's President Obama, you will be someone's Lebron James, you will be someone's entertainer, someone's dancer, someone's comedian, someone's clown, someone's fool, someone's thug, someone's gangster, someone's nigga, and someone's nigger. You will have to decide on who you are everyday when the path is unclear and that is unfair. White men in this country get to be white men and own it. Sure there are various types and they can try on cultures, but ultimately the default white male culture is a natural fit in America. As a Black man you will have to forge your existence despite evident pulls in other directions. You will have to take responsibility for your growth and development and not simply say you are who you are. Stop asking for something you won't get, build, and be strong and lead the community.

Ask yourself, are you who you were destined to be or are you a product of who society has created you to be? Is there more to you? This isn't a question regarding status or finances, but are you happy? Are you fulfilled? If not, then change. Work hard and develop a solid base under you and chase the vision. Yes, you will have challenges and no it won't be fair. Yet, you are everything you need and you will find your network to help you along the way. It will take strategy and a strong mindset, but never be someone else's puppet or fool. Never fall into a narrative that has been provided to you. Animals react and you are not an animal. You have the same DNA that has established this country good, bad, and ugly and you have the same DNA that raised empires in other lands. You have the heart of a warrior and the ability to rationally offer leadership for the betterment of all. You can change the world as long as you monitor the change in self.

Finally, please remember, you are like a river. Sources are provided and pour into you and you should mind the sources that do. Your sources should build you to be strong and full. And like a river, you will flow into others. Offer your flow to specific areas and be mindful of your energy. You may one day be the river that changes the lives of the next generation or maybe one member of the next generation, but you can't do either positively unless you respect your own flow.

That's all I have for you, my son. Rise and be the king you are. Wait no longer. You are the movement and you are all the leader you need. This is your calling. I love you. Go get 'em!

Made in the USA
Middletown, DE
29 October 2023